the high school
in a changing world

the high school
in a changing world

THIRTY-SIXTH YEARBOOK, 1958
AMERICAN ASSOCIATION OF SCHOOL ADMINISTRATORS

FOREWORD

THIS VOLUME goes to the printer in November 1957 when the American people are making a fresh appraisal of all their public services, including education. They are doing this in the light of startling new evidence, flung into the sky, of Russian scientific progress. As our Yearbook Commission now reviews its manuscript, approved at our final meeting in September, we find no reason for changing interpretations or recommendations.

The value system which has long been the foundation of American education continues to stand. The proper business of American schools is not to change course in confusion at every fresh alarm but, in full awareness of the tensions and the promise of our times, to pursue with foresight and resolution the historic purposes to which our people are committed.

Our Commission was charged to take a new look at American secondary education and to consider what its role should be in the fabulous era now opening out before mankind. We have looked forward as far as we could. We have examined the current situations in our schools and in our culture. We have tried to point out how our junior high schools and senior high schools may help young people to strengthen themselves and use their cultural heritage in order to live well with themselves and all mankind.

Those who search these pages for spectacular proposals will be disappointed. We advocate no revolution, we offer no panacea. We do express our confidence in the American high school for we believe that this unique instrument of democratic education has served our nation well. To be sure, our schools are imperfect; the need to improve them is urgent. But the way of progress lies in doing more of the good things already under way, in refining procedures now in the pioneering stage, in making available to more students the advantages currently enjoyed by those enrolled in the best of our schools. We need new ideas, too, but the surest paths to better secondary education are most likely to be blazed, not by those whose zeal exceeds their insight, but by teachers, administrators, and school boards who approach the future with the strength of experience and the momentum of steady accomplishment.

We reaffirm in these pages the belief of this Association that our schools must be dedicated to the sound education of every youth, whatever his talents or his handicaps. We must be concerned with the development of every student's full intellectual capacity, but we must pay adequate attention also to the other aspects of his growth.

Our high schools are precious to us as symbols of democracy, but their chief value lies in their power as instruments for strengthening our people one by one and so carrying forward for another generation the endless struggle to liberate and dignify the human spirit.

As members of this Commission we are indebted to the Executive Committee of the American Association of School Administrators for the opportunity to work on a problem of great importance. Further, we owe special gratitude to:

Worth McClure, who as Executive Secretary, full of experience and wisdom, saw that we got off to a good start.

Finis E. Engleman, named Executive Secretary after we were under way, who brought us a fresh outlook, a rich background, and a generous spirit of helpful encouragement.

Henry L. Wright, who thru his firm, Kistner, Wright & Wright, contributed the talents of Frank T. Sata, who created the symbolic decorations which add so much to the cover and to the title pages of the chapters.

Hazel Davis, assistant director of the NEA Research Division, who helped us in countless ways, beyond the call of duty, as editor and coordinator of production.

6

CONTENTS

COMMISSION ON THE HIGH SCHOOL
IN A CHANGING WORLD

pressures and prospects

1

pressures and prospects

IF WE COULD LISTEN to a group of citizens talking about the local high school in Anytown, USA, we would soon learn that they take the school for granted as part of community life. They are pleased when the football team is on the winning side; they like to hear the band play; they show the new high-school building to visitors. Their local taxes help to pay for the high school. They want it to do a good job; they want to be proud of it. They are not likely to question the high school's existence nor its usefulness, but they may express some fears and misapprehensions. These concerns might include:

    • The fear that high-school graduates are poorly prepared for college entrance, especially in mathematics, science, and English, and that they are insufficiently prepared in these areas to enter the world of work.

    • A feeling that the "good old days" of strict discipline, hard work, and long hours of homework have been replaced by a "get by" attitude; that too many students are taking it the easy way.

    • A concern that the attainments of American high-school youth may not compare favorably with those of his counterpart in Europe, and that in physical fitness he may also be below European standards.

11

Along with these apprehensions, many of the same citizens are aware of the positive aspects of the high school's work. They might express the following:

• Satisfaction that so many high-school graduates do so well in college, and that their local boys and girls were able to win many scholarships.

• Awareness that the high school has to provide an adequate program for all students, those who will go directly to work as well as those who go to college.

• Confidence that high-school students generally are able to get along well with others, and that the basic causes of delinquency lie in home conditions.

• Gratitude for counseling and other evidences of the school's concern for giving each student the opportunity to make the most of his abilities, whatever they are.

• Knowledge that the faculty is underpaid and the school is understaffed, and that more money is needed for the school to do its big job better.

The concerns of Anytown's citizens regarding their high school, whether based on fact or fallacy, are human problems which can be solved by purposeful effort and deeper understanding. The implications of the questions raised are nationwide and worldwide in their scope, but decisions at the community level determine the direction that secondary education will take. The local decisions are not completely free choices—social forces, governmental policy, world affairs all have their influence—but there is still a significant range of decision making at the community level. Those who are served by the schools and those who staff the schools all should share in these decisions.

Community Controls of Secondary Education

The community controls the shape and form of its schools. A county, a state educational authority, a regional accrediting body, or a national organization can issue directives, give advice, conduct surveys, impose sanctions, even withhold money, but these exercise only partial controls. As the com-

munity decides, the school may be well organized or
ill organized; supported adequately, or barely, or luxuriously;
be housed in good buildings or historical relics; have a community program, or content itself with teaching the
Three R's. Depending on the amount of responsibility it
exercises, the results it will accept, the amount of money it
will pay, and the effort it will put into planning and organization, the community has control.

The controls which a community exercises over its school
system are of two orders—the controls of men and the controls
growing out of social and economic forces operating within
the community.

Controls by Men

The controls exercised by men are specific and tangible.
They are the controls of voters in electing members of the
school board and the town council, in approving or defeating
school bond issues. They are the controls of pressure groups
that would censor schoolbooks, of PTA meetings struggling
to reduce school problems to a common denominator of understanding, of teachers and administrators within the system
reaching for new opportunities and urging better facilities.
These are controls which express themselves ultimately in the
school budget and the school buildings, the salary schedule,
and in the year-to-year quality of the school program.

In the operation of the school these controls are paramount,
for they determine the relationship of the school to the community. A school which cannot win and hold community support, including financial support, must inevitably regress toward mediocrity, while a community which will not accept
responsibility, including financial responsibility, for its school,
is failing in its obligations to itself, and particularly to its young.

Controls by Community Evolution

Yet these controls of men, important as they are, operate
within the limits of the pattern established by the community

and must change as those patterns change. Communities add or lose industry, increase or decrease in wealth, add or lose population as the pattern of livelihood changes, draw closer to other communities as transportation and communication change, draw apart from other communities that are affected differentially by new developments. All such changes, in their turn, change the schools. Four such forms of change may be recognized:

Change in the nature and size of the community—Few communities remain static. Changes in population come with technological change, with the arrival of new activities or the departure of old ones. Farming communities tend to lose population as farms become increasingly mechanized and small units are merged into larger and more efficient ones. In such cases school districts should grow larger as the population grows smaller, and the tax base should become larger and firmer in relation to the number of children. Communities near cities become suburbanized and in time urbanized, so that a school may develop from a country school into a suburban school, and on to a raddled existence on the edge of an encroaching industrial slum, all within the active lifetime of a teacher in the system. Some communities leap directly from farm land to industrial backyard as when the United States Steel Corporation erects a new plant along the Delaware River. In such cases the tax base per child may grow smaller as the school population increases without commensurate increase in per-capita income, while the demands on the school system grow larger as it is forced to extend itself over wider ranges of ability and multiple objectives.

Changes in the concentration of school children—As communities change, the concentration of school children changes. A military base will bring a flood of transient children in the early primary grades; an upper-class suburban development will put pressure on the junior and senior high schools. An industrial community will demand industrial and vocational schools; a community which lives by commercial and service activities will demand a whole spectrum of services including adult education and eventually community-college programs. Demands for school services in a changing community can easily outstrip its legal capacity to pay for them.

Changes in the distribution of wealth—Larger in their scope than the community are social forces that tend to reduce extreme differences in wealth among the residents of a community. The organization of labor has brought about a degree of uniformity in wage scales which crosses both industrial and geographical lines. Taxation affects both accumulations of capital and the ability to accumulate capital. Thus the distribution of wealth, at least as it is expressed in power to purchase commodities and take advantage of opportunities, tends to approach a community norm. This means that communities have tended to become much more homogeneous with respect to family ability to purchase advantages—including educational advantages—for their children, and much more homogeneous with respect to the advantages they do purchase. Hence the schools are under constant pressure to provide equal opportunities for all of their pupils.

Changes in the bases of social mobility—As the community is affected by industrialization, concentration of population, and the distribution of wealth, it offers new opportunities for social mobility. The variety and availability of such opportunities are products of the emphasis on specialization and on professional occupations which result from industrialization and the concentrations of populations. The difference in kind of such opportunity is the difference between social movement thru the accumulation of personal wealth and social movement thru education. The latter is based on the equalization of educational opportunity, the broader distribution of wealth as translated into purchasing power, and the scarcity of trained specialists and professional men. Such social movement may require two generations to accomplish, whereas personal wealth may accomplish the same degree of social movement in one generation.

In sum, then, the trends within the community are all trends which tend to emphasize and develop education, both in and beyond the community.

Statewide and Nationwide Social and Economic Influences

Beyond the community, the workings of another set of background trends in American life become apparent. Seven such trends are important in their effect on education:

The Continuing Expansion of Credit

The enlargement of credit—consumer credit, commercial borrowing, and government borrowing—has been the basis for a steady rise in the American standard of living and for a steady increase in the cost of living. The effect of these increases upon education has been to develop the demand for enlarged opportunity before the money is available to pay for it.

The Continued Expansion of Scientific Knowledge

Perhaps the most important effect of the expansion of scientific knowledge upon our schools is the continued broadening of opportunity available to the secondary-school graduate. Until now, this expansion has had relatively little effect upon either the curriculum or the outlook of our secondary schools. There is no doubt that eventually both of these will be enlarged as the impact of the new knowledge is felt in our daily lives.

The Continued Expansion of Population

The effect of the rise in population is, of course, felt directly in terms of need for physical facilities and additional personnel.

So far it has not had a noticeable curriculum or methodological effect altho needs for changes in these areas to accommodate increasing numbers of students are felt and are being studied.

The Continued Reduction of Intercultural Discrimination

Because all cultural and economic groups meet in the secondary school, the long-time trend in the United States toward removing discriminations against certain religious and ethnic groups affects the school program. Since there is resistance to lowering the bars of divisiveness, deep emotions and explosive forces may be released that have repercussions in the high schools. Serious problems arise; the learning experiences within the school should in the long run help to resolve these problems.

The Steady Increase in the Productivity of the American Worker

Altho studies of productivity have so far been unsuccessful in assigning an exact value to increased productivity as distinct from the results of increased capital and raw materials, and improvements in distribution, there is evidence of a continuing increase in productivity which has had its own discrete effect upon the creation of additional national wealth and, in turn, upon the standard of living. There is also abundant evidence that the increase in productivity has been at least in part a result of the raising of the mean level of education of the labor force, a fact demonstrated by the decreasing percent of the labor force drawn from youth of school age and the increase in the percent of school-age youth actually in school or college. Hence, the use of our educational system, and particularly of our secondary schools, as a means of increasing per-capita productivity represents a trend of utmost importance in planning the future of our schools.

An important corollary to increasing productivity is increasing automation, which replaces industry's demand for unskilled manual labor with the need for highly skilled workmen to run complicated machines. The falling market for unskilled labor completely changes the role of the school with respect to individuals of low-average mentality. The school at one time sent such individuals into the labor force by the simple expedient of failing them, but now it must retain them in school and try to prepare them for some type of vocational usefulness.

New Forms of Occupations

Industrialization and concentration of population have already been noted as national trends which have their immediate effect at the community level. They also have had a national effect in forcing the development and expansion of specialized occupations at all levels—nonprofessional, semiprofessional, and professional. The development of these occupations has been accomplished largely thru the expansion of our educational system, on both the secondary and higher levels. In the process, there has been much redefinition of educational programs, resulting in new courses of study and the admission to education of new groups of students.

This process—the creation of new forms of education and the consequent opening of opportunity to new groups—has been under way for most of this century and has been responsible for much of the expansion of education. It is still under way and may be expected to bring about further expansion.

The Lengthening Span of Education

The statistics on increased enrolments in secondary schools and colleges may be summarized in the single fact that the average American who completes his schooling today has had at least four more years of attendance in school than his counterpart of 1900. The lengthening of the average number of years of education completed—already over 12 years for the population aged 20-24 years—is now invading the years set aside for higher education. The question then arises as to whether Grades XIII and XIV are to be defined as extensions of secondary education or the introduction to higher education. The decision on that question will be of major importance for both secondary and higher education.

The trends outside the community have an indirect relationship to education, but in terms of the effects they produce their influence is massive and formidable. It is to be noted that the first three of these trends—credit, science, population —are causes of educational change, while the last three— productivity, professionalization, and the lengthening of the educational span—are products of education which, in turn, have a feed-back effect by developing further emphasis on education which, in turn, produces more changes.

Controls Due to National Policy

Beyond these trends, which are the products of our society and its organization, are yet other trends which are a direct result of the official concerns of our government. Three such concerns are reflected in our secondary schools.

Defense

Defense as a primary concern of government has a direct effect upon our secondary schools. It creates job opportunities, thus enlarging the employment market and raising salary levels. For male youth, it represents the probability of service in the armed forces immediately after high school or immediately after college. Further, it opens an important number of specific careers in the armed forces, most of which include educational opportunities.

Recently we have had occasion to question the form that our future defense concerns will take. The United States is perhaps the only country in the world which can now afford to maintain both a full-sized defense establishment and a full-sized social development program including education, health, and welfare. The question must necessarily arise as to whether we can in fact continue to afford both without readjustments in our tax structure. An ancillary question is the inflationary or deflationary consequences of any change in our defense program.

Research

The concern of our government for the advancement of scientific knowledge is perhaps the most important single factor in the present effort to emphasize mathematics and science in both secondary school and college. To the extent that it has been a successful effort, it has changed the career plans of an undetermined number of secondary-school students. Its continuance is certain to have important effects upon higher education, both by supporting scientific research and by drawing more science students into higher education.

One present barrier to effective use of the federal government's interest in science teaching and research has been the fact alluded to earlier—that the consequences of recent developments in scientific knowledge have had little effect on the secondary-school curriculum.

Americans Overseas

As part of our effort to maintain world peace by maintaining world prosperity, Americans now serve as technicians, advisers, managers, and planners in many countries. Since we have no program of training for overseas service, other than limited programs for career diplomats, the task of educating for overseas service has devolved upon our regular educational establishment. So far, this is a problem which has not touched the secondary schools, or at any rate has not been recognized by them, but the number of Americans serving overseas is now sufficiently large to warrant attention at the community level.

The Brooding Disaster

Our governmental leaders, like our military leaders and, indeed, most of the population, are concerned with the threat of extinction resulting from the grim armaments of the atomic age and space warfare. To counteract these generalized fears or to allay their effects, strong efforts are made toward the greatest possible use of the manpower we have. Hence, the emphasis on talent and talent searches, the possibility of federal aid to education, and the development of scholarship programs. Perhaps these would have evolved under any circumstances tho it is doubtful that all would have reached their present extent. Whatever the cause, the federal government recently has been concerned with education and the expansion of education as never before in its history.

Four circles of trends have been outlined here as sets of influences affecting educational developments. Their exact effects are impossible to determine; yet, in a sense, these and related trends and movements are powerful controls of education. One or another of these trends affects every educational decision we make. In other words, they control the items that are considered in the final three sections of this chapter —the goals of secondary education, the tasks of the modern secondary school, and current provision for youth education. They must be recognized in making all our plans and decisions.

The Goals of Secondary Education

The controls of men and of their social units are the major determinants in the destiny of secondary education, but education in turn modifies the controls themselves. A lesser appraisal of the influence of institutional education in the history of our nation would be both inaccurate and deceptive. The reciprocal relationship is inevitable if we would subscribe to the great documents which so clearly crystallized the dreams and convictions of the founders of our nation and to the public statements of those who gave direction to its evolution. The hopes and dreams of people determine the goals toward which their institutions will move.

The goals of secondary education have undergone several major changes in the course of our history. The concept of free public education beyond the simplest rudiments of literacy was not generally accepted until well into the nineteenth century.

The earliest establishments of secondary education provided only for a few highly selected and favored young men who might be readied for college and the pulpit. This phase was followed by a reaction characterized by Franklin's concern for a more "practical" school, the demise of which has often been ironically attributed to the dearth of "practical" teachers. In turn, and with dramatic expansion as its most significant early attribute, there emerged the high school, conceived as free, public, and largely a steppingstone toward further and higher education.

This new institution, however, was not to be limited to this purpose, as the highly selective grammar school had been, nor was it to be privately controlled and privately supported as most of the academies had been. The American high school, greeted by success in its earliest form in the 1820's, and with legal provision for its support and control in the hands of the public, slowly and surely found itself during the century.

This institution was indigenous to this country, yet related by tradition to various institutions in Western Europe. It was unique in that it was open to all, regardless of circumstance of birth; served all thru adapting its program as the controls permitted; and worked to preserve and extend the rights and opportunities of each student within the framework of our social philosophy.

The goals of such a school are its very cause. The dream of education for all, enhanced by the vision of more and better education for all, was an inevitable outcome of the emerging social philosophy of a healthy, expanding democracy. The controls of men and their communities allowed for a better life, and in this better life was the necessity as well as the privilege of more extensive and meaningful education for all.

Yet goals, as such, are often only vaguely identifiable in the forms and functions of institutions. From our heritage of Western civilization there had come documents on the nature of the free man, his opportunities and his responsibilities.

There were clear statements concerning the responsibility of the school for preparing certain young people for further formal education. There was ample evidence of the increasing complexity of responsible citizenship in an expanding, industrial, democratic society. The role of formal educational institutions, as contrasted with informal sources of learning and particularly in relation to the home and the church, as positive influences in the lives of youth, has obviously changed as those institutions and influences have changed. Yet, as late as the first decade of this century there was no one basic statement of goals adequately representative of the new, expanding, amorphous, uniquely American program of education for youth —the modern American high school.

The Cardinal Principles

A committee of the NEA's Department of Secondary Education, dealing with the articulation of secondary schools and colleges, submitted a report to its sponsoring body in 1911.[1] It urged that college admission be based solely on the completion of any well-planned high-school course. This recommendation underscored the conviction that the high school had its own distinct function in a democratic society, and that it should plan its program to meet the needs of its students.

In 1913, a Commission on the Reorganization of Secondary Education was established by the National Education Association. Sixteen committees of this group prepared reports dealing with secondary-school administration and various subject fields. A reviewing committee consisting of the 16 chairmen and 10 members at large was organized. Following extensive correspondence and frequent meetings, the reviewing committee published its historic report in 1918.[2]

---

[1] Kingsley, Clarence D. "Report of the Committee of Nine on the Articulation of High School and College." *Proceedings, 1911*. Washington, D. C.: National Education Association, 1911. p. 559-67.

[2] National Education Association, Commission on Reorganization of Secondary Education. *Cardinal Principles of Secondary Education*. U. S. Department of the Interior, Bureau of Education, Bulletin 1918, No. 35. Washington, D. C.: Superintendent of Documents, Government Printing Office, 1918. 32 p.

Discussing the goals of education in a democracy, the report included this statement:

It is the ideal of democracy that the individual and society may find fulfillment each in the other. . . .

The purpose of democracy is so to organize society that each member may develop his personality primarily through activities designed for the well-being of his fellow members and of society as a whole.

Consequently, education in a democracy, both within and without the school, should develop in each individual the knowledge, interests, ideals, habits, and powers whereby he will find his place and use that place to shape both himself and society toward ever nobler ends.[3]

Recognizing changes in society, in the secondary-school population, and in educational theory, the Commission stated the now-familiar Cardinal Principles of Secondary Education. The main objectives of education in our society were listed as:

1. *Health*
2. *Command of fundamental processes*
3. *Worthy home membership*
4. *Vocation*
5. *Citizenship*
6. *Worthy use of leisure*
7. *Ethical character.*

The remainder of the report consisted of a development of the role of secondary education in contributing to the achievement of these objectives.

That this distinguished Commission should have published such a statement in 1918 was in itself significant. Most of the deliberations of the group were taking place during the height of a world war and at the peak of this nation's involvement in that conflict "to make the world safe for democracy."

Educational Policies Commission

Twenty years afterward, during the latter days of a catastrophic economic depression, the Educational Policies Com-

---

[3] *Ibid.*, p. 9.

mission published a major document on the goals of education. Its title, *The Purposes of Education in American Democracy,* indicates its wide scope.[4] It is based upon an analysis of what an "educated" person is and does. Drawing upon considerations of the social setting in which Americans live, their rights and responsibilities within that setting, and the role of education in contributing to the preservation and enhancement of the privilege of such citizenship, the Commission clustered the objectives of education, while not separable, under four headings for analysis:

1. The Objectives of Self-Realization
2. The Objectives of Human Relationship
3. The Objectives of Economic Efficiency
4. The Objectives of Civic Responsibility.[5]

Under each heading idealized descriptions are given of the skills and behavioral qualities of persons who have achieved these objectives. Forty-three such items are listed, with explanatory text elaborating on each one.

By implication, the statement of goals has special meaning for secondary education, for the degree of accomplishment of each objective will be a function of the degree of maturity of the individual and the amount of effective education which he may have experienced. In terms of its lucidity, its sound scholarship, and its pertinence to the problems of the times, this statement has been accepted as a second highly significant contribution to the clarification of the legitimate goals of American secondary education.

Imperative Needs of Youth

Among more recent reports that have had impact upon curriculum planning for secondary schools, a significant statement was issued by the National Association of Secondary-

[4] National Education Association and American Association of School Administrators, Educational Policies Commission. *The Purposes of Education in American Democracy.* Washington, D. C.: the Commission, 1938. 157 p.

[5] *Ibid.,* p. 47.

School Principals.[6] It states the imperative educational needs of all youth, and affirms that the school should meet these needs, which become the modern goals of education:

1. All youth need to develop saleable skills and those understandings and attitudes that make the worker an intelligent and productive participant in economic life. To this end, most youth need supervised work experience as well as education in the skills and knowledge of their occupations.

2. All youth need to develop and maintain good health and physical fitness and mental health.

3. All youth need to understand the rights and duties of the citizen of a democratic society, and to be diligent and competent in the performance of their obligations as members of the community and citizens of the state and nation, and to have an understanding of the nations and peoples of the world.

4. All youth need to understand the significance of the family for the individual and society and the conditions conducive to successful family life.

5. All youth need to know how to purchase and use goods and services intelligently, understanding both the values received by the consumer and the economic consequences of their acts.

6. All youth need to understand the methods of science, the influence of science on human life, and the main scientific facts concerning the nature of the world and of man.

7. All youth need opportunities to develop their capacities to appreciate beauty, in literature, art, music, and nature.

8. All youth need to be able to use their leisure time well and to budget it wisely, balancing activities that yield satisfactions to the individual with those that are socially useful.

9. All youth need to develop respect for other persons, to grow in their insight into ethical values and principles, to be able to live and work co-operatively with others, and to grow in the moral and spiritual values of life.

10. All youth need to grow in their ability to think rationally, to express their thoughts clearly, and to read and listen with understanding.[7]

---

[6] National Association of Secondary-School Principals. *Planning for American Youth.* (Revised edition; original printing, 1944.) Washington, D. C.: the Association, a department of the National Education Association, 1951. p. 9.

[7] *Ibid.*, p. 9.

Recapitulating Our Goals

In each of the above documents there is a stress upon the intimate relationship between the purposes of education and the social environment of the learner and the school. Each commission developed its statement during a time of national and international crisis. Despite the dramatic worldwide changes in the past half century and the consequent modifications in the function of our schools, there is an impressive constancy in the goals we seek. The paths we tread may alter to a disturbing degree, but our ultimate destination does not change.

In reviewing these and other statements of the goals of modern education, we find two common threads woven thru them all. There is concern that each individual shall have an opportunity to realize his maximum potential as a person. There is a parallel concern that the society of all men shall consequently be enhanced. These concerns are mutually supportive and basic to the goals of modern American education.

It is therefore appropriate that those responsible for this Yearbook state unequivocally the goals for secondary education as they accept and use them thruout the succeeding pages of this publication. After careful study and discussion the following statement has been accepted for this purpose:

> This Commission is concerned that this nation might fail to realize its greatest destiny because of inadequate provision for the education of our youth. Its members believe that American youth represents our greatest national resource and that if such a resource is to be a firm foundation for the future greatness of this nation, a program devoted to the development of American youth must have great goals, the achievement of which will tax our clearest thinking and demand our maximum efforts.
>
> This Yearbook Commission acknowledges and supports, as the legitimate and critically important goals of our secondary schools:

The maximum development of all the mental, moral, emotional, and physical powers of the individual, to the end that he may enjoy a rich life thru the realization of worthy and desirable personal goals, and

The maximum development of the ability and desire in each individual to make the greatest possible contribution to all humanity thru responsible participation in, and benefit from, the great privileges of American citizenship.

We are aware that times and circumstances provide many agencies, including the home, the church, and a multitude of means of communication thru which young people may develop these powers.

We nevertheless hold that the *public secondary school,* open to all and available to all, and representing the public, as it is supported and controlled by all, has the responsibility for guaranteeing to each American youth the opportunity for achieving *self-realization* and *social effectiveness.*

The goals of the school may never be fully achieved; yet the commitment to strive for their accomplishment is binding upon all who would faithfully serve the cause of American secondary education today.

Tasks of the Modern Secondary School

Basic agreement on the goals of education leads to the next consideration. What must the secondary school do to contribute its legitimate and reasonable part toward the achievement of these goals?

Chapter II of this volume states the task as a whole—meeting the needs of all—in terms of a humane philosophy of education. Chapter III sets forth the task in some detail in terms of the range of functions thru which the secondary school advances in a variety of realistic efforts to achieve its goals.

Basic to the whole question of the task are questions as to the scope, jurisdiction, and methods of secondary education. The final answer is still in evolution, to be worked out by the American people in their thousands of communities. The thinking of the Commission is expressed in the paragraphs that follow.

Scope

Contrary to the old concept that the high school was to serve only those who sought its services and conformed to rigid requirements, it becomes increasingly clear that the clientele of the school must include all youth within the community and that the school cannot be excused if it abdicates this position.

Changing forces in each community may complicate this task, and changing times may vary its nature, but those responsible for secondary education must courageously persist in serving all, at least to the extent of awareness and action in furthering their progress toward self-realization and social effectiveness. This includes youth who may never actually be enrolled in the public school; it involves threats to moral and mental health which may be extant in the community.

If the secondary school is to serve all youth, it is obvious that it must shed any residual coloration as a selective institution. This change in the role of the secondary school often leads to serious misunderstanding even on the part of well-informed adults. Continued interpretation of the school's responsibility is needed.

Such an awareness should lead to a working relationship among all institutions and agencies, public and private, which serve youth. This cooperative relationship must be shared among homes, churches, social agencies, custodial institutions, service clubs, recreation councils, museums, commercial recreation centers, and a host of volunteer organizations and governmental agencies. The role of each must be agreed upon.

The public high school, as the one institution open and available to all youth, regardless of family background, is the logical center for coordinating all efforts to contribute to the welfare of all youth. The absence or inadequacy of other youth-serving agencies in the community mandates aggressive work on the part of those who administer the school to encourage the community to create needed agencies to fill vacuums which are not legitimately the province of the school. And it forces frequent reconsideration of just what is the school's province.

The Problem of Jurisdiction

Just how far into the lives of youth should the public schools reach? This question, of course, is one which has no simple answer. Yet a balance must be achieved among the services for which the school must be held clearly responsible, the resources available to the school, and provisions for the welfare of youth available outside the jurisdiction of the school. And herein lies the confusion which often accompanies any discussion of the "functions" of the school.

The truism that no two American schools are alike has its parallel in that the specific tasks of no two schools can be identical. The youth population, the community in which they live, the range of other institutions, the very mores of the adult and youth populations will inevitably condition the tasks of the school. Thus, in a large city, liberally endowed with many institutions and agencies available to youth, the public secondary school must avoid trespassing into areas already served by others. In contrast, for a less sophisticated community, where the school may be the only organized agency common to the youth population, the tasks of the school will rightly cover a much wider range.

The Problem of "How"

A cavalier "statement" of goals without commitment to them can be more dangerous than useful. It is the actual and whole-hearted acceptance of goals by the faculty and by those who support and control education that is so important to the task of the school. Anything less leads to confusion or hypocrisy or both. Thus, constant restudy of the goals and the related tasks is a basic professional obligation.

The degree of successful accomplishment of these tasks will be gauged by the behavior of its products. In an effort to help schools assess their work, a recent study conducted by the National Association of Secondary-School Principals and the Educational Testing Service, with the assistance of the Russell Sage Foundation gives great promise of specific clarification of the critical tasks of the modern high school.[8]

Current Provisions for Youth Education

American secondary education has long been recognized as serving youth aged 12 thru 17. Those below age 14 are in school almost as universally as are children of elementary-school age. Those aged 14 thru 17—the traditional high-school years—are also in school, to the extent of 88.2 percent of the age group, or nearly 9 out of 10. And over a third—35.4 percent—of the next group, aged 18 and 19 years, are in either high school or college.[9]

[8] French, Will, and associates. *Behavioral Goals of General Education in High School.* New York: Russell Sage Foundation, 1957. 247 p.

[9] In October 1956, the percents of the population enrolled in "regular" schools, of the age groups from 10 thru 24 years, were as follows:

10 thru 13 years	99.2 percent	18 and 19 years	35.4 percent
14 and 15 years	96.9 percent	20 thru 24 years	12.8 percent
16 and 17 years	78.4 percent		

The 9,540,000 aged 14 thru 17 years were distributed as follows:

Enrolled in "regular" schools:

Below Grade IX	1,050,000 or	11.0 percent
In Grades IX thru XII	7,196,000 or	75.4 percent
In college or professional school	167,000 or	1.8 percent
Total enrolled	8,413,000 or	88.2 percent
Not enrolled	1,127,000 or	11.8 percent

Of those not enrolled, a small fraction, which amounted to 1.6 percent of the total population aged 14 thru 19 years, were in "special" schools outside the regular school system, such as trade schools or business colleges.

See: U. S. Department of Commerce, Bureau of the Census. *School Enrollment: October 1956.* Current Population Reports, Series P-20, No. 74. Washington, D. C.: the Bureau, April 30, 1957. 11 p.

Some of these young Americans are in school because the law requires their attendance; others, because the family expects it. Some are there because their friends are in school and they seek the social warmth of doing things with their peers. Some have specific plans for their future and the hope and faith that the school will contribute to those plans. Others are there because in our industrial society there is no other place for them.

With the growth of American secondary education, the tasks and accomplishments of the school have changed. Individual leaders, who courageously pioneered programs of more meaningful learning, brought about successive steps in such changes, and various professional commissions and study groups have had impact as well. In fact, citizens who may not have been inside a high-school classroom during the past 50 years are surprised and bemused at what is to be witnessed in the course of a visit to a modern high school. This change has occurred because of changes in the world outside the school, in the nature of the school population, and in our knowledge of how learning takes place; and because of the activities of professional leaders in encouraging the adaptation of the school to conform to these changes. This latter activity has included efforts to influence the controls of men to the end that individuals and communities shall support and require an increasingly effective educational program for youth.

A complete inventory of the contributions of such leadership would be impossible, but it is well to recall certain major and conspicuously effective legislation, studies, and movements which during the past half century have helped to improve secondary education in America:

1. Provisions for specific vocational education were encouraged by the enactment of the Smith-Hughes Act of 1917. Subsequent additional acts not only involved the federal government in supporting certain broader aspects of the programs of secondary education, but by example encouraged such schools as did not participate directly in the federal program to provide instruction in agriculture, homemaking, distributive education, and various trades and industrial arts.

2. The influence of the Progressive Education Association, altho usually acknowledged as having had most influence on childhood education, did directly and indirectly affect method and morale within our better secondary schools. Controversial in retrospect and subject to much misinterpretation, the Association nevertheless championed and made possible practices based upon research and philosophical inquiry to the end that our teachers, parents, pupils, and general public work in a more cordial, encouraging, and intelligent relationship than might have been the case had the Association never come into being.[10]

3. The Eight-Year Study, sponsored by the Progressive Education Association and financed by the Carnegie Corporation and the General Education Board, helped to improve relationships between high schools and higher education.[11]

The cooperating secondary schools were in effect freed from specific college entrance requirements for a period, to permit curriculum adaptations which the schools felt were desirable for their students; a high degree of success of graduates from these high schools in their subsequent college careers was reported by the study. The findings were published in the early 1940's, when their importance was overshadowed by preoccupation with World War II. But the study did result in some modifications of college entrance requirements, and also more realistic relationships among schools and colleges whose officers are aware of the implications of the Eight-Year Study.

4. The Cooperative Study of Secondary School Standards, initiated by the North Central Association, was begun in 1934, with the six regional accrediting associations as collaborators. More than the development of the Evaluative Criteria as a mere instrument for gauging accreditation, this study encouraged local school staffs to accept the procedures for use of the instrument as a continuous basis for improvement of the school.[12] Such evaluations have contributed much to the liberalizing of secondary education and to the confidence of school faculties in self-study.

---

[10] Meyer, Adolphe E. *An Educational History of the American People.* New York: McGraw-Hill Book Co., 1957. 444 p.

[11] Progressive Education Association, Commission on the Relation of School and College. *Adventure in American Education.* (Five volumes.) New York: Harper and Brothers, 1942, 1943.

[12] Cooperative Study of Secondary School Standards. *Evaluative Criteria.* 1950 edition. Washington, D. C.: the Study, 1950. 305 p.

5. *Education for All American Youth* and its revision sub-titled *A Further Look* were published by the NEA-AASA Educational Policies Commission in 1944 and 1952, respectively.[13] Here are fictional descriptions of the solutions to very real problems of providing meaningful education for the great variety of American youth. These two works, drawing on the best creative thought, set a standard for all those who have responsibility for secondary education to use. As a vision of an ideal, they told the story of what may become, one day, a sound and comprehensive program for rural and urban youth. How much influence these books have had on the thinking, hoping, and planning for better high schools is difficult to estimate, but that it has been great is certain.

6. Growing in influence thruout recent decades has been the National Association of Secondary-School Principals, which in its continuing program has contributed to the professional leadership of the school administrators most directly concerned with the high schools. Its Committee on the Orientation of Secondary Education, with financial help from the Carnegie Foundation, published reports on the issues and on the function of secondary education.[14] Its statement of the 10 imperative needs of youth has influenced practice in many secondary schools.[15]

7. The U. S. Office of Education has maintained a continuing program of leadership and research on varied aspects of second-ary education. Two major projects were the comprehensive research studies by the National Survey of Secondary Education, which reported in 1932,[16] and the sponsorship of

[13] National Education Association and American Association of School Administrators, Educational Policies Commission. *Education for All American Youth.* Washington, D. C.: the Commission, 1944. 421 p.

National Education Association and American Association of School Administrators, Educational Policies Commission. *Education for All American Youth, A Further Look.* Revised edition. Washington, D. C.: the Commission, 1952. 402 p. $2.

[14] National Association of Secondary-School Principals, Committee on the Orientation of Secondary Education. "Issues of Secondary Education." *Bulletin of the Department of Secondary-School Principals* 20: 1-364; January 1936.

"Functions of Secondary Education." *Bulletin of the Department of Secondary-School Principals* 21: 1-263; January 1937.

[15] National Association of Secondary-School Principals, Committee on Curriculum Planning and Development. "The Imperative Needs of Youth of Secondary-School Age." *Bulletin of the National Association of Secondary-School Principals* 31: 1-144; March 1947.

[16] U. S. Department of the Interior, Office of Education. *National Survey of Secondary Education.* Bulletin 1932, No. 17. (Reported in 28 monographs.) Washington, D. C.: Superintendent of Documents, Government Printing Office, 1932, 1933.

the National Commission on Life Adjustment Education for Youth.[17] Probably the greatest value derived from the life-adjustment program lay in the creation of state committees, including persons from without as well as within the profession of education, to take a careful and critical look at the provisions by each state for the education of its youth. In many states the actions of these committees modified to an appreciable degree the controls of men and of communities in demanding and supporting more extensive provisions for youth education.

In addition to the above, evidence has been gathered thru many studies of young people who have left school before graduation. On national, state, and local levels, these disturbing findings have provoked many schools to action on curriculum offerings, special provisions for the gifted and the mentally deficient, and a more serious concern for accurate knowledge about the youth to be served by the school.

Study and experimentation continue, whether by unheralded individual teachers thru action research, or nationwide programs generously underwritten by industrial foundations. The high school of today is a vital and changing institution, and is becoming increasingly responsive to the complex demands placed upon it.

From this inheritance, then, we can briefly indicate the provision for youth thruout America today. Thru our faith in the importance of education beyond childhood, we have created many schools of great variety.

Some 30,000 separate attendance units for secondary education blanket this land. About 4000 are nonpublic high schools. There is the highly selective independent school which aims to prepare boys for admission to a limited number of highly esteemed older colleges and universities. The parochial secondary school, seeking to weave the tenets of a specific reli-

---

[17] Federal Security Agency, Office of Education, Commission on Life Adjustment Education for Youth. *Vitalizing Secondary Education*. Bulletin 1951, No. 3. Washington, D. C.: Superintendent of Documents, Government Printing Office, 1951. 106 p.

Cummings, Howard H., and others. (For the Second Commission on Life Adjustment Education for Youth.) *A Look Ahead in Secondary Education*. U. S. Department of Health, Education, and Welfare, Office of Education, Bulletin 1954, No. 4. Washington, D. C.: Superintendent of Documents, Government Printing Office, 1954. 105 p.

gious faith thru its total instructional program, represents another type. The military school, the girls' boarding school, the country day school, and other forms occur. Some 11 percent of secondary-school students are in nonpublic schools.

The remaining 89 percent are to be found in 26,000 tax-supported and publicly controlled schools, each part of a state plan for youth education. Among these are one-room schools serving sparsely populated areas and, because of their size, limited in the quality and variety of program offerings available to each youth. At the other extreme may be found the urban high school enrolling thousands of youth, who may be penalized thru loss of personal attention. Between these extremes lie the thousands of public high schools—junior, junior-senior, four-year "regular," rural consolidated—each with its own program emphasis, expenditure level, special services, and teaching talent, and each varying in the extent to which it meets the educational needs of all the youth within its area of service.

Altho we are far from the achievement of our ideals concerning youth and altho critics continue to remind us of our real as well as imagined failures, the high schools of this land are continuing to serve more youth better, decade by decade. Today, nearly 9 out of every 10 young people of high-school age are in school. Of this large group, at least half will continue to seek some form of post-high-school education. More money is being spent for youth education than ever before in our history, and much more is needed. More parents and adult nonparents are contributing to the control of youth education than ever before, and more teachers are teaching youth. The American high school has come of age.

reaching

the needs

of all

reaching the needs of all

TODAY'S YOUNG American must grow to maturity and find his place in a bewildering world. Helping him in that process is the secondary school. Chapter I describes some of the characteristics of the setting and some of the requirements which the secondary schools should meet.

Many divergent pressures impinge on the school, some of which seem to be unreconcilable. For the administrator and the classroom teacher the age-old problem of finding unity in diversity is more complex now that nearly 90 percent of the boys and girls aged 14 thru 17 are in school (as compared with less than 10 percent in 1900). Teachers and administrators feel the mounting pressures of demands from many quarters. The values of the past must be appreciated and preserved, while the needs of the explosive present and enigmatic future must be foreseen and met. For each student, there is the ever-present task of being one's own individual self when everybody is being pushed into patterns. Adolescents are in the middle. They feel, but do not yet understand, the pressures upon them. Somehow, they must be helped to find their own places and to learn to deal with the continuing tensions of our times.

39

Essentially the problem with respect to American youth of secondary-school age is this: How can the school help each individual to discover and develop his best potentialities so that he may be personally happy and socially useful? To realize the goal, the educator must know the material with which he works.

An ancient proverb says, "A man of knowledge increaseth strength." The administrator must know what society's needs are and how individuals respond to them. He must know youth and be able to identify and reckon with the forces which affect them. He must be able to understand and appraise individual differences. Constant effort must be exerted to humanize educational institutions which have been adapted to mass education. The school exists for the student, not the student for the school.

When the school meets the needs of all, it will do so by meeting the needs of *each,* and no two are alike.

An Operational Concept of Student Needs

The school will be effective in proportion to the degree to which society's needs and each individual's needs are appraised and met by the school program.

It is easy to be confused in thinking about student needs.[1] During one of the projects sponsored by the Cooperative Program in Educational Administration, several administrators were exploring possible changes in programs based on student needs. Fortunately, because they were doing a thoro job, they came to realize that they were not discussing purely student needs. They were thinking also of what the students "needed" to do in order to make administration easier and so were viewing student needs thru the bias of their own desires.

We have long accepted the fact that students have biological needs and that the school should concern itself with them.

---

[1] Brink, William G. "Introduction: The Youth-Needs Motive in Secondary Education." *Adapting the Secondary-School Program to the Needs of Youth.* Fifty-Second Yearbook, Part I, National Society for the Study of Education. Chicago: University of Chicago Press, 1953. p. 3.

However, many students suffer from physical defects which are not apparent to the teacher, and which are ignored by the school. These defects decrease the pupils' ability to learn. Medical science continues to demonstrate that mind and body are inextricably related.

In recent years knowledge of human behavior has been extended so that workable theories have been constructed about "psychological needs." These needs are even less obvious than physical needs, but they may be identified, and their potency understood.

Some needs take precedence over others, while some needs depend upon other needs for fulfilment. Some individual needs are universal. The individual must know how to respond to a great variety of social pressures, many of which are in conflict with his individual needs. Needs change as the individual develops. The tenth-grader decides he will drink orange juice because he believes it will both add to his competence in athletics and improve his complexion so that his girl will respond favorably to him. The successful pursuit of the girl modifies his vocational goal, thereby changing his academic needs, and so on, ad infinitum.

Any schematic design of human motivation is somewhat arbitrary and artificial. This is especially true of a listing of the highly interrelated needs of youth. However, the administrator needs some operational concept of student needs if he is to provide leadership in reaching the needs of all. Therefore, the administrator may find it useful to view his task in serving students under three headings:

1. Needs imposed by the culture—developmental tasks
2. Societal demands
3. The individual.

Requirements of the Culture—Developmental Tasks

One of the most promising developments of recent years is our increasing awareness of the part culture plays in shaping an individual. The ways of living built up by a group of human beings do much to shape his behavior, character, and personality. Benedict has written that "until we are intelligent as to its [culture's] laws and varieties, the main complicating facts of human life must remain unintelligible." [2] Since we believe that cultural pressures are so crucial during adolescence, we place developmental tasks first in three types of student needs.

Havighurst has called the goals imposed by the culture the *developmental tasks*.[3] The term *developmental* is significant. The tasks, or the skills, attitudes, and understanding essential to the task, must be learned at the appropriate time. The individual is ready to learn specific skills in relation to his correct "task" at the stage of his development when the task is important to him. For instance, when being able to dance is essential for learning a new relationship to his age mates, a youth will learn this skill more readily than at any other time. Furthermore, the sequence of these tasks is about the same for all adolescents altho it may vary with individual boys and girls. "When the body is ripe, and society requires, and the self is ready to achieve a certain task, the teachable moment has come."[4] In order that the timing be right, it is essential that the student personnel services, with full participation by teachers, be functioning adequately.

If an individual bypasses a task at the proper time, he may be more or less handicapped for the rest of his life. If a teen-ager fails to establish a mature give-and-take relationship with his age mates of both sexes, he may resort to childish patterns of behavior in adult life. In fact, successful negotiation of adolescent tasks may neutralize the harmful effects of prior failures in adjustment.[5] Failure to become adequately adjusted to the requirements of adolescence may be a serious matter

---

[2] Benedict, Ruth. *Patterns of Culture*. Boston: Houghton Mifflin Company, 1934. p. 2.

[3] Havighurst, Robert J. *Human Development and Education*. New York: Longmans, Green and Co., 1953. 338 p.

[4] *Ibid.*, p. 5.

[5] Sullivan, Harry S. *The Interpersonal Theory of Psychiatry*. New York: W. W. Horton and Company, 1953. See Chapters 16, 17, and 18 for a discussion of the crucial nature of adolescence for success in "the business of living."

because this may be the last and most vital failure in a series of failures to make reasonable progress in developmental tasks. In working at tasks with his own age group, a youth has the supporting context of others in the same boat, who, busy with their own development, are less apt than otherwise to be critical of him.

The Tasks

What are the developmental tasks? Havighurst lists six tasks for younger boys and girls, and 10 for adolescents.[6] A statement of five tasks, made by Corey, may be functionally adequate for all schools except those well advanced in the use of this framework for developing their programs.[7]

1. *Coming to terms with their own bodies*—Adolescence is the time when bodily changes are not only pronounced but are perceived by adolescents as such. This is the period when boys and girls begin to take on the physical characteristics of adults. Growth is irregular, one part of the body maturing before another. Awkwardness and sometimes painful adjustments accompany the many changes.

This is also the time when appearance becomes extremely important. Adolescents are much concerned over such matters as overweight, skin blemishes, and wearing eyeglasses. Any irregularity in physical feature or lack of ability in physical prowess may be a source of much discomfort to boys or girls because they believe that it is a handicap in their social relationships.

2. *Learning new relationships to their age mates*—Anyone familiar with the special vocabulary of the adolescent can hardly fail to recognize the closed-shop character of this age. Few things mean more to adolescents than group acceptance

---

[6] Havighurst, Robert J., *op. cit.*, p. 159-76. (Discusses implications for the curriculum.)

[7] Corey, Stephen M. "The Developmental Tasks of Youth." *The American High School: Its Responsibility and Opportunity.* Eighth Yearbook of the John Dewey Society. (Edited by Hollis L. Caswell.) New York: Harper and Brothers, 1946. Chapter 5, p. 70-99.

and approval, and they will go to any length to win them. Quarrels with parents become frequent as youth try to meet the requirements of both the group and the home. Parents do not understand why the adolescent is rebellious one day, then loving and thoughtful the next. It is in this period that the youngster develops heterosexual relationships. Both boys and girls are concerned with being attractive to the opposite sex and are eager to learn the skills which move them along successfully toward this goal. American youngsters have difficulty in making a satisfactory heterosexual adjustment because there is still much that is unrealistic in the way in which sexual matters are discussed in the home. With the changing nature of masculine and feminine roles in American society, much more attention should be given to the demands of this developmental task.

3. *Achieving independence from parents*—Eventually boys and girls must go it alone, without the aid of parents. The process of moving from dependence to independence is a gradual one, which is often painful to parents. Wanting to stay out late, resenting supervision, and wanting the family car are focal points of tension. But these, as well as some forms of overt rebellion, are usually nothing more than the adolescent's only means of showing that he is growing exactly according to plan. He must break away from the parental home, and, in our complex and ever-changing society, he cannot just be shoved out of the nest and made to fly in a few days. The process of gaining independence is slow and ambivalent. Parents often unwittingly hold on to the adolescent, making it difficult for him to achieve independence. The increasing necessity for economic dependence on parents makes achievement of this task difficult.

4. *Achieving adult social and economic status*—This task is related to achieving independence from parents. Adolescents are more or less preoccupied with the need to have their own spending money. Having a job, so that it is not necessary to ask parents for money, is important to them, and a sign of growing up. Yet the economic system makes it increasingly

difficult for an adolescent to achieve any kind of economic independence.

In order to show their adulthood, they drive fast, stay out late at night, and are somewhat extreme in dress; girls use too much make-up. Their actions often arouse parental disapproval; yet, all these forms of behavior are symptoms of the adolescent's effort to become what adults profess they want him to be—an independent citizen.

5. *Acquiring self-confidence and a system of values*—All persons need to feel adequate; they need to feel that the world will not overpower them. During adolescence, boys and girls are trying themselves out. To be a self-respecting individual means to be able to stand on one's own feet. Much of the activity of adolescents is in the nature of self-discovery and establishing self-confidence.

During this period, given opportunity, they ask profound questions about the good, the true, and the beautiful; idealism reaches new heights. Commitments are made. In some ways it is a dangerous time in that choices are made on inadequate understanding. Nevertheless, the idealism of the adolescent has not yet been dulled by experience, and he gives himself wholeheartedly to a cause. Boys and girls should have many opportunities to raise serious questions and to explore their meaning. It is dangerous to take for granted that because we live under a democratic form of government, all citizens understand the implications of democratic principles. Insights into concepts such as the dignity and integrity of man must be gained anew by each generation. Boys and girls need opportunity to explore the rationale which supports our value system.

How Students Work on the Tasks

The thoughtful administrator will observe that adolescents *do* work at these tasks, and that boys and girls must become skilful in performing those tasks which the culture holds essential. As Corey so well puts it, these "are tasks at which adolescents insist upon working much of the time *irrespective of what adults think they should be doing.*"[8] *Actually, the school is the adolescent's social laboratory.* Here, with his own age mates, he works on these tasks. Unfortunately, many teachers, driven by their own needs, cannot either accept these tasks as legitimate goals for the pupil or recognize the dynamic power with which the student is motivated to work on them.

Altho the Seven Cardinal Principles are somewhat related to developmental tasks, there is a subtle but highly important difference. The Cardinal Principles are expressed in the future tense. Developmental tasks stress the present tense. The student cannot be satisfied with studying "about" his body which he will someday know how to use effectively; he is currently involved in making vital adjustments to major bodily changes. He may find satisfaction in choosing an occupation into which he will some day enter, but even in this respect, he must make progress now in the process of moving toward his selection. If questioned, he would like work experience now. Again, he cannot be contented with the promise that some day he will be able to conduct himself well at a social affair—this he wants to be able to do now!

The administrator who wishes to learn firsthand about the students' involvement in these tasks may do so with ease. For instance, having students write anonymous compositions on such topics as "How it feels to be growing up," or "If I had three wishes," or "If I had $500," will reveal some of their preoccupations. The teacher may then note the nature and frequency of adolescent problems. A checklist or inventory given to adolescents will yield valuable information on specific problems related to developmental tasks.

With rapidly growing enrolment in high school, the administrator must pay increasing attention to the problems created by postponement of function. For instance, delayed marriage and delayed entry into an occupation, which are recent cultural developments, have created tension for all concerned. However, at this writing there appears to be a trend

---

[8] *Ibid.,* p. 84.

toward earlier marriage. Popular writings about adolescents suggest that "going steady" (or "steadily") vs. "playing the field" presents a major problem of youthful choice. This may create a whole new set of problems for the administrator. While achieving emotional independence from parents and other adults is a continuing process, begun long before adolescence, it becomes critical during these years. When an individual is ready to function on his own, our society makes it difficult for him to do so.

For the administrator, the important fact to note is that boys and girls *must* become skilful in performing those tasks which the culture holds to be essential. Whether thru organized education or by other means, these are goals toward which they should move. Developmental tasks are real. Meanwhile, adults tend to view activities of children and youth as "preparation for life" or as play.

Few things would serve young people better than for adults to take them seriously and to realize that play for children is their work and that whatever adolescents are involved in is held as seriously in their value system as the work and other problems of adults. Furthermore, working at the tasks imposed by the culture will take up much of the adolescents' time and energy.

The curriculum is not only what the school prescribes; rather it is what the pupil extracts from it on the basis of what he needs. Cultural tasks are essential for survival. In this time of rapid change, tasks viewed by youth as important may not make sense to adults in the light of their own experience. It is essential to realize that they *do* make sense to the adolescent and that he behaves in terms of *his value system*. The individual's self-respect is deeply affected by the way he feels he is performing these tasks.

Contrary to popular opinion, which tends to charge youth with irresponsibility, experience with one group of talented students shows that they are eager to think thru and discuss the basis and implications of value systems.[9] More opportunity

---

[9] Morris, Glyn. "A Stimulating Seminar for Rural Youth." *Journal of the National Association of Women Deans and Counselors* 21: 31-34; October 1957.

is needed for them to formulate serious questions and to follow thru on the ramifications which go with answering them. It seems clear that a system of education closely geared to a textbook—where answers are given, and therefore the questions already raised—does not provide the opportunity for students to ask important questions.

A wide-range picture of the adolescents' viewpoint can be found in a recently published summary of an extensive study of high-school student opinion on everything from politics to parents. The findings add support to the "developmental task" approach in building a program for secondary-school youth. It also presents some thought-provoking data on the ineffectiveness of citizenship training as practiced in our schools, and supports the emphasis expressed in this Yearbook for greater concern with the individual pupil.[10]

Administrative Approach

Altho the home, the church, and other community agencies have important parts in helping youth become skilful in their developmental tasks, the school has a major responsibility as society's most thorogoing institution for training youth. In this respect the administrator can work along these lines:

Help teachers become familiar with developmental tasks— At best the task of developing a unified point of view among the faculty will be difficult. Teachers come from different backgrounds and bring to their teaching a variety of experiences. It is not safe to assume unity of purpose or understanding. Commonly-held attitudes may be worked toward thru a systematic child-study program of high-school students, similar to that outlined by the Institute for Child Study, University of Maryland.[11] Where it is accepted, the concept of developmental tasks offers an operational framework for thinking and planning.

---

[10] Remmers, H. H., and Radler, D. H. *The American Teenager.* Indianapolis: Bobbs-Merrill Co., 1957. 267 p.

[11] Prescott, Daniel A. *A Child in the Educative Process.* New York: McGraw-Hill Book Co., 1957. 500 p.

Utilize the motivational value of developmental tasks— Teachers usually want to find ways of motivating students. Many lessons or projects are started with efforts to stimulate student interest. Much material in the literature studied in school relates to developmental tasks. Discussions can be enlivened by relating topics to a developmental task or tasks. For example, the psychological realities of a situation in a piece of literature should be made real, and fully explored. Such a work as *The Forsyte Saga* involves conflict between two generations and offers excellent opportunity for discussing current attitudes of adolescents toward adults. Many novels and plays offer similar opportunities. Of a character, the teacher can ask the class, "How do you think he feels?" thereby opening up the psychological implications of the situation.

Provide experiences in the developmental tasks in subject areas—Homemaking courses, already more or less geared to developmental tasks, might be expanded to take in more students, especially boys. More opportunity to carry on community projects is necessary. There is scarcely a community which could not benefit from the guided endeavors of high-school students. Unsightly spots may be beautified, services provided, and goods manufactured. Students can do much to improve the surroundings of their schools, especially in small communities. The Citizenship Education Project of Teachers College, Columbia University, has listed hundreds of worthwhile school and community projects which are possible for students, together with materials which can help teachers organize and carry out these projects effectively.[12] The projects are listed on a chart which shows the subject areas to which each might be related. This is a rich and stimulating source of ideas for secondary schools in need of laboratory practice in citizenship. Work-study programs, now in existence in a number of schools, especially in the South, provide students with valuable training and a corresponding feeling of maturity.

---

[12] A descriptive price list of publications is available on request to the Citizenship Education Project, Teachers College, Columbia University, New York, N. Y.

Develop and strengthen the small guidance unit—Unlike the elementary school, where each class is a homeroom, the formal curriculum of the high school does not lend itself to providing for experiences of immediate concern to the students. For this reason a small guidance unit, such as the homeroom, is essential. When the daily homeroom period is long enough and when the teacher is trained to conduct it, students can participate in many worthwhile activities related to their developmental tasks. This is a neglected potential in many high schools primarily because teachers lack the skills and administrative support necessary for leadership in their homeroom responsibilities.

The homeroom is not necessarily the only small guidance unit; certain types of "core" programs may also serve this purpose. As school programs are currently operating, however, the homeroom seems the most likely arrangement for meeting the need for the small guidance unit.

Develop and strengthen the student activity program—The school council, clubs, and intramural athletics are all reservoirs of experience for youth in terms of their developmental tasks. These should be examined from time to time to make certain that all potentialities are being utilized. Far too many student councils are nothing more than adjuncts to administration. One would hesitate to assign a class of students to a teacher not trained in his subjectmatter area. Yet, learning the "art" or "process" of democracy by way of a school council is presumed possible without skilled leadership. It needs a teacher skilled in the subtleties of group technics, and having an understanding of the meaning and place of democratic procedures as applied to the maturity level of students and the limitations and potentialities of self-direction in a public school. The skills students need to learn in order to operate successfully in such a complex activity as a school council require at least the same teaching effort as does mathematics or language.

Broaden the concept of guidance—Each teacher has opportunities to relate the formal curriculum to the needs of youth. However, to do this successfully, teachers need help in becoming sensitive to individual needs and potentialities. Too often, they perceive guidance as the work of only the specialist. The administrator can support the teachers in all situations where they are striving for flexibility of program and appropriate experience for youth. Guidance can be effective only where there are opportunities for boys and girls to do what is necessary for all phases of their growth and development.

View discipline thru developmental tasks—Adolescents whose behavior seems inappropriate may be working on their development tasks. Rebellion and insubordination may simply be signs of reaching out for independence and maturity. The principal may find his disciplinary measures more judicious and appropriate if he keeps this in mind and brings his teachers along with him in his growing understanding of the principles of good discipline.

Society's Needs

Reference has been made to the changing nature of society and to the pressures resulting from the new demands imposed upon modern man. Youth must find his place in a world of rapid communication, mobility, and technological change. While it is essential for the administrator to know and respond to the developmental tasks of youth because these are tasks which youth view as important, he must also see youth in relation to specific aspects of society's needs and *help each youth accept these responsibilities as his.*

It is the administrator's responsibility to give leadership in translating the developmental tasks of youth into specific learning experiences. In this process youth is helped to see the relationship between his goals and society's. He "accepts" them as his "needs." The starting point is the individual's needs. Beginning with these and the motivation they provide, the skilful teacher helps students to become articulate about expressing them as specific goals, immediate and remote. Also he helps to develop the necessary skills for achieving in them. There is continuing evaluation of progress and redefinition of goals in the light of new insights and achievements. Practically speaking, it is to this end that schools are established—that society may be preserved. Preservation, however, is contingent on a balanced relationship between individual and societal needs.

In these days of rapid mobility and interdependence, it may be helpful for the administrator to view societal needs geographically: local, state, national, and international. Local communities should see themselves in a wider context. For instance, the problem of migration could form the core of a program for the study of many societal needs.

Any statement of what modern society in the United States requires of its members is likely to be incomplete and soon to become obsolete. Who could have predicted in 1938 that the United States in 1958 would have armed forces stationed all over the globe? One might generalize by stating that the United States needs "healthy, useful, thinking citizens"; but in shaping an inclusive and complicated program of education, the administrator requires a more specific blueprint.

Always it must be said that society requires of its members the development of their maximum potentialities in the basic skills necessary for communication: reading, writing, and computation. The school has long since accepted these as major goals. Unfortunately, they have often been viewed as goals in themselves, unrelated to the ends for which they are means, or they have been taught en masse, rather than to individuals. Interestingly enough, in 1950 in response to the question: "What is the most important thing young people should get out of high school?" Elmo Roper found that only 13 percent of parents declared "academic background" to be the ultimate goal of education.[13] Proficiency in the skills of communication may be increased by relating them wherever possible to the "tasks" of youth. The enthusiasm with which "nonreading" adolescents read *Teen-Age Tales*[14] demonstrates this point. However, there are other societal needs which many

[13] Remmers, H. H., and Radler, D. H., *op. cit.*, p. 129.

[14] Strang, Ruth, and Roberts, Ralph M., editors. *Teen-Age Tales*. Boston: D. C. Heath and Co., 1954.

administrators have not yet recognized as important. It is to these we call attention.

Technological Skills

The demands of an industrial economy will continue to strain resources everywhere even as it adds to them. Inventions are bringing changes in geometric progression. A simple device, such as the transistor to replace the vacuum tube, makes possible improvements in electronics which stagger the imagination. Workers are being upgraded so that the proportion of unskilled workers is declining rapidly. In 1950 the proportion was about one-fifth compared with one-third in 1910.

Some critics of public secondary education claim that science courses are not being taught to as many students as in former years. This claim is unfounded, as Eells has so adequately shown.[15] However, if schools are to meet current needs, attention must be given to the qualitative aspect of the science program, especially as this relates to what is required for successful performance in science courses in college and university. Rural schools, particularly, continue to suffer from inadequate resources for teaching science.

Many secondary schools provide little or no opportunity for their students to learn about the practical aspects of electronics. Manpower shortages in certain occupations, such as those of skilled machinists, toolmakers, and diemakers, have persisted for several decades. The question of how much of this training should be given in secondary schools is unsettled, but it is safe to say that there is generally too little, not too much. Teachers and students should be taken on extended tours of industrial plants. Teachers should be given a better orientation to the world of work as it now is. All educators should be familiar with the occupational structure of the United States; that is, the percent of workers in the major job classifications. United States Census reports on characteristics of the population will help the administrator get an accurate picture of his local com-

---

[15] Eells, Walter C. "Let's Talk Facts!" *School Executive* 76: 41-46; March 1957.

munity and state in this respect. Finally, educators must now learn to think in terms of "career patterns" instead of specific occupations. Many persons now move thru a series of related careers; and, with change as the order of the day, this tendency will no doubt increase.

Adaptability to Mobility

During the six years of 1950 thru 1955, a *yearly* average of 1.6 million persons moved from farms to nonfarm areas (or to the armed forces) and 597,000 persons moved from nonfarm areas to farms.[16] Year after year the studies show that nearly 20 percent of all the people—at least 30 million—have moved to a different house during the preceding 12 months. From 6 to 7 percent have moved to a different county.[17] And yet, the problems connected with mobility have hardly found a place in the curriculum. These problems are not yet clearly defined, but we do know that moving about creates insecurity, particularly for persons moving from rural to urban areas. Harlan County, Kentucky, is currently working on a program of this kind. One major trucking company has issued a pamphlet giving suggestions to parents on preparing children for moving. Students should be helped to plan for settling in a new community and for finding the resources there which can contribute to their well-being. Rural youth should be taken to adjacent cities and made acquainted firsthand with social and civic institutions and especially with the services of the state employment offices. Contacts with local offices of these types will provide a useful first step.

Carefully planned follow-up studies will give the administrator specific information on this problem. The National Association of Secondary-School Principals, the U. S. Office of Education, and many state departments of education can pro-

---

[16] U. S. Department of Agriculture, Agricultural Marketing Service. *Farm Population Estimate for 1955.* Washington, D. C.: the Department, 1955. p. 1.

[17] U. S. Department of Commerce, Bureau of the Census. *Current Population Reports.* Series P-20, No. 73. Washington, D. C.: the Bureau, March 12, 1957. p. 9.

vide patterns for these studies.[18] No school can function adequately today without a "feedback" such as this.

Administrators of both rural and urban schools are challenged to give attention to this problem. One large city, Cincinnati, has been concerned with the difficulties of its citizens who have come recently from rural areas. Urban schools can do more to provide orientation for newcomers.

World Responsibilities

Traditional courses in history and civics apparently have not developed mature understanding and acceptance of our nation's larger role in world affairs. At a time when our national economy has bounded far ahead of predictions of a decade ago, the people have not convinced their leaders that they want their government to assume a larger obligation for helping other nations bridge the gap between their economy and ours. Understandings and attitudes can be modified in this direction. High-school students should have maximum contact, direct and indirect, with peoples of other lands. They can organize programs for sharing their own resources with others less well provided than they and thereby find an outlet for the idealism so much in evidence during adolescence. The United Nations must become real to them.

The Armed Services

Present policy requires that a large proportion of the youth now in high school will serve some time in the armed forces. Those responsible for developing a more effective liaison between the armed forces and the school are dismayed by the general lack of interest shown in the problem that this policy creates. One study of 500 high-school students in a rural area showed that 30 percent of them were deeply concerned with their own part in this program. As many went into the services as went on to higher education. Much can be done to

---

[18] Landy, Edward, and others. "Occupational Adjustment and the Schools." *Bulletin of the National Association of Secondary-School Principals* 24: 1-154; November 1940.

acquaint students with the services and the part such experience might play in their educational program. Furthermore,
students need clarification regarding a citizen's responsibility
to his country in this respect. Tho this period of military
service may be a necessary evil, a mature person can utilize
such an experience creatively. When we consider how much
time will be allotted to this experience by many young people,
it seems clear that the schools should give serious consideration
to orientation for it.[19]

Family Living

Follow-up studies reveal that many students wish they had
had more training in skilful family living. Young people need
more understanding of the changing roles of men and women
in our society. When given opportunity, youth show considerable eagerness to discuss family life; also, they point out that
the present curriculum includes little on this topic. To be
sure, disjointed aspects of the present curriculum are related
to family living, but what is needed is integrated experience.
Rarely do teachers of social studies, English, and home economics, for instance, plan together for teaching. Furthermore,
while English and social studies may be required of all students thruout their high-school experience, regardless of the
need, homemaking is usually elective after the ninth grade.
Despite what seems to be a necessary trend for women to enter
the labor market, homemaking continues as a major occupation. If the family is to remain the basic unit of life in our
culture—certainly a desirable prospect—much can be done
to help youth resist disintegrative forces now in operation.

Skill in Working in Groups

Whether it be as a member of a trade union, the local PTA,
or the U. S. Senate, an American citizen is usually a member of

---

[19] Help is available thru the U. S. Department of Defense, Washington, D. C.
See also: North Central Association of Colleges and Secondary Schools, Defense
Committee. *Your Life Plans and the Armed Forces.* Washington, D. C.:
American Council on Education, 1955. 149 p. (*Teacher's Handbook,* 23 p.)

one or more organized groups. Because he normally belongs
to several, he needs understanding of his role in a group and
skill in the methods by which groups accomplish their goals.
This is a practical grass-roots aspect of democracy. Teachers
and administrators who are proficient in group problem-solving
skills are in the minority.[20] Boys and girls need to learn how
to formulate group problems and how to organize themselves
to solve them. They need to understand the concept of revolv-
ing leadership, to feel comfortable in putting forth ideas and
suggestions, and to learn to serve in whatever capacity is
best in the group. Relatively few schools offer genuinely
creative experience in this area.

Emotional Maturity

Emotional maturity is a by-product of numerous experiences,
many of which are beyond the school's control. If we are to
recognize the growing pressures upon individuals, systematic
attention must be given to this need. A mature person is
a "free" person, who can act on the basis of thought. He has
had experience in coming to terms with himself, in making
choices, and in formulating judgments. He is not afraid to
stand alone, and he accepts the responsibility for his decision.
He recognizes and accepts his limitations. He participates in
groups, making his wishes known.

To provide one kind of experience which contributes to
maturity, the school should explore every possibility for permitting students to know self-direction. Certain areas of the
curriculum lend themselves to this: social studies, general
science, English, and homemaking. Such a question as "What
are some of the things we'd like to learn this year?" could start
students thinking about their problems and often can result in
a well-rounded, vital learning experience. Homeroom and
student-activity programs can also contribute appreciably to
this end. Students need opportunities under guidance to discuss
their mutual concerns intelligently. Care must be taken not to

---

[20] See also Chapter XI, p. 312-14.

make these experiences just another course, but rather to utilize fully every possible opportunity for such activity within the entire school program.

Creative Thinking

Creative thinking should not be confused with what is presumed to follow if a student is well grounded in the "fundamentals." Even when a marked ability to think critically and creatively is innate, this ability can be enhanced by training and practice, just as musical talent is enhanced by training in theory, harmony, and composition. However, the analogy is imperfect. In music, the student may be urged to compose on his own but in school the student is so often encouraged only to vote Yes or No on decisions already arrived at in history, literature, and other subjects. The curriculum is closed. He needs opportunity to formulate curriculum by asking questions and planning the experiences by which the answers, if any, may be found. An excellent example is seen in the film, We Plan Together.[21] He needs many opportunities to understand and appreciate his heritage, but he also needs opportunity to challenge its assumptions. This is not the best of all possible worlds! Students must learn to understand and to protest against the mass manipulation of people by the use of psychological tricks.[22]

The individual personality may be shaped largely by society; but if societal pressures become too great, he loses his individuality. Let us not forget that many of society's greatest gains have come from individuals and minorities who resisted society. Much of the Bible, for instance, might be considered a "minority report." The same is true of other great scriptures. Perhaps there was never more need for the prophetic dissenter than today. But the pressure for conformity in our culture is

[21] We Plan Together. 16 mm, sound, black and white, 20 min. Teachers College, Columbia University, New York, New York.

[22] Fromm, Erich. "Man Is Not a Thing." Saturday Review. March 16, 1957. p. 9.

Packard, Vance O. The Hidden Persuaders. New York: David McKay Co., 1957. 275 p.

almost irresistible.[23] Everywhere the peer group is "looking over our shoulder." Boys and girls need help in establishing a balance between legitimate societal demands and psychological regimentation. Remmers and Radler present evidence that the high-school student is incapable of asserting his individuality; such a finding offers a disturbing prospect for a nation which depends so much on individual initiative.[24]

Making Decisions

Today's citizen is called on to throw his weight, one way or another, on tremendously complicated issues of far-reaching significance. For instance, the question of danger from fall-out as a result of the continued testing of hydrogen bombs makes even the most complicated political issue of the last century seem insignificant. The survival of the human race may hinge on the solution of this problem. The way in which the question of trade with Communist China is settled has a bearing on the attitudes of a billion people toward the free world of which we are a part.

Today's citizen must make more decisions, and more rapidly, than any of his forebears. These decisions require accurate information, carefully evaluated for its implications. Youth need training in this. In many sections of America only one newspaper is available. One need only examine a half dozen different newspapers for any given day to realize what this means by way of emphasis or omission, especially when we keep in mind that even in the United States a majority of newspapers tend to support one political party which may not be the majority party. It would be instructive to know to what extent the typical high-school student has any sophistication regarding the reading of newspapers and of appraising the material which comes to him by way of mass communication mediums.

[23] Riesman, David, and others. *Lonely Crowd*. Garden City, N. Y.: Anchor Books, 1953. 359 p.

Whyte, William H. *Organization Man*. New York: Simon and Schuster, 1956. 429 p.

[24] Remmers, H. H., and Radler, D. H., *op. cit.*, Chapter IX, p. 222-38.

Too few average citizens understand the power structure, sometimes used upon them with irresistible force, of the economic system whose products they enjoy. For instance, how many laymen are remotely aware of the implications of the fact that organizations may be incorporated in states where they conduct no business nor have holdings while operating extensively in other states? How many realize the extent to which the natural resources of some of the "poor" states of the union are contributing annually to the vast income reported for some of the "wealthy" states? Much that goes on is remote from the average citizen because it does not appear to touch him directly. At best, it will be hard to develop objectivity on many topics of vital importance, but the school should continue striving to provide students with understanding of this complex system and skill in making fair decisions.

Using Money Wisely

As has been pointed out in Chapter I, high-school graduates will find themselves in possession of much more money than their parents had at the same age. Many a parent is amazed to find that the starting salaries of his children may be almost equal to what the parent has arrived at after 20 or more years of faithful service. More and more blue-collar workers are earning wages higher than the salaries paid to white-collar workers in many responsible posts. This wider distribution of wealth calls for education in the use of money. To know how to spend wisely may be a more important goal than is currently realized.

Even as society makes more provisions for the security of its citizens thru group hospitalization, social security, and private retirement plans, the citizen needs help in planning for the wisest distribution of his financial resources.

Such matters as improved safety and comfort in automobiles, the use of credit, hospitalization, insurance, the use of alcohol and tobacco, and quality buying will be of vital importance to future citizens, and the school might well include more opportunity to study these matters in the curriculum.

The Individual

One person's needs and society's needs are integrated in each individual personality. If these are brought into reasonable balance, the individual becomes a mature person. The successful completion of his developmental tasks at the appropriate time will contribute to the fulfilment of his need to succeed, to belong, to be accepted, to be loved, and to grow in the ability to direct himself. Then he "feels" useful; he counts as a person. Full self-realization is the result of many experiences, beginning at birth, by which the individual has gained a favorable impression of himself. There has been a fair balance between success and failure.[25]

When an individual fails to acquire the skills required to meet the demands of society, various unfortunate reactions take place. For instance, a boy who cannot succeed in school may simply quit. If he cannot find a ready-made reason for doing so, he will invent one, or behave in such a manner as to be required to quit. If his relationships with his age mates of the opposite sex are not satisfactory, he may resort to fantasy or other inappropriate behavior. In any case, where progress in the developmental tasks and in meeting societal needs is slow, there will be accompanying frustration, and danger of emotional breakdown.[26]

The individual boy or girl is the arena where the Carnegie Unit and the sometimes vaguely stated goals of secondary education must be reconciled, where the cultural heritage and the individual's need to be self-sufficient must be brought into balance. It is in this arena that the inclination to satisfy one's personal ambitions clashes with pressures of family, of neigh-

---

[25] Prescott, Daniel A. *Emotion and the Educative Process.* Report of the Committee on the Relation of Emotion to the Educative Process. Washington, D. C.: American Council on Education, 1938. p. 119.

[26] Ivins, Wilson H.; Fox, William H.; and Segel, David. *A Study of a Secondary School Program in Light of Characteristics and Needs of Youth.* Bulletin of the School of Education, Vol. 25, No. 6. Bloomington: Indiana University, November 1949. 68 p.

Segel, David. *Frustration in Adolescent Youth.* U. S. Office of Education, Federal Security Agency, Bulletin 1951, No. 1. Washington, D. C.: Superintendent of Documents, Government Printing Office, 1951. 65 p.

borhood, of community. Here the battle is joined between the needs and abilities of the individual and the sometimes unrealistic ambitions of parents. If each individual is to bring order out of these divergencies, if his needs and society's needs are to be brought into a constructive relationship, the school must help him thru understanding him.

Myths That Make Trouble

Administrators, teachers, parents, and adults in general know that different people are different. But all too often we keep on acting as if they were alike. Even our efforts to study the traits of individuals may backfire. We give achievement tests and consider only the average scores; we give intelligence tests and do not analyze the results; we group by grades and assume that grades are homogeneous.

The myth of the average student—The danger in using the term *average student* is that it tends to confuse the thinking and working of teachers. It refers to a mythical composite of individual human beings, but no one boy or girl is what the average purports to show. The average represents an abstract evaluation of achievement around which individual evaluations tend to cluster. Because it indicates a central tendency it dominates the scene but in a distortive way. It has characteristics of the lowest common denominator. The indiscriminate use of such a measure tends to make us discount those who achieve less than it defines or to injure those who have gone beyond, by inducing complacency or false superiority.

The greatest danger in using the term *average* is that it may induce teachers and others to violate the integrity of individuals by relating them to depersonalized standards. It detracts *from individual uniqueness by making pointless comparisons*. It forces conformity beyond the point where conformity is essential for the common good. A great forward stride in reaching the needs of youth might be effected if each secondary-school administrator could accept the implications of the statement, "There is no average student," and adequately develop those implications. Our tardiness in meeting the needs of talented youth is due in part to this insensitivity to the abstract nature of the "average."

The myth of the IQ—The intelligence test measures many different abilities. "The new doctrine of infant damnation" are words that John M. Brewer is alleged to have used to describe the misuse of standardized intelligence tests. By this he probably meant that a child was indelibly tagged with an intelligence quotient regardless of its accuracy and without knowledge by the teachers and others of the meaning of the score.

Intelligence testing is a two-edged sword. Like the X ray, intelligence tests can bless or burn. Used out of context, severed from related factors, a standardized test score may serve only to compound confusion. Children and teachers tend to play out the roles assigned by an IQ regardless of its accuracy. Boys and girls may undershoot the mark on a single test, partly because of previous imperfect appraisal of their abilities by some teachers, and for the rest of their school years be undervalued. It is morbidly interesting to speculate on how much human potential is unrealized in the United States for this reason alone.

Intelligence—that is to say, the kind of intellectual performance measured by standardized tests administered to groups or individuals—consists of a number of *different* kinds of abilities, more or less related, depending on the test. The important thing to realize is that when two children each make a total score of 100, there may be two entirely *different* patterns of subscores on as many as 11 different subtests.

Somewhat as the designs differ in snow flakes, *individual boys and girls have different kinds of intelligence* even tho their test scores add up to the same figures! Two high-school students each received an intelligence quotient of 109 on a *Wechsler-Bellevue Intelligence Scale* (Adult). Student A scored 119 on the verbal tests and 94 on the nonverbal or performance tests. Student B scored 109 on both the verbal and nonverbal section. In no pair of the 11 subtests did A and B have identical scores. Such patterns of difference could be demonstrated countless times. To deal with two students on the assumption that because their gross IQ's were identical, they could do the same kind of work and profit from the same program, would be wrong. It is important to remember this fact when formulating a program designed to reach the needs of all.

It is especially important to avoid making major decisions regarding an individual student, or a group for that matter, on the basis of group tests. The results of careful observation by several persons over a period of time are also needed in this respect. Often unrealized potentialities have been discovered by skilful psychological examination when all other evidence indicated lack of ability. Whenever there is any doubt regarding a student's potentialities, the school should make it possible to have an individual test administered by a competent person.

A group of administrators in one system found it highly profitable to devote a series of meetings to investigating the implications of testing in their schools. They met under the leadership of their superintendent and various experts to review and broaden their knowledge of standardized tests and the ways to use them. Teachers in their schools were helped to extend their horizons on the uses and values of tests. When teachers continue to appraise students by using an unqualified reference point, there is a serious lack of administrative leadership.

The myth of the "grade level"—Theoretically, a grade denotes a collection of students who are at a common stage of achievement. The book-centered, subject-centered course of study which prevails in most American secondary schools is designed with this in mind. However, a bad theory leads to bad results. With a little examination it will be found that the theory of grades is almost completely untenable. The logical and inevitable outcome of universal education is universal promotion, except in a few cases where the child, after careful evaluation and due consideration by all concerned, will benefit by remaining in the same grade.

"The high school teacher will find a range of from eight to ten years in mental age at each grade level; and these conditions will be found to exist whether the school enforces strict policies of promotion and failure or promotes entirely on the basis of chronoligical age." [27] In general, the same range of achievement, especially in reading ability, will be found among students in nearly all subject areas.

A principal may find this out for himself by arranging the scores from high to low on any section of an achievement test, or reading test, for any grade. Ninth-grade students in a typical central school in New York State showed a reading range from Grade 5.4 to Grade 10.6. Only one-third of the group read at ninth-grade level. The distribution of ability in verbal reasoning for the 13 seniors in a small high school was as follows:

> One at the 15th percentile
> Three at the 50th percentile
> Three at the 55th percentile
> One at the 60th percentile
> One at the 70th percentile
> Two at the 75th percentile
> Two at the 80th percentile.

The other seven areas tested showed a similar or even greater range.

These differences are not unusual, they are typical. *"Since the beginning of educational measurement no fact has been more frequently revealed, and its implications more completely ignored."* [28] [Italics added] Variability in achievement is much greater in high school than in elementary school. Secondary-school authorities may find cold comfort in the fact that an extensive study reported by Learned and Wood showed that the same condition prevailed in higher education.[29] If

[27] Cook, Walter W. "The Functions of Measurement in the Facilitation of Learning." *Educational Measurement.* (Edited by E. F. Lindquist.) Washington, D. C.: American Council on Education, 1951. p. 10.

[28] *Ibid.*

[29] Learned, William S., and Wood, Ben D. *The Student and His Knowledge.* New York: Carnegie Foundation for the Advancement of Teaching, 1938. 406 p.

anyone is looking for escape thru the door of more rigid promotion policies, this is closed, for the evidence points to the fact that the mean achievement is as high for schools with low retardation rates as for those where low-ability students are retained longer.[30]

It must always be remembered also that trait differences within an individual reveal the same picture of variability. *The Differential Aptitude Test* battery which measures eight different abilities often reveals a wide range of competency for one individual. One ninth-grade girl was at the 90th percentile in verbal reasoning and the 85th percentile in abstract reasoning, but at the 26th percentile in space relations. Facts such as these, coupled with variations in other personal qualities, such as physical size, stamina, energy output, and clarity of goals, can make a tremendous difference in a student's response to the school program, hence in its value for him.

Self-realization comes only when a student feels that he counts as a person in his group. What he has to contribute must be appraised not only in comparison with the contributions of others, *but for its intrinsic worth*. This suggests that current symbols of success and methods of evaluation be examined for their implications. Care must be taken not to level down, but there should be a better balance between perfection in achievement as measured by absolute standards and the contribution of an individual in relation to his ability to perform. Boys and girls need to feel that any useful work is valued for its own sake. This question is increasingly raised: How can boys and girls accept this ideal if at commencement time only those having native ability in abstract thinking are honored, and if honors are distributed on the assumption that all students could have won them if they had really tried hard enough?

[30] Coffield, William H. *A Longitudinal Study of the Effects of the Non-Promotion on Educational Achievement in the Elementary Schools.* Doctor's thesis. Iowa City: State University of Iowa, 1954. 150 p. Abstract: *Dissertation Abstracts* 14: 2291-92; No. 12, 1954.

Wallihan, Robert S. *A Comparative Study of Retardation in the Primary Grades of the San Diego, California, City Schools.* Doctor's thesis. Boulder: University of Colorado, 1956. 181 p. Abstract: *Dissertation Abstracts* 16: 1418; No. 8, 1956.

The administrator must clarify his understanding of democracy as this relates to education. To deal with all students as tho they were equals would be a grave injustice—if by equality is meant similarity. In a democracy the goal should be that of making it possible for each person to participate to the extent to which he is capable—of helping each individual meet all his legitimate needs as long as they do not conflict with the best interests of the group. To achieve is a basic need.

Steps Toward Individualizing Instruction

Only as teachers work increasingly with students on an individual person-to-person basis, can administrative ideas about meeting the needs of each young person become fully effective. Whatever the administrator learns and tries to do about meeting individual differences will lack vitality except as he shares his learning and his efforts with his colleagues on the faculty. While many teachers tend to be emotionally polarized around a departmentalized subject-centered high-school program, they also respond warmly to the needs of students as persons. When the administrator is providing leadership in meeting the individual needs of all students, such practices as the following prevail.

The principal helps the teacher to cope with the situations presented by individual differences. Either with individual teachers or in group meetings, and with the aid of supervisors, he can take certain steps that will help teachers and students in working toward individual growth. He assures the teacher that he understands the range and depth of the teacher's problem. Both teacher and administrator accept the tentative picture of the range of abilities in a specific classroom as these are reflected by the standardized tests. Such reassurance will help free the teacher for more creative effort.

The principal helps the teacher discover and use the resources available for dealing with the varied abilities in the classroom. For instance, he will make certain that the library is equipped with books and other resources which are adequate for high-school youth of limited ability in reading and that the teachers have access to them. Lists of such books are available and are constantly being developed.[31]

He helps the teacher organize and develop experiences that are in keeping with the varied needs and abilities of the students. In working with a young teacher, an administrator can go thru the chapters of a textbook and help the teacher to distinguish between essential and nonessential materials, suggest experiences within and outside the school which would vitalize the textbook material, and arrange for joint efforts by teachers of different subjects.

He makes provisions for more realistic evaluation procedures in order to escape the present dilemma created by trying to appraise students by two conflicting standards: (a) according to success in mastering the subject, and (b) according to effort and ability. This, in itself, is a long-range task which is basic to any program designed to meet the needs of today's youth.

He makes certain that teachers know something about the personal characteristics of each student and encourages them to expand their knowledge. Administratively this can be done by insuring that teachers have time and opportunity to systematically examine the students' cumulative records. Guidance has developed in response to the pressing necessity to know and respect individual differences. Too often, however, the information available on a student is never, or only partly, utilized. This is especially so in high schools, where individual teachers meet many more students in a day than does the elementary-school teacher and are discouraged by the prospect of trying to examine many scores of individual student records.

The administrator might make sure that each teacher has time, for which he is paid—either before school opens in the fall or during the school day—to examine records and abstract

---

[31] Strang, Ruth, and others, editors. *Gateways to Readable Books.* Second edition. New York: H. W. Wilson Co., 1952. 148 p.

For an extensive list of sources of materials for slow and retarded readers, see: Blair, Glenn Myers. *Diagnostic and Remedial Teaching.* Revised edition. New York: Macmillan Co., 1956. Chapter 8, "Reading Materials and Practice Exercises," p. 173-211.

pertinent data on each student. Or the counselor may do this. For instance, the exact level at which a student is operating in various subject areas is essential information for each teacher. Details about his health are important. It is only by knowing students that teachers become sensitive to their individual requirements. It may be reasonably safe to assume that only a small percent of high-school teachers in the United States have identified the retarded readers among their students. Many do not recognize the difference between the slow reader and the retarded reader.

The administrator recognizes and encourages the use of the case conference, as an effective method for responding to individual needs that should never be overlooked. (See the discussion on pages 73-74.)

Insight by the Administrator

An important feature in the administrator's concept of the individual is his understanding of hidden needs. The administrator is not a psychiatrist, but if he fails to recognize the function of the subconscious in human behavior, his grasp of the situation may be quite superficial. A boy in trouble because he chronically defies authority is not himself apt to realize that he may be reacting to a maladjusted home situation. The administrator will not realize it either if he deals only with the symptom of overt hostility. The administrator can be effective only if he recognizes that there are underlying causes.[32]

One of the striking developments of recent years is the extent to which commercial organizations have systematically capitalized on current knowledge of the subconscious reactions in order to manipulate public opinion. This may or may not be a legitimate use of this knowledge about motivation of human beings. However, school administrators can and should use this knowledge, in order to help boys and girls be their best selves.

---

[32] Saul, Leon J. *The Hostile Mind.* New York: Random House, 1956. 211 p. An excellent and readable discussion of the basis and effect of hostility.

In addition to accepting the wide range of abilities found among students in the secondary school, the administrator knows that sociological and economic factors are to be taken into account. Each student comes from a home in the community. In one home, the family eats its meals in a family group; in another, food is eaten on a nonschedule, catch-as-catch-can basis. In one home, the boy's father holds the door open for the mother to enter; in another, the father is likely to go first. In one family group the aged grandfather is a revered and valued member of the family; in another he is a tiresome old has-been, treated as such by adults and children alike. Thus each student exists in a matrix of unique customs and values.

The students whose Hungarian grandparents settled on the poor soil of a farming community are responding to subtle but quite different values and pressures from their classmates whose English great-great-grandparents settled earlier in the more favorable spots. Even where all are of the same racial origin, there will be differences in status and prestige of which the school must be aware.

Deep in the personality of each student the values of his home prevail to influence his perception of himself and his outlook upon the world around him. The student's background will affect the way in which he responds to the school and, as Hollingshead pointed out, the way in which the teachers respond to him.[33]

The wise administrator tries to keep in mind not only the needs of youth imposed by the culture and the specific requirements of society—he must also see learners as unique individuals, each with his own needs, reacting to the requirements imposed upon them. He safeguards the individual, not only by intelligent use of the knowledge of individual differences referred to earlier, but by recognizing that each person has his own measure of needs, both biological and psychological. He not only strives to provide satisfactory experiences for boys and girls, but he also responds to the individual as a

---

[33] Hollingshead, August de B. *Elmtown's Youth.* New York: John Wiley and Sons, 1949. Chapter 8, "The High School in Action," p. 163-203.

person, a person who may be currently failing at one or more important developmental tasks thru no fault of his own.

In dealing with individual students, the administrator brings to bear all his knowledge of human behavior. He does not abrogate his function of maintaining control in the school but, for the time being, he emphasizes his basic role as a teacher. He becomes a counselor with all that this implies. He realizes that no student deliberately chooses to be stupid or a nuisance, and that his behavior, however illogical it may seem, is the logical outcome of factors and situations, many of which are unknown to the student and beyond his control. No matter how inappropriate the student's behavior may be, the administrator knows the student is striving for integrity. So he asks himself such questions as: How does this student see himself as a person? Does he feel inadequate? What need or needs is he trying to fulfil? What is keeping this student from achieving his goals? Whose approval does he value and work for? What is the effect of frustration on his behavior? What inner conflicts does he have? How much does this student lose in effectiveness because his energy is going into his emotional problem?

The principal recognizes that when he confronts a student he is in effect confronting all that has happened to that student since birth, and that current frustrations may be extensions and elaborations of earlier ones. He recognizes that when a student is in difficulty the student is probably trying to meet some legitimate need in an inappropriate manner, or that the student's perception of his need is distorted. As far as possible, the principal deals with an individual in terms of his needs because he realizes that these are the motivating forces around which the person grows. The individual becomes his best self in an environment which is somewhat in tune with his unique requirements, but which also helps him feel at one with the group.

Reaching the Individual thru Guidance

In meeting the challenge implied in this chapter, the administrator needs the support of an adequate guidance program, now sometimes called student personnel services. The Educational Policies Commission's report, *Manpower and Education*, states, "Guidance services, uniquely characteristic of American education, should be further improved, and so increased in scope as to involve all who teach and to reach all who learn." [34]

Guidance is synonymous with the title of this chapter. It is "a process of interaction in which every individual is helped through his own efforts, to discover and develop his own best potentialities for his personal happiness and social usefulness." [35] It will be noted that this definition is broad and inclusive. It suggests that guidance has to do with any aspect of the student's experience which either advances or obstructs his growth and his ability to profit from the school program.

An adequate guidance program meets student needs in many ways. It provides a systematic procedure for identifying individual characteristics, resources, and limitations. This is done thru careful selection, administration, and use of standardized tests and thru systematic collection, interpretation, and use of information about the student's history, his home and background, his changing goals, his out-of-school experiences, his attitudes, and his feelings about himself and key persons around him. A thorogoing program makes it possible for teachers to gain skill in accurately observing and recording data on a student's character and personality traits. Autobiographical material is gathered; checklists and inventories are wisely used. The student's health is checked thru observation by the teacher and periodic examination by the physician and the school nurse. All this information is carefully compiled in a cumulative folder which shows his developmental history, and reflects the trends and changes in his growth and achievement in a meaningful way. The information in this folder is

---

[34] National Education Association and American Association of School Administrators, Educational Policies Commission. *Manpower and Education*. Washington, D. C.: the Commission, 1956. p. 126.

[35] Strang, Ruth. *The Role of the Teacher in Personnel Work*. Fourth edition. New York: Teachers College, Columbia University Press, 1953. p. 31.

always used in any situation where a student is being appraised or discussed.

Guidance provides for coordinated effort by the faculty. One guidance device which can be a powerful integrating force in the school program is the *case conference*. In this, the individual student, the information about him, the curriculum, and the teachers are brought together in a dynamic way. The conference provides for an inclusive look at the student, by the adults in the school setting most closely related to him, and sets in motion nuances of empathy on the part of all concerned which might not otherwise be released. Frequently this may turn the tide so that teachers view the student in a more favorable light and find ways to help him. The case conference proceeds as follows:

Step one—The chairman, either the counselor or some other person, explains the reason for the conference and presents the student's history and other pertinent data about him.

Step two—Each member of the group (usually all teachers concerned, or who know him, together with the nurse and other specialists) present information which they have in addition to that already given.

Step three—The chairman asks the members to analyze the problem, that is, What is causing the student to act this way? At this point care should be taken to discuss the problem only; no suggestions are made as to the solution, or changes which ought to be made.

Step four—The chairman summarizes the discussion of causes.

Step five—The chairman asks each member to make suggestions as to changes in program, remedial procedures, and so forth. Sometimes, it appears necessary to get more information.

Step six—A program is agreed on, and persons are designated to carry it out.

Step seven—A date is set for re-convening to discuss progress and make further proposals if necessary.

The case conference is most effective when the above procedure is followed carefully.

By this method, community as well as school resources are tapped. Social agencies and other resources are inevitably brought into the situation and utilized in helping a student succeed.

This conference method has been found by some to be the one most effective procedure for helping teachers both to make use of and to see the value of a thoro guidance program. It is also effective in bringing about changes in the curriculum. Having seen how useful the information on a student becomes, teachers are more willing to take responsibility for collecting and recording such facts in the future. If he has not already done so, the principal will do well to look into the case-conference approach to understanding individuals.[36]

Where the climate is favorable, guidance helps students to create experiences meaningful to them. For example, a homeroom program, under adequate leadership, can provide for experiences not otherwise possible in the school schedule. When administrator and teachers view the homeroom in this way, they will encourage the students to indicate areas of concern which they wish to discuss. Here, for instance, students may gain experience in social skills and graces, so important to adolescents, and other worthwhile projects are initiated.

Guidance helps individuals to assume responsibility for self-direction. Today's citizen needs all the experience in decision making that is possible. The guidance movement has been developed on the assumption that individuals have both the ability and the right to make choices, and that this right should be exercised at every point commensurate with the individual's maturity. It respects the integrity of the individual. It also assumes that choices are most appropriate when they are based on adequate information.

Counseling, which is an important part of guidance, provides opportunity for an individual to discuss his problems with a person trained in this function. In this face-to-face relationship students are helped to appraise their potentialities, discuss their plans, gain insight about themselves, and if the counselor is trained to do so, to re-educate themselves with respect to attitudes and understandings about themselves. In

---

[36] For a detailed account of the case conference and other ways by which the principal may facilitate guidance practices thru inservice training, see: Morris, Glyn. *Practical Guidance Methods for Principals and Teachers.* New York: Harper and Brothers, 1952. Chapter 7, "We Study the Individual," p. 163-88.

today's complex world, counseling is an essential part of the school program. Only the scarcity of qualified counselors keeps many more students from seeking help than are now doing so.

Guidance not only provides unity to the student's efforts but it can help to unify an otherwise fragmented school program. Each student needs someone who "knows him as a whole." In the high school, where he moves from teacher to teacher, this is especially necessary. Either the counselor or the homeroom or core teacher can do this. Too often, however, the counselor has too many counselees, or the homeroom teacher accepts the assignment under duress, with the result that many students do not have the advantage of guidance in this respect.

In today's rapidly changing world every student must have early, frequent, and systematic appraisals of his abilities in relation to both requirements and opportunities in advanced education and the world of work. Helping youth select and enter an occupation commensurate with his talents is a major concern of guidance. Even at best, there are gaps in this service, and eternal vigilance is necessary to keep abreast of the times. For a large proportion of students this service is still below even a minimal level. For many boys and girls considerable counseling is essential, not only to help them in making realistic plans, but also to help them in dealing with the limitations and frustrations of their own situations.

One formidable gap in the guidance program of many schools is the failure to involve the entire school staff. To be sure, counseling is a specialty, but most classroom teachers can do much to help guide students in one way or another. Many do informal counseling. They play an essential part in gathering valuable information about individual students as they are observed in the classroom. Most teachers are eager to make their contribution to the guidance program, and under effective leadership will do so.[37] The English teacher collects information on the student thru essays and autobiographies

---

[37] For a full description of the classroom teacher's role in the guidance program see Strang, Ruth, *op. cit.*

and utilizes the rich resources of literature to help students gain self-understanding, the art teacher contributes valuable aid by giving special attention to students who need creative experience, and the social studies teacher develops projects in citizenship, while others perform like services.

In reaching the needs of all, the administrator is constantly confronted with the problem of making each classroom situation more responsive to individual differences. The job of grouping students so that teaching may be more effective will be ever present. Too often this is perceived as possible only in terms of intellectual ability. However, student needs and interests are also dynamic focuses for grouping. This suggests that not only must we modify the dimensions and direction of our thinking regarding grouping, but also we must prepare to be more flexible about this. For instance, to suggest only one of many possibilities, interest in jet airplanes, common among youth of high-school age, might lead to advanced study in aerodynamics by intellectually gifted students on the one hand, and, on the other, the construction of models by those who may be limited in ability to deal with theory and mathematics.

Making the Institution Human

Institutions for human betterment—and the school is one— must be on guard against themselves lest the ends for which they are established become subordinate to the means. Nothing is more important than a human being, but many young humans have been caught up and damaged in rigid, subject-centered school curriculums.

A gifted and mature man, now professor in an American university, quit high school in the tenth grade because of economic pressure outside the school and misunderstanding by teachers within. During his army career in World War II, fortunately for society and for him, a watchful and thoughtful officer recognized his ability and suggested that he take some correspondence courses to qualify for a high-school diploma.

To his own amazement he discovered he had a gift for mathematics, and the journey toward self-realization was resumed and successfully completed.

His experience is different from many others only in degree and outcome. His very creative ability, which the school should have nurtured, forced him to protest blindly against the inflexible atmosphere of his school. No one can adequately estimate the loss suffered by the nation and by individuals themselves because the potentialities of so many people go unrealized. Here is a challenge of the highest order to the administrator.

Much attention is currently directed toward meeting the needs of exceptional children, particularly those who are intellectually superior. However, the nation has need of *all* talent found in its youth. This includes talent in leadership, the arts, dramatics, manual dexterity, music, and the kind of general talent possessed by some individuals which does not express itself noticeably in any one area of achievement. Furthermore, the term *exceptional* includes all students whose minds and bodies are such as to require special consideration, including the handicapped, whose potentialities require nurture of a special and sustained kind. We cannot afford not to utilize all the potentialities of all our people.

Between June and September 1957, some 200,000 high-school graduates who placed in the top 30 percent of their classes were lost between high school and college thru lack of guidance, motivation, or finance. Many of them should have continued their formal education. Only a part of this number would have been sufficient to fill the present gap in scientific and technical manpower. Undoubtedly, the causes for their failure to enter college are multiple. Early identification of their ability together with adequate guidance might have reduced the number. This process should begin long before secondary school, and the cooperation and understanding of parents should be enlisted at an early date.

The nation is now feeling the results of an educational program which has, in effect, been polarized around the mythical "average." In the years of rapid expansion, more than this may not have been possible. But for several decades we have given allegiance in theory to individual differences. Looking back, we can say that had we done so in practice, the present hue and cry about our failure to provide for the gifted might not have arisen. The same can be said about provision for slow learners and handicapped children; *when individuals are cared for, all are cared for.*

In conclusion: The administrator recognizes and accepts the range of the problem; then, building on the findings of those who have systematically observed and pointed out the needs of youth, he in turn develops systematic procedures for refining these discoveries in his own situation and makes provision for meeting student needs.

programs for unity and diversity

III

programs for unity and diversity

SECONDARY EDUCATION—available to all, enrolling all, and meaningful to all—has long been a part of America's hopes and aspirations for its youth. Many high schools have made significant progress toward school programs to serve all youth; others serve the needs of only a small proportion of young people. The need for reorganizing the secondary-school curriculum is pressing; it grows out of the belief that it is an obligation of the school to youth and to American society.

The Comprehensive Secondary School

The Commission on the Reorganization of Secondary Education redefined the goals of the secondary school and advocated the comprehensive high school, combining all curriculums in one unified organization, as "the standard type of secondary school in the United States."[1] Since that in-

---

[1] National Education Association, Commission on Reorganization of Secondary Education. *Cardinal Principles of Secondary Education.* U. S. Department of the Interior, Bureau of Education, Bulletin 1918, No. 35. Washington, D. C.: Superintendent of Documents, Government Printing Office, 1918. p. 24.

fluential Commission made its pronouncements some four decades ago, our schools have been offering an ever broader program in their efforts to meet the educational needs of an increasing percent of the youth of their communities. Gradually the multipurpose secondary school has come to be recognized as the agency most capable of serving all youth.

A number of specialized high schools exist in large cities, and in certain other communities, usually those dominated by one trade or industry. These special-purpose public vocational schools—business, trades, aviation—still require a common program of general education. Many of these separate institutions are strong schools and are making significant contributions to youth education. They appear to have served a useful purpose in broadening the content of public youth education, but the present trend seems to be against their expansion. Highly specialized programs that cannot economically be provided in all high schools in a large system may each be centralized in one comprehensive high school, open to qualified students from all sections of the community. Thus each comprehensive school may have its specialized program.[2]

Conant states that "if one accepts the ideal of a democratic, fluid society with a minimum of class distinction, the maximum of fluidity, the maximum of understanding between different vocational groups, then the ideal secondary school is a comprehensive public high school."[3] French calls the comprehensive school "one of our best means for creating social unity without crushing individuality and for developing individual diversity without cultivating social cleavages."[4]

Basic Functions

The programs of the most effective high schools in America have largely consisted of adjustments and modifications in

---

[2] French, Will; Hull, J. Dan; and Dodds, B. L. *American High School Administration: Policy and Practice.* Revised edition. New York: Rinehart and Co., 1957. p. 91.

[3] Conant, James Bryant. *Education and Liberty.* Cambridge, Mass.: Harvard University Press, 1953. p. 81.

[4] French, Will. "The Role of the American High School." *Bulletin of the National Association of Secondary-School Principals* 39: 10; February 1955.

an increasingly broad range of subject requirements. A cursory examination of the requirements for graduation reveals the functions which such practices reflect. This Commission supports as a basic level of effectiveness such functions as:

1. Provisions for exploring and expanding the unique talents of each student in terms of both immediate goals of further education, and of life goals of a vocational type

2. The development of an awareness of the heritage of our Western civilization and the history of the land in which we live, with stress upon many of the social problems now confronting citizens of America and the world

3. A program of physical education and health education (including an awareness and practice of good safety habits) geared to the individual's own physical endowments and personal requirements

4. The development of skills and appreciations in the use of the English language as a means of communication and a source of enjoyment

5. A knowledge of the world in which we live thru a study of the tools and basic principles of the physical and life sciences and their impact on the modern world

6. The development of the skills of computation and of an understanding of some of the principles and procedures of mathematics

7. The provision of experiences touching upon the fine arts to the end that some degree of understanding of what constitutes quality in the fields of music, drama, poetry, literature, painting, and sculpture shall be part of the student's personal equipment

8. The development of attitudes and skills of social responsibility as a youth and as a future adult citizen

9. Experience in working with peers and adults in informal and formal settings thru which the individual develops some of the skills of teamwork without a loss of personal identity within the social setting.

Functions of an Enriched Program

The forward look at secondary education presupposes that the comprehensive school is the institution best qualified to meet the challenging demands of our modern society and the educational needs of a rapidly increasing youth population. While the present program in the typical secondary school is inadequate, there is a distinct trend among many comprehensive schools toward an expanded and enriched program. Schools which have developed such programs have done so on their acceptance of most of the following functions, either as their sole responsibility or as a joint responsibility with other agencies and institutions of the community:

1. Guidance to each student in assessing and employing his own strengths and weaknesses, interests, and ambitions relative to the life plans of each youth, whether such plans involve further formal education or not

2. The meaningful teaching of the great events and issues which constitute the history of our country and the world so that the lessons learned may help each youth contribute, to the best of his ability, to the future dignity and peace of all mankind

3. The development of the skills of literacy for each youth up to his maximum potential, regardless of that potential's relationship to any arbitrary norm, and likewise regardless of any deficiency or precocity which he may bring to the school as a new student

4. The provision of health services which will insure the achievement of the goals of education, insofar as physical and mental health may play a critical part, including health examinations, referral services, and provision for special education for the handicapped youth

5. Constant and carefully planned coordination with the homes of each youth so that the combined influences of home and school shall work in harmony for the best interests of all

6. Careful articulation with schools from which the young person comes and to which he may go so that the total program will be a meaningful educational experience resulting in the achievement of the goals of education (This is especially significant in terms of the uniqueness of the functions of each level of education.)

7. Provision for specialized education of great variety, as distinct from the minimal program of general education, with awareness of the importance of such variety to the identification of career goals, life plans, preparation for further education, and personal development

8. Acceptance, as a major function, of responsibility for constant and continuous follow-up of all its graduates and drop-

outs so as to contribute to their adjustment to post-school life and to guide the school in modifications of its offerings and methods.

Functions in a Shared Program

Other suggested functions, which some schools have accepted as a joint responsibility, or in the absence of collaboration, as a sole responsibility, include:

1. Encouragement and guidance of young people in active civic service thruout the school and community (Such experience will be part of the general program for all students and will assist them in developing the skills and knowledge requisite to sound, responsible citizenship.)

2. Provision of recreational centers for youth and families, including facilities and staff at times when needed (Students will participate in the supervision of recreational activities for younger children as part of their civic service experience.)

3. As part of its responsibility for all youth, providing a welcome to former students, whether graduates or not, who seek counsel and specialized or general education which may contribute to their further self-realization

4. Provision of guided and meaningful work experience for all youth as part of their program of general education.

The foregoing list of functions should be expanded and revised in the light of local conditions, changing resources, and new knowledge of the individual and of the society which may emerge. It is the conviction of this Commission that any improved and challenging program of secondary education can result only from the identification and acceptance of functions determined to be of greatest significance in the local school and its community.

This approach to program development was the basis for the prescriptions and recommendations contained in the remainder of this chapter.

Unity and Diversity

The unique role of the comprehensive secondary school has been defined as that of creating social unity and also of developing the individual to his maximum potential. The idea of unity with diversity and diversity within unity characterizes this advanced level of the common school.

The democratic secondary school must provide both unified and differentiated education. Such provision will be accomplished thru mutually supportive programs of general and specialized education.

A well-balanced program of secondary education must include as one of its two main ingredients a unified curriculum to meet the needs of all youth and of society. The "imperative needs" of youth are one important source of common curriculum content.[5] Persistent problems and common interests of young people are guides to essential learning experiences for all. Because youth from all segments of American life attend our schools, provision must be made for the development of social competencies and attitudes in our program. There are many issues and problems in our adult society that each citizen must face, understand, and attempt to solve. Youth should learn to understand and to deal effectively with them as a vital part of the process of growing into responsible citizenship. These are recognized bases for a program of general education that should control decisions on the curriculum.

Our democratic society derives great strength, however, from its diversity. The varying abilities, interests, and aspirations of youth require a wide variety of educational experiences. Specialized learnings "represent ways in which a person fulfils his personality needs, develops his talents, and finds his own particular niche in society."[6] Ours is an age of specialization. The industrial economy and the changing social structure also demand a diversified program of secondary education. Specialized education, available for each student and fitted to his needs, must be an integral and coordinated part of the secondary-school curriculum.

---

[5] See Chapter I, p. 25-26.

[6] Anderson, Vernon E. *Principles and Procedures of Curriculum Improvement.* New York: Ronald Press Co., 1956. p. 298.

Guiding Principles in Program Design

Many factors—economic, social, political—have led to changes in the high-school curriculum during the past 10 years. Continued changes and a better understanding of the needs of youth point the way to further revisions now and in the near future.

There must be a logical and defensible basis for planning curriculum improvement in terms of guidelines that give design and direction to the educational program and thus make possible the performance of the essential functions of the modern secondary school. This Commission believes that such guiding principles would include these:

1. The secondary school has the responsibility for providing a balanced program of general and specialized education. For most youth, the early years of secondary education will largely be devoted to general education, while in the later years more emphasis will be put on specialized education. The change in emphasis will occur as the unique interests, talents, and goals of each student are determined.

2. The grade placement and content of general education should be governed by such factors as: (a) basic needs of all youth; (b) the individual's future role as a citizen, homemaker, and worker; and (c) behavioral evidence indicative of his social, emotional, and intellectual maturity.

3. The grade placement and content of programs of specialized education for each student should be determined by such factors as: (a) his maturity; (b) the nature, specificity, and immediacy of his educational and vocational goals; and (c) an awareness of his peculiar interests and abilities, and the need for their development.

4. School organization and curriculum practice should discourage rather than encourage social stratification.

5. Learning experiences should be provided in many different forms (inside and outside the school) so that progress is possible in terms of each individual's needs, abilities, and interests. Such experiences should be provided in ways other than by adding to the number of courses.[7]

---

[7] Adapted in part from: Work Conference on Life Adjustment Education. *Why Do Boys and Girls Drop Out of School and What Can We Do about It?* U. S. Office of Education, Federal Security Agency, Circular No. 269. Washington, D. C.: Superintendent of Documents, Government Printing Office, 1950. p. 41-42.

These guides to curriculum structure, and others adapted to the local school situation, should characterize the program design of the modern secondary school which makes adequate provision for the education of all youth in our complex, democratic society.

General Education

The Harvard Committee described general education as those learning experiences which will provide for the educational needs which all responsible persons have in common in our democratic society. It also referred to general education as "that part of a student's whole education which looks first of all to his life as a responsible human being and citizen." [8] In secondary schools, *general education* usually refers to the courses and activities which are required of all students. It is the "constant" element of the student's program. The term *common learnings* is frequently used to connote a more precise concept of the basic program of general education at the secondary level and to distinguish it from the college program.[9] Either *general education* or *common learnings* may be used to designate the basic educational experiences that should be provided for all youth.

Aims of General Education

What purposes are to be served by a program of general education? The literature on general education reveals many statements of purposes. McConnell and others, writing in *A Design for General Education,* say that "general education refers to those phases of nonspecialized and nonvocational education that should be the common possession, the common denominator, so to speak, of educated persons as individuals

[8] Harvard Committee on the Objectives of a General Education in a Free Society. *General Education in a Free Society.* Cambridge, Mass.: Harvard University Press, 1945. p. 51.

[9] Saylor, J. Galen, and Alexander, William M. *Curriculum Planning for Better Teaching and Learning.* New York: Rinehart and Co., 1954. p. 307-308.

and as citizens in a free society." [10] Johnson describes general education as "that part of education which is concerned with the common knowledge, skills, and attitudes needed by each individual to be effective as a person, a member of a family, a worker, and a citizen." [11]

French and others analyzed these statements and concluded that general education itself has both an individual and a universal purpose:

> Underlying these statements are two correlated purposes for general education: one concerned with the person as an individual, the other concerned with him as a citizen. The first proposes that general education help each young person realize his fullest potentialities. . . . The first purpose of general education, therefore, is based upon the proposition that the various common capabilities of young people should be developed as fully as possible through education so that they will be able to utilize them as needed in the planning and the living of their own lives. . . .
>
> The second of the two coordinated purposes of general education . . . is concerned with the growth of youth toward responsible citizenship. The words "responsible citizens" are used in their broadest sense to include the common relationships one has with other people in face-to-face situations, as well as those arising as one cooperates on a less personal basis in political, social, economic, or cultural organizations. That education in this country should be designed to help all young people become responsible citizens in this sense, is as essential as that it should help each to realize his individual potentialities. The very existence of the democratic state demands it. Without the universally shared willingness and ability of each citizen to act as intelligently as possible upon matters of public concern, democratically oriented societies are bound to fall far short of their declared purposes. [12]

---

[10] McConnell, T. R., and others. *A Design for General Education for Members of the Armed Forces.* Series I—Reports of Committees and Conferences—Number 18. Washington, D. C.: American Council on Education, 1944. p. 7.

[11] Johnson, B. Lamar. *General Education in Action.* A Report of the California Study of General Education in the Junior College. Washington, D. C.: American Council on Education, 1952. p. 20.

[12] French, Will, and associates. *Behavioral Goals of General Education in High School.* New York: Russell Sage Foundation, 1957. p. 27-28.

In a further analysis of the aims of general education, French and his associates raised a question as to whether individual development and active citizenship may not be two aspects of the *same* purpose. They reason that:

> Only in a democracy do the ends sought by the society from education and the concern of each person for full growth and development tend to coincide. Only in a democracy is it so evident that if one throws himself freely into the affairs of his time, he does not thereby lose his opportunity for his own full and free development—but gains it for himself and others. So these two correlated purposes of any program of general education for all youth in the United States can be said to merge almost into one purpose. This fact accounts for the presence and importance of a required, "integrating" program of "general education" in our high schools. It makes the evaluation and improvement of the existing general education program in each high school the most important responsibility of its professional staff.[13]

The staff and the lay public should study the purposes of general education in their school and their community. A statement of the desired goals of the program should receive general acceptance as an essential step in evaluating what the school is now doing and as a basis for proposed changes.

There is less disagreement on the aims of general education than on the means of achieving them. Problems and issues arise when schools, in planning or improving programs of general education, seek to determine what content should be selected, how the program should be organized, and what methods should be used. The development of a program of general education that will lead to the kinds of behavioral outcomes that reveal growth toward self-realization and responsible citizenship for all our youth is the most crucial curriculum problem facing our secondary schools.

The Content of General Education

The program in our elementary schools is almost entirely within the scope of general education and so, increasingly,

---
[13] *Ibid.*, p. 31.

is that of the junior high school. Altho many differences exist, approximately half the required work in the typical high school is in the constants. The vast majority of secondary schools use systematized fields of knowledge, organized as subject courses, as the basis of general education. Most of the content is from the fields of English, social studies, mathematics, and science, usually in that order. There is increasing concern that the content in each course be not merely an isolated body of knowledge, but an essential phase of a unified program that contributes significantly to the development of the common, unspecialized competencies of youth as persons and as citizens.

Other areas of study designed to produce the kinds of competence sought for all youth would seem to require content in social-civic education, family-life education, economic education, health and safety education, moral and spiritual education, and vocational information and counseling. Some instruction in each of these areas and on a sequential basis should be given to meet many of the important common needs of youth.

The traditional subject course as the basis of general education is being questioned by many secondary schools. Other bases upon which to build an improved program of common learnings are being examined. One approach is thru the "common needs of youth"; another is thru a study of "presentday problems." Some schools, using these and similar methods of content selection, provide learning experiences drawn from any and all subject fields that will aid the students to attain those abilities and attitudes that every youth should possess.

In addition to the more formalized, organized content of required courses, there are other rich and rewarding experiences that are considered an important part of general education. Participation in all-school activities, such as assemblies and school elections, has significant educational value and contributes to the aims of this phase of the program. These activities are a part of the content of general education to the extent that they are available and open to all and meet common needs.[14]

---

[14] See later section of this chapter, "Student Activities," p. 117-22.

The educative force of the atmosphere or tone of a school may also be included in the substance of general education. Efforts to develop a democratic environment thru cooperative planning and action by the administration, faculty, parents, and students, and the responsibilities assumed by students for the reputation and welfare of their school, are learning experiences and influences that can result in the kind of general education that contributes effectively to the desired behavioral outcomes.

A fully developed program of general education will provide for every student a series of planned activities and experiences thru which he will develop to the fullest: the desire to continue to learn and to make contributions of his talent to the betterment of his fellow men; knowledge and attitudes contributing to his physical and mental health as an individual; preparation as a young person for present and future roles as a member of a family including an awareness of the changing role of the family and its indispensibility as our basic social unit; a sharpening of his awareness and enjoyment of beauty, both as a creator and consumer; skills in and knowledge of the tools, materials, methods, and products of our technical and industrial economy and its relationship to the other cultural and economic units thruout the world; the methods of problem solving, involving both the problems of traditional sciences and those of the social sciences; and the acquisition of basic information which will help each youth face and solve such problems as are identifiable in his own immediate future.

The Organization of General Education

The conventional curriculum organization for general education is based upon separate subjects, each taught independently. The Carnegie Unit is the measuring instrument of acceptability and respectability in the organization of the program of studies. Course offerings in English, American history, first-year mathematics, general science or biology, and physical education and health are the usual requirements.

Approximately one-half of the usual 16 units required for graduation are in this group. These prescriptions and others added locally comprise the usual general education program.

This was the program design in 1949 in about 97 percent of the high schools. It was estimated that not more than 15 to 20 percent of the junior high schools used a less traditional organization.[15] In 1956, Bossing found in a study of 1000 schools that 9 percent of the undivided and junior-senior high schools, 6 percent of the regular high schools, and 7 percent of the senior high schools reported some form of core curriculum.[16]

Emerging practice—There is a slight trend to the inclusion of some of the so-called "undeveloped" areas of general education, such as social-civic education, economic education, and home and family education, within the content of required subjects as short units on a sequential basis, particularly in Grades VII thru X. The sparsity of good instructional material is one serious barrier to many teachers who might otherwise include content from these needed areas in their required subjects.

A number of secondary schools have developed problems courses, usually for Grades X and XII, which provide unifying experiences not included in the traditionally required courses. Such offerings may be part of the prescribed program or available to some students on an elective basis.

Another organizational pattern provides parallel courses or "tracks" in various common subjects to meet the varying abilities of students.

Other program designs which deviate from conventional practice in curriculum organization include:

1. Informal and systematic correlation of subjects
2. Fused and unified fields of knowledge
3. Core organization based partially or exclusively upon teacher planning.

[15] Wright, Grace S. *Core Curriculum in Public High Schools.* U. S. Office of Education, Federal Security Agency, Bulletin 1950, No. 5. Washington, D. C.: Superintendent of Documents, Government Printing Office, 1950. p. 5-6.

[16] Bossing, Nelson L. "Development of the Core Curriculum in the Senior High School." *School Review* 64: 224; May 1956.

All these unconventional plans of organization appear to lay stress upon instruction that is oriented to the concerns of youth. Priority is placed on the school's obligation to develop in youth a competence to deal with the practical, persistent problems they face in everyday affairs.

The Random Falls idea illustrates a curriculum redesign which proposes drastic changes in both purpose and structure. In outline, the plan calls for schools of not more than 300 students. Each school is to include all high-school age groups, enrolled for full-time work except for brief vacations, and is to be staffed by a variety of teachers and coordinators. In large centers the schools may be grouped as schools-within-a-school. The program is in three parts. One is *development of the individual's resources*, centered chiefly at the school itself. *Citizenship development* is furthered thru vocational and service contracts with employers. *Community service* is provided thru students' volunteer service on community projects, and in reverse, thru consultation and advisory services from individuals and community groups.[17]

The individual school faculty should undertake a thoro study and analysis of what each required subject and unconventional grouping of common studies can contribute to the attainment of the aims of general education, as a step toward designing a curriculum to realize the desired outcomes.

Some administrative considerations—Within the general education program, adaptations should be made to individual differences.[18] The term *general education* does not mean that all students should have the same educational experiences or achieve at the same level. Broad desired outcomes are common to all programs of general education, but individual experiences may vary. These outcomes should be achieved by all students within the limits of their capacities.[19] The ability

---

[17] Shaw, Archibald B., and Reid, John Lyon. "The Random Falls Idea." *School Executive* 75: 47-86; March 1956.

[18] Spitznas, James E. "General, Special and Vocational Education: An Exploration of Distinctive Differences." *What Shall the High Schools Teach?* 1956 Yearbook. Washington, D. C.: Association for Supervision and Curriculum Development, a department of the National Education Association, 1956. p. 197.

[19] Saylor, J. Galen, and Alexander, William, *op. cit.*, p. 55.

of the individual student is the only fair standard to measure his progress and achievement.

Programs of general and specialized education operate concurrently at all grade levels in the high school, and in the same subject field, and even in the same class. The distinguishing feature is that in general education students relate their own peculiarly individual experiences to the common purpose, while in specialized education they relate these experiences to their own purposes.[20]

Behavioral Outcomes of General Education

Just as there are many different statements of the basic aims of general education, there are many ideas on the specific objectives that must guide the design, content selection, and methodology of general education. Light may come from the recent study of behavioral outcomes of general education in high school.[21] The study seeks to determine the kind and level of behavior, stated as outcomes of general education, which it is reasonable to expect from a well-matured high-school graduate. It is believed that the competence to behave in certain ways is essential if all youth are to live effective, satisfying lives in our society and culture. This competence is needed and exhibited in the aspects of life which are shared by all youth and in which it has seemed most important that certain common standards of behavior be established. When this study is completed and a statement of expected behavioral outcomes of general education is available, each secondary school should be assisted in discharging its proper function of revising its own objectives, of evaluating its present design and program, and of making such changes in content and procedures as are indicated.

Such a study and its follow-up in local schools may reveal that there is no established pattern of common studies that

---

[20] Spitznas, James E., *op. cit.*, p. 182.

[21] French, Will. "A Survey of the Behavioral Outcomes of General Education in High School." *Bulletin of the National Association of Secondary-School Principals* 40: 9-14; September 1956.

French, Will, and associates. *Behavioral Goals of General Education in High School.* New York: Russell Sage Foundation, 1957. 247 p.

contribute to these outcomes for all youth, and that certain courses and experiences may possess high potential and others contribute little. The influences of home, church, and community may have greater educative value in developing these behavioral outcomes than schools generally recognize. The study will provide help to local schools, and communities will find help in working more effectively toward any desired behavioral outcomes which are not being achieved thru their present general education program.

Significance of a Functional Program

Leonard affirms that the developing programs of general education represent the first significant fundamental change in the curriculum of secondary education during the past 50 years. He believes that the break-thru is especially important for these reasons:

> First, they recognize the need for common skills, attitudes, behaviors, and understandings among all youth in a democratic society. Second, they are centered in the social and personal needs of youth. Third, they are related to goals deemed desirable rather than to subject disciplines. Fourth, they are orderly and carefully planned, worthy in themselves, and pupils recognize their significance for their own living and education. Fifth, they give a truly significant purpose to universal secondary education and relate to its proper place the development of special interests and aptitudes for college entrance, occupational competence, and personal development.[22]

These observations serve as appropriate criteria in efforts to improve the common, required program at the secondary-school level.

The stakes are high, and the need for a functional program of general education is pressing if we are to move forward. Our quest is for young people who are able and eager to assume the obligations of responsible citizenship. What should be the structure and program of general education in your secondary school? What is your concept of a unified curric-

---

[22] Leonard, J. Paul. *Developing the Secondary School Curriculum.* Revised edition. New York: Rinehart and Co., 1953. p. 394-95.

ulum for all youth? How will you proceed to develop common learnings that will develop the desired behavioral outcomes in youth?

> The general must come to carry a connotation of richness and spirituality more than the academic now does. Time was when common learnings were designed for a privileged elite; it is now high time that a curriculum of general education be created for *all* youth in a democratic society. The general— whether it be a course to take, an atmosphere to be striven for, a heritage to be glimpsed, an outcome to be achieved, a need to be fulfilled, a problem to be solved, a vision to be shared, a heart to be stirred—must be so conceived by a faculty that all pupils have a chance to participate in it. No other meaning of general education is sufficient for the task facing the American high school.[23]

Specialized Education

A well-balanced program should not only provide for the general education which gives our society stability and balance, but should also provide broad offerings of specialized education which would stimulate the development of each individual youth to his maximum potential by providing him with opportunities to meet his individual needs, to develop his special talents, and to make progress toward his vocational goals.

> The specialized offerings in the secondary school are roughly of two types: courses organized into a defined sequence of work in preparation for a vocational field or for entrance into an institution for further study, and more flexible courses that satisfy avocational or personal interests.[24]

The scope and extent of the school's program of specialized education should be as great as the needs and interests of the students, but in practice the resources of the individual school

---

[23] Henry, George H. "Foundations of General Education in the High School." *What Shall the High Schools Teach?* 1956 Yearbook. Washington, D. C.: Association for Supervision and Curriculum Development, a department of the National Education Association, 1956. p. 172.

[24] French, Will; Hull, J. Dan; and Dodds, B. L., *op. cit.*, p. 215.

determine the program. Generally speaking, the program of special education shows scope and variety in the junior high school, while depth is more typical of the offerings in the upper years of the secondary school when an increasing amount of time is given to special education. A broad, elective program of specialized education should discover and develop the educational, vocational, and avocational needs and interests of each student.

Students should have opportunity to elect courses in which they have a special interest or for which they have a particular need. For students preparing to enter college the school curriculum should include advanced courses in academic fields not included in the general education program. Some of the college-bound group need to meet specific entrance requirements; all of them need to develop special competencies that make for success in college.

Students planning to go from high school into employment need special courses which may include initial training and background experiences for an occupation. Those who have demonstrated real ability in one or more subject fields also should have the opportunity to take advanced courses.

A wide variety of possibilities should be open to all so that they may explore special interests for leisure use and other individual needs. An expanded program of specialized education will insure diversified experiences and educational services that will meet the unique educational needs of each youth to a greater degree than is now present in most secondary schools.

Some Administrative Considerations

Practices in subject organization, marking standards, and teaching procedures, different from those in general education, may characterize the specialized part of the curriculum.[25] Recognized need, individual interest, and desire to achieve

---

[25] *Ibid.*, p. 191.

may call for standards not justifiably required in general education. Greater flexibility in scheduling is essential in offering specialized courses. Adequate guidance and counseling services should be developed so that each student may have suitable learning experiences for the realization of his vocational, educational, and avocational goals.

Education for Further Study

More than 700,000 young people enrolled as freshmen in American colleges in the fall of 1957. These college students comprise over 50 percent of the total number in their high-school graduating classes. The estimate has been made that in the fall of 1967 nearly 60 percent of the graduates will enter college.[26] Preparation for college is a major function of most high schools and is growing in importance.

On the basis of past experience, more than 1 out of 4 of these freshmen will not return for their sophomore year to the same college. Great stress is being placed upon the problem of getting into college; the attrition rate in many higher educational institutions reveals that making good in college should also be a problem of concern to the high schools.

The program of specialized education thus includes preparation for advanced education. Most high schools have a schematic arrangement of courses in English, social studies, mathematics, foreign languages, and sciences which is termed the college-preparatory curriculum. The concept of specialized education presented in this chapter holds that courses in these various subject fields which are not required of all students and which are taught to meet special needs are part of specialized rather than general education. These courses have long been presumed to be essential for entrance to and success in college altho numerous studies, the best known being the Eight-Year Study, have shown that the particular pattern of subjects taken in high school has little to do with success in college.[27]

---

[26] Based on unpublished estimates of the U. S. Office of Education.

[27] Aiken, Wilford M. *The Story of the Eight-Year Study: With Conclusions and Recommendations.* Adventures in American Education, Vol. 1. New York: Harper and Brothers, 1942. 157 p.

Instead of depending upon a definite sequence of specific high-school subjects, success in college is more likely to be based upon high achievement in high-school work, high level of interest and ability, adequate verbal skills, and effective study habits. Douglass suggests several objectives that schools may pursue to enhance the possibilities of success of their students in college:

1. Development of a large vocabulary, with specific and precise meanings of words.
2. Development of the ability to express oneself orally and in writing.
3. Developing the ability to find materials and to organize them from a considerable number of sources.
4. Development of study habits and skills.
5. Developing skill in arithmetical and simple algebraic computation and problem solving.
6. Development and maintenance of intellectual and other cultural interests—in science, in public affairs, in good reading, in music, in art, in writing, and in history.[28]

Emphasis upon a pattern of subjects is being replaced by greater concern about the ability of the student, as measured by aptitude and achievement scores, the high-school record as a whole, and qualities of character and personality.

The high school should also provide opportunities for its college-bound students to elect subjects in the specialized program in which they have special interest and aptitude. Special offerings in the arts, music, practical arts, and academic fields should be available to students who have demonstrated interest and ability to progress satisfactorily in such courses.

Vocational Education

Vocational education trains people directly for useful employment and aids in keeping them employable. It is concerned with the development of skills, understandings, attitudes, working habits, and appreciations needed by workers to enter

---

[28] Douglass, Harl R. *Modern Administration of Secondary Schools*. A revision and extension of *Organization and Administration of Secondary Schools*. Boston: Ginn and Co., 1954. p. 251.

and to make progress in employment on a useful and productive basis. Vocational education as discussed in this chapter is limited to the high-school level.

Vocational education in our changing times—There appear to have been more changes in the ways of doing things during the last 50 years than in all previous history. Many more changes are in sight. Vocational education plays an important role in preparing people to adjust to these changes, particularly as they pertain to work.

Nearly 90 percent of the youth of ages 14 thru 17 receive some high-school education. By the time they reach 18 and 19, about one-third are in college or still in high school. The percent staying in high school is rising, but a majority of the boys and a high percent of the girls enter gainful employment immediately upon leaving high school. Since these young people obtain their first jobs without further training, the secondary school makes the major educational contribution in preparing them for jobs.

When young people enter the labor market, they find their services in much the same category as other salable products, for employers and buyers are alike in that they pay for the product in terms of quality, demand, and supply. Youth with marketable skills and abilities are in greatest demand, and their services are bid for at the highest price. Youth with lesser skills and abilities come next, and the unskilled take whatever jobs they can get at low pay.

With the increased demand for skilled manpower, secondary schools have an opportunity and, indeed, a responsibility to offer vocational education programs which will aid youth to develop their abilities to the maximum as potential workers under changing conditions in industry, on the farm, and in the home.

Skilled manpower is needed—Skilled manpower has helped to make the United States a highly productive nation. The productivity per worker in this country is several times greater than that of workers in many other countries. Whereas a hundred years ago it required 85 percent of the productive workers to produce the food and fiber needed by our country, today only 13 percent are so engaged. At present, the average farm worker is producing twice the amount of food and fiber that a worker did as recently as 1940.[29] Skill and technology, when applied to machines and the sciences underlying production, have made this possible.

One skilled worker in some industries with automatic machines may now produce as much as did 100 workers a decade ago. Highly specialized scholarship and skill are needed to produce these machines, and their maintenance and operation require a high degree of technical understanding and skill.

Electronics and automation will bring further major changes. The industrial revolution due to steam and electricity may seem small in comparison with the new developments now unfolding.[30]

Increases in basic production have increased the opportunities in distributive and business occupations. At present more workers are engaged in distribution than in basic production (exclusive of agriculture). The demands for skilled workers in the distributive fields are increasing.

The intricate manipulations and decisions underlying effective family living, household management, and family relationships now require highly skilled homemakers. Perhaps never before have the social, cultural, technical, and economic aspects of our society made such heavy demands on the abilities of women in the home.

Skilled manpower is, therefore, a growing need, and vocational education has a responsibility for supplying training to meet the demands.

Educational objectives and procedures should be clearly understood—Vocational education is an integral part of a total

---

[29] U. S. Department of Agriculture, Agricultural Research Service. *Changes in Farm Production and Efficiency: 1956 Summary.* Washington, D. C.: Superintendent of Documents, Government Printing Office, 1956. p. 45.

[30] Stern, James. *Automation and Vocational Education.* Speech delivered at Annual Summer Conference of Local Administrators of Vocational Education and Coordinators of Apprentice and Cooperative Occupational Training at Leland, Michigan, June 18, 1956. Lansing: Michigan State Department of Public Instruction, June 1956. 12 p.

education program. It presupposes the existence of a program of general education which has as its objective not only the acquisition of basic skills of learning, but also the development of patterns of conduct, values, and attitudes necessary for effective living in our democratic society. Vocational education, on the other hand, is geared primarily to the specific objective of fitting persons for useful employment in designated fields.

Vocational education and general education have much in common. Too often the differences are magnified disproportionately, in view of the similarities. The following comparison of procedures and objectives in two secondary courses may aid in clarifying concepts in this regard.

A high-school senior, thru guidance, has decided on a career in merchandising. He registers for a course in chemistry and a course in distributive education. The chemistry course is designed to give basic understandings and appreciations about the chemical phenomena the students may encounter in their everyday experiences, thereby enabling them to live more satisfying lives. The course enrols students who are going on to college as well as those who plan to enter productive employment upon leaving high school.

The distributive education course is geared to a specific occupational objective. While taking the course, the student is employed part time in a retail store. He receives on-the-job supervision from his high-school distributive education teacher and also from his employer. He registered for the course for the purpose of learning the skills and abilities basic to successful entrance into the occupation of his choice.

Common elements in the instruction in both courses are:

- Both instructors take into consideration the factors in volved in orientation and learning readiness.
- Both instructors impart and develop basic understandings and appreciations for the subjectmatter involved. In addition to subjectmatter understandings, the student concomitantly acquires attitudes, interests, and ideals in both courses.

The course in distributive education at this point has not been completed; it is concerned with two more elements which the course in chemistry does not involve:

   • Student participation in work (here and now) under a
practical and productive situation which is related to the classroom instruction
   • Supervision and evaluation of the work experience by the
teacher and the employer for the purpose of aiding the student
in improving his merchandising abilities. This includes on-the-
job instruction.

Learning by doing is, therefore, an essential facet of vocational education. The four elements of instruction just enumerated apply to all fields of vocational training: business occupations, distributive education, homemaking, trade and industrial
education, and vocational agriculture.

The *Dictionary of Occupational Titles* lists over 50,000 specific jobs and describes over 35,000 of them. A high percent of
these jobs are found in the five occupational fields listed above.
Obviously the school cannot give specific preparatory vocational instruction in all of them. For this reason the school, the
office, the factory, the farm, and the home should work closely
together in all programs of vocational education. This makes
it possible for students to receive up-to-date instruction and
experience in the use of modern facilities in industry coupled
with the preparatory and related training which schools can
provide. Classroom and on-the-job instruction, therefore, are
given cooperatively by the school and industry.

The analogy of "round pegs fitting into round holes" has
been emphasized so much that some young people get the fal-
lacious idea that their native abilities fit them within narrow
limits only for certain jobs or professions. With thousands of
jobs to choose from, most individuals may succeed in many job
categories. Native and acquired abilities, coupled with attitudes and interests, furnish predictable clues for success in
broad vocational fields.

Students should be encouraged to seek the counsel of teachers, parents, workers in their fields of interest, and others who
may give them information basic to making wise decisions concerning occupational choices. Guidance counselors cannot be
expected to do the whole job of occupational counseling by
themselves.

Where should vocational education be taught?—School administrators and others often express divergent opinions on the "how and where" of conducting vocational education in the secondary schools. Various opinions in this regard are reflected in the following five plans (it should be noted that Plans 1, 2, and 3 involve shop training in trade and industrial occupations for at least one-half of each school day):

Plan 1—For the juniors and seniors in comprehensive high schools, devote about one-half of the school day to general education and the other half to specialized education which would include college-preparatory courses for college-bound students and vocational courses in various fields for those who are interested.

This plan operates in comprehensive high schools in urban and suburban communities in many states. Vocational students meet the basic curriculum requirements for all students and also obtain trade-preparatory training in school shops, usually in the eleventh and twelfth years. In this plan, decisions concerning occupational choice (at least the fields of interest) have been made by the eleventh year. A limitation of the plan is that the high cost of facilities restricts the number of trade courses that can be offered. Even so, many of the larger schools provide preparatory training in 25 or more trades. Such a plan cannot operate in small schools because of prohibitive costs; however, business, distributive education, and home economics courses fit well into this plan.

Plan 2—Establish vocational high schools in urban and suburban centers for those who desire such training. Programs in such schools are not usually college preparatory in scope or content.

The program enumerated in Plan 2 is common in the larger communities and cities in the Northeast. The citizens in Baltimore recently provided the buildings and facilities for the Mergenthaler Vocational-Technical High School. Students at this school must meet relatively high qualifications as determined by intelligence and achievement tests.

Central High School in Cincinnati is another example of such a program. The recently erected commodious building is located on a large campus five miles from the center of the city. It replaced several smaller trade schools which operated for many years. Students enter Central High as ninth-graders and may pursue trade training in 10 occupational fields.

Students in such vocational high schools must choose their occupational field early. For the equivalent of a half day they receive general-education courses in English, citizenship, mathematics, science, health, and physical education. They receive orientation in the trades for the first two years and specific trade training for the last two years. In the twelfth year, many students participate in a cooperative program with industry. Proponents of this program like it because, they say, it adds purpose to their training in the minds of students. A dedicated loyalty to their chosen trade is found in many students. Opponents of this program declare that students in Grades VIII, IX, and X are too young to make a specific occupational choice and that it is difficult for them to matriculate for college if they change their minds somewhere along the way.

Plan 3—Establish area vocational schools in urban and suburban centers, encourage juniors and seniors in the surrounding high schools to enrol on a part-time or full-time basis if they can profit by such instruction, and open the schools also to post-high-school enrollees. If high-school students enrol on a part-time basis, they receive instruction in general education in their own high schools. The area-school work is evaluated in terms of high-school credit, and the students are graduated with their own high-school classes. An example is the Salt Lake Area Vocational School at Salt Lake City, Utah.

Plan 4—Conduct courses in vocational agriculture, home economics, diversified occupations in the trades and industries, business education, and distributive education in comprehensive high schools; these courses usually require less than one-half of the student's time.

This fourth plan, with many modifications, is the most prevalent program in the country. Ten thousand rural and suburban high schools have programs in vocational agriculture. Vocational home-economics courses are conducted in a large percent of both rural and urban high schools. Vocational business and distributive education programs are increasing. Most of these programs require less than a half day of students' time (usually not more than two hours a day) and may be conducted effectively in comprehensive high schools. Trade training requiring shop facilities is prohibitive in small rural high schools. However, a program of diversified occupations in the trades, operating cooperatively with industry, may be conducted in areas where there are sufficient industrial establishments. This type of trade training has been in operation for many years in the Southern states and elsewhere.

The diversified-trade-occupations program at Gaffney, South Carolina, is an example. Here the teacher-coordinator devotes approximately one-third of his time to the program. He usually has about 20 students in the course involved with 10 or 12 occupations such as television repair, photography, meat-cutting, laundering, dry cleaning, nurses' aides, and several different trades in the textile industry. The students are given directly related occupational instruction in the high school and are employed in selected business agencies for approximately 20 hours per week.

Pilot programs for training in diversified occupations on an area basis are currently under way in a number of rural high-school districts in Illinois.

Changed marketing and processing procedures in agriculture are requiring fewer farmers but are providing many more job opportunities in occupations related to farming. High-school vocational-agriculture courses offer basic training for farming and also for occupations related to farming.

Plans 1 thru 4 all place vocational education within the framework of the high-school years. Proponents of vocational education at the high-school level call attention to many contributions it makes, notably these:

1. It gives purpose to school studies in the minds of many students who otherwise would not have such purpose.

2. It provides marketable skills and abilities for many students who seek employment immediately after leaving high school.

3. It reduces the percent of high-school drop-outs.

4. It adds to the productivity and economy of the country and, therefore, to the national welfare.

The different patterns have been developed to meet varying local needs and as expressions of varying philosophies of vocational education. In developing new programs, school administrators should reconsider community needs and objectives, and should recognize still another pattern of organization, which is typified in Plan 5.

Plan 5—A fifth plan is to conduct no vocational education requiring extensive shop or laboratory training at the high-school level. Trade and industrial courses which meet acceptable standards are postponed until after high-school graduation and then obtained in post-high-school area vocational schools, community colleges, or technical institutes.

Proponents of Plan 5 usually maintain that good programs of industrial arts in the upper years of high school are desirable. Specialized one-hour-period unit courses in industrial arts at this level have definite prevocational implications and are effective orientation programs for trade training at the post-high-school level. These advocates believe it is too expensive to equip trade shops in high schools. They also believe that students need more time to make a vocational choice and that the period in which we live requires more time for basic general education for successful living.

This concept of vocational trade training is prevalent in a number of the Western states. In California, in particular, about two-thirds of such training is conducted at the post-high-school level, mainly in junior colleges. With trade technical programs becoming more prevalent because of the need for trade technicians in the chemical industry, in electronics, and in automation, it is anticipated that trade and industrial education offerings patterned after this plan will increase thruout the country.

Student vocational organizations an integral part of vocational education [31]—Three dynamic youth organizations, national in scope, are associated with secondary vocational edu-

---

[31] See also "Student Activities," p. 117-22.

cation—the Distributive Education Clubs of America (DECA), the Future Homemakers of America (FHA), and the Future Farmers of America (FFA). Each organization holds state and national conventions. Each emphasizes training in leadership, cooperation, community service, and the proper application of specific training to actual work situations on a productive basis. *Learning by doing* underlies all programs of activities. The U. S. Office of Education personnel in vocational agriculture and homemaking are professionally identified with the Future Farmers of America and the Future Homemakers of America.

Once regarded as extracurriculum, these activities are now definitely an integral part of the curriculum. A dedicated devotion to the ideals of these organizations is observed among most members.

Many school administrators believe that the personal development and leadership training offered thru these vocational youth organizations may be as important as the vocational skills and abilities acquired in classrooms and on-the-job instruction. A wholesome respect for the dignity of the work around which each organization is centered is an observable outcome.

School administrators have definite responsibilities for keeping the programs of local clubs and chapters in line with sound educational policies. Commercial and recreational activities may be carried to extremes unless there is proper guidance and supervision.

The local administrator and vocational education—Public-school administrators seem to be increasingly aware of their responsibilities and opportunities for conducting programs of vocational education. This requires an understanding of the philosophy and the administrative policies needed in providing vocational instruction that is geared both to individual interests and to community needs.

School superintendents and high-school principals cannot be expected to keep up with the intricate training demands of the various programs in vocational education. They are, however, responsible for appointing competent vocational directors and for seeking the counsel of advisory committees of representatives from the major vocational groups. These committees aid in keeping administrators and directors informed about needed programs in terms of both national and community interests. It is important that the committees understand their function to be advisory rather than executive.

Administrators in comprehensive high schools may have to make a number of adjustments in scheduling vocational education programs. The class periods in any vocational course must provide sufficient time for the teacher to do an adequate instructional job.

Students should be registered in these courses in terms of ability and interest. There was a time when vocational education was limited to the training of the hands for operative skill. This concept should have vanished with the horse-and-buggy days. Yet, some administrators still direct into vocational courses many students who have failed elsewhere, on the theory that such enrollees can succeed with their hands where they do not have to use their heads. This idea is a misconception of the role of vocational education. Administrators who attempt to make vocational education courses the "dumping ground" for the misfit or the incorrigible are usually heading for trouble. Such students, in the presence of costly equipment and instructional supplies, often cause grief to all concerned, and the educational outcomes are usually nil.

Vocational education at the state level is under the general direction of a state board for vocational education. Vocational education plans, approved by state boards, provide standards under which most local programs operate. Local administrators usually find it advantageous to make extensive use of the professional services of state directors and supervisors of vocational education in upgrading local programs.

Making a living or living a life?—"I am not interested in education concerned with making a living, but rather with that which will aid youth in living a life," remarked a leading citizen in a public meeting. Statements of this kind will bear scrutiny. Making a living involves an occupation. Most adults depend upon themselves or members of their family for providing a living. They normally spend from one-fourth to one-third of their time on a job or in a profession. Here they are associated closely with other people who greatly affect their lives. They, too, affect the lives of others with whom they work.

The method of making a living may determine the kind of house in which the worker and his family live, the caliber of friends he makes, the clubs or associations with which he affiliates, and the amount of education his children will receive. It also may govern his opportunities for rendering service to others, his recreational activities, and the extent of his enjoyment of the spiritual and cultural environment.

All high-school youth should learn to realize that the kind of life to be lived is predicated to a great extent upon the method of making a living. In our country this is determined largely by the individual himself, and the wisdom of the choice may depend upon the vocational education available in high school.

Trends in Vocational Education

Administrators, supervisors, and classroom teachers should be constantly alert to trends in business and industry, on the farm, and in the home, and adapt vocational training programs accordingly. This will require that they collaborate closely with leaders in these fields.

Following are some probable trends which will affect all the fields of vocational education and with which administrators should be concerned. It is anticipated that:

• Consulting personnel from industry, agriculture, and the home will be used to a greater extent to aid vocational education teachers in making courses contribute more effectively to the needs of enrollees.

• New combination programs will evolve, uniting two or more fields, such as agriculture and business, homemaking and business, homemaking and the trades, and trade training and distributive occupations or business.

• A closer collaboration will prevail between vocational teachers and guidance counselors at the high-school level in providing students with adequate occupational information as an aid for making more intelligent vocational choices.

• Future vocational programs in terms of length of training time, course content, and instructional procedures will be geared more closely to the current needs of industry, the farm, and the home as determined by surveys, research, and help from consulting committees, instead of being based on traditional patterns.

• There will be increasing demands and increasing response to demands for specific training programs to meet both emerging and long-term specific needs.

• Cyclonic changes in industry will require extensive retraining programs for unemployed workers displaced by automation. High-school students in preparatory courses should be appraised of this possibility.

Predictions as to trends in the future concerned with specific sections of vocational education include the following:

Business Education

• More attention will be devoted to the vocational facets of business training, and cooperative programs will increase in scope.

Distributive Education

• Cooperative programs in comprehensive high schools will increase in scope in urban centers as a result of improved instructional procedures and better liaison activities of distributive-education coordinators with business establishments.

• High-school cooperative programs will emphasize on-the-job training in the jobbing and wholesaling fields of distribution as well as retailing, which to date has been given major consideration.

Home Economics

• As proportionately larger numbers of women are being gainfully employed sometime during their lives, it is anticipated that more guidance and training will be directed to occupations related to homemaking in high-school courses in home economics.

• With earlier marriages, larger families, decreasing divorce rates, and increasing demands by the homemaker for prepared and packaged food, home-economics programs at all levels will devote more emphasis to sound credit, consumer education, home-and-family living, child development, and problems of parenthood.

Trade and Industrial Education

• Vocational-technical high schools in urban centers will in the future be established only after careful studies and surveys have been made to determine that training for the trades can be done more effectively in them than in comprehensive high schools. This will place responsibility on comprehensive schools for more effective vocational programs than in the past.

• Future trade and industrial education programs at the high-school level will be concerned relatively more with breadth than with depth. The "know-why," based on science and mathematics in a trade field, will be given more emphasis than the "know-how" in manual skills of a specific trade.

• Cooperative programs in diversified trade and industrial occupations, requiring close collaboration between school and industry, will increase in comprehensive high schools located in both rural and urban communities.

• Trade and industrial programs of the "general-industrial-course" type will increase in comprehensive high schools. There will be a tendency for certain comprehensive schools in large communities to be assigned as area vocational schools for training in designated trade fields.

• The impact of electronics and automation on industry will increase the demand for trade technicians, many of whom will require training at the post-high-school level in technical institutes and community colleges.

Vocational Agriculture

• Vocational-agriculture courses at the high-school level will be recognized by school administrators and others as offering basic vocational training for those preparing for occupations related to farming, as well as for those who intend to become farmers.

• Vocational-agriculture teachers will devote considerable emphasis to orienting farm boys to job opportunities in related farming occupations.

• Farm mechanics will receive greater emphasis in the total training program, not only in shop skills, but in rural electrification, farm structures and appliances, farm power and machinery, and in the mechanics associated with conservation.

School administrators and others concerned with vocational education should be aware of the importance of modifying programs to meet training needs. If these programs are not continually modified, they rapidly become obsolete and ineffective. Vocational programs must be flexible and adaptable to meet the demands for new skills and understandings in a rapidly changing economy.

Education for Avocational Interests

Both vocational education and special preparation for college are phases of specialized education that contribute largely to occupational success. But the secondary school should contribute also to the development of constructive personal interests and skills that may be used only in hobbies or recreation. Self-realization may be achieved thru a variety of personal interests and social skills—the school has an obligation to help. Sometimes a recreational interest may be aroused in an academic subject or special phase of it; sometimes it may be found in some form of art, or a sport, or in the clubs and civic activities of the school.

Traditionalists who regard as educational frills those learnings which do not fall within academic patterns should take a fresh look at the purposes of secondary schools. A well-rounded curriculum offering in the secondary school is concerned with all aspects of personality development.[32] A variety of avocational and hobby interests may be regarded as good insurance for both physical and mental health. The therapeutic values of wide interests should never be overlooked. The skills and understandings underlying the intelligent use of leisure hours may be as valuable to the welfare of the total personality as are the vocational skills and understandings basic to the job or the profession.

Administrators, teachers, and guidance counselors should ever be on the alert to see that high-school students keep a balance in their activities. A student may become so obsessed with a hobby that he fails in his schoolwork. Some high-school boys develop "jalopy fever" in their eleventh and twelfth years

[32] Jones, Anna May. *Leisure Time Education.* New York: Harper and Brothers, 1946. p. 68-99.

in school, and want to spend all their time overhauling or racing their souped-up treasures. Others may involve themselves in all the details of a club or group of clubs so that no time is left for rest and study. Such students need the steadying hand of adult counseling to keep them on the track of purposeful activity.

While a few individuals may go overboard with a hobby or hobbies, others need encouragement in the development of personal talents for physical and emotional outlets. A desirable balance is a goal to be attained.

What, then, shall be the role of secondary schools in aiding students to develop avocational interests? It resolves itself into a personalized problem.

The question is often asked as to whether one subject is more valuable than another in aiding the development of avocational interests. Almost any course may arouse the personal fancy of a student, but those in music, art, drama, industrial arts, general homemaking, interpretive dancing, literature, and geology are usually regarded as having rich potential for the development of such interests.[33] But courses in general education should also make a contribution.

As with all instruction, the power behind the course is the teacher. A course in music appreciation may deal so intensively with the theory of harmonic and melodic technics that students will develop an antipathy toward good music instead of delighting in it.

A physics teacher may be so involved with the intricacies of his subject that physics becomes abhorred by his students. Another teacher may make the same course so exciting that many of his students will become dedicated science hobbyists.

English courses properly taught open doors to a world of lifelong enjoyment. Skills and understandings acquired thru physical education may lead to hobbies in hunting, hiking, boating, golf, and spectator sports.[34]

---

[33] Shulman, Gerry, and Shulman, Will. "The 'How To' of Mineral Collecting." *Recreation Magazine* 47: 358-59; June 1954.

[34] Mitchell, Elmer D., and Mason, Bernard S. *The Theory of Play.* Revised and enlarged edition. New York: A. S. Barnes and Co., 1948. p. 193-217.

Hobby clubs and activities are often organized by students who develop a liking for doing things in regularly scheduled courses. Administrators, teachers, and counselors should always be alert to provide opportunities where students may give expression to their hobby interests. Annual demonstrations in various fields give such opportunities, thru hobby shows, student assembly programs, stunt nights, fairs, concerts, plays, and other occasions which offer a means of exercising personal talents. Advising and counseling with students who participate in these activities should be as integral a part of a teacher's assignment as class instruction is.

For many persons the fondest memories of high-school days are of teachers who took a personal interest in their avocational talents. One test of the effectiveness of the tools of learning and of the attitudes and ideals acquired in secondary school may be the avocational pursuits of former students. Every administrator, teacher, and counselor should be aware of his opportunity and his obligation to help students in this area of personal development.

Special Handicaps, Special Talents

Secondary schools are increasingly concerned with meeting the needs of exceptional children. Physically handicapped students, including the blind, the partially seeing, the deaf, the hard-of-hearing, the crippled, the speech handicapped, and those with health problems, may need services and training to lessen or overcome their defects. Whenever possible, these boys and girls should be given the opportunity to take part in the normal activities of the school. Many of them, with only a slight program adjustment, can follow a regular schedule in school.

The mentally retarded and the slow learners are a part of the student body of most secondary schools. These students should have the chance to perform up to their level of ability, and they will, if the school provides adequately for their peculiar needs. These provisions include special counseling, suitable course offerings, individualized instruction, and appropriate instructional materials.

Some students are handicapped by social and emotional problems. They, too, require special counseling, modification in course requirements, lighter work loads, and sympathetic and understanding attitudes on the part of teachers. The total number of youth in these various categories and the commitment of the school to serve their needs will determine the nature and extent of the special adjustive program and services.

It is estimated that approximately 15 to 20 percent of the students in the typical secondary school possess personal talents of such a high order that special attention should be given to their development. It should be recalled that not only is the youth of high average IQ in this group, but anyone whose abilities are uniquely high in any field. Enrichment in regular classes is a common practice. Some schools have policies permitting the acceleration of the most able students. Other schools section talented students in special classes or honor courses. A few high schools have introduced college-level courses in their program of specialized education.

The secondary school has an obligation to provide appropriate educational opportunities for all youth; more and more schools are meeting this responsibility.

Student Activities

Among the most interesting and challenging areas of the high school's entire instructional program are those items that come under what may be called the activities program. These activities are given many different labels such as extra-class, semicurriculum, noncredit, curricularized activities; co-curriculum; extracurriculum; super-curriculum; all-campus curriculum; activities curriculum. The discussion here refers to this whole area of the school's program as "student activities."

Both general education and specialized education gain strength from student activities. Student councils, class organizations, and experiences as committeemen and officers in other student organizations help students toward the civic and social competence at which general education aims. Such

selective student activities as the varsity football team, the
senior play, or the Latin club serve the purposes of specialized
education in developing individual talents and perhaps in giving vocational training as well.

Talk with any secondary-school principal for a few minutes
concerning the program of his particular school and you will
soon detect that one of his chief concerns is the student-activi-
ties program. It is of so much importance that the principals of
the larger schools have found it desirable to employ directors
of student activities. These directors give full time to planning,
coordinating, and leading in such a fashion that each of the
student activities will provide worthwhile experiences.

Educational periodicals contain articles on many phases of
student activities. A national magazine, *School Activities*, is
published monthly from September to May.[35] The National
Association of Secondary-School Principals has appointed a
Committee on National Contests and Activities. This committee studies the many applications received from sponsors in
business, industry, government, and the professions, and annually prepares an approved list of national contests and activities that meet educational standards. One value of the committee's approved list is that it reduces somewhat the number
of contests in which a school is asked to take part.

A New Development in Secondary Education

Athletic contests between schools have a long history and
are probably the first student activities to win a recognized
place in school life. There was a time when principals looked
upon the voluntary joint enterprises of students as anticurri-
culum, but that day is far in the past. The year 1920 has been
mentioned as the turning point from regarding student activities as a problem of discipline to recognizing them as a part of
the curriculum problem.[36]

---

[35] School Activities Publishing Company, 1041 New Hampshire Street, Lawrence, Kansas.

[36] Miller, Franklin A.; Moyer, James H.; and Patrick, Robert B. *Planning
Student Activities.* Englewood Cliffs, N. J.: Prentice-Hall, 1956. p. 9.

Elbert K. Fretwell is often referred to as the father of the modern philosophy concerning the activities program. In 1919, at Teachers College, Columbia University, Fretwell was the first to offer a professional course in extracurriculum activities. The real credit for this change in philosophy, however, should be given to those many unnamed teachers who saw education not merely as a memorization of facts, but rather as the building of personalities, and saw that student activities were a means of growth.

These enterprising teachers saw many unfulfilled needs that athletics alone could not satisfy. Orchestra, dramatics, glee clubs, journalism, and hobby clubs of various kinds often began thru the spontaneous enthusiasm of a teacher and a group of students who shared an absorbing interest. These extra activities became so significant in promoting educational values for the students that the administrators soon began assigning sponsors and making them available during the regular school day.

We have come a long way in modifying our attitude toward the activities program because in many instances we are incorporating these activities into the school program and are giving Carnegie credits for the work.[37] Some educators believe that in time there will be so complete a fusion of student activities with the regular curriculum that the student activities program will lose any separate identity. Certain activities, however, do not fit well into the pattern of class instruction, and these are likely to remain as extracurriculum interests, for the worthwhile opportunities for learning experience that they provide.

Within the past decade the number of activities appears to have increased appreciably. The implications of this great increase are not quite clear at the present time. Perhaps the regular curriculum described under the two preceding headings of this chapter as general education and specialized education is failing to meet the total needs of students. Or perhaps the school is merely reflecting the growing complexity and variety of the society around the school.

[36] Miller, Franklin A.; Moyer, James H.; and Patrick Robert B. *Planning* can Book Co., 1941. 400 p.

Certainly student activities have multiplied in many schools without a corresponding growth in the number of teachers. In trying to do all things for all students, we may be trying to do more than the school is equipped to do. Administrators who are concerned with the morale and growth of their teaching staffs are appraising the time and energy required in sponsoring student activities. They are seeking ways to keep the size of the activity program and the size of teaching staff in balance.

The Purpose of Student Activities

The size of the school and the interests of the students will largely determine the number and types of student activities to be offered. But certain guiding principles should govern the activities program in any size or type of school.

One recent statement[38] recognizes four contributions that should be aimed for thru student activities: First, they contribute to the personal development of students. Established interests may be pursued; new interests may be discovered. They lead to good citizenship thru opportunities for leadership, fellowship, cooperation, and the use of initiative. Student activities develop school spirit, meet the needs of youth for being in groups, and help to widen student contacts. They encourage moral, spiritual, and social development; promote mental and physical health; and give an outlet for creative capacities.

Second, student activities contribute to curriculum improvement. They supplement and motivate the work of the classroom; they make it possible to experiment with new learning experiences that may be later incorporated into the curriculum, and they make it possible to give individual and group guidance thru informal contacts.

Third, student activities may lead to more effective school administration. They provide a channel for teamwork shared by students, faculty, and administrators; they give young

[38] Miller, Franklin A.; Moyer, James H.; and Patrick, Robert B., op. cit., p. 13-19.

people a variety of ways to make worthwhile use of spare time, and they make it possible for teachers to get better insights into the reasons for students' reactions to problems.

Fourth, student activities can promote good relations with the community by arousing the interest of parents and other adults in the life of the school and by gaining their informed support of the school program.

Evaluation of Student Activities

Too little attention has been given to the evaluation of student activities. Quite often a school will overemphasize one activity and by this very action limit the provision of other and possibly more worthwhile interests. Sometimes the activities program grows by imitating the programs of other schools. This is a mistake. The activities of each school must grow out of the needs and the desires of its own students and out of opportunities afforded by the community. A plan of evaluation is needed in which the entire school participates.[39]

The tendency is to place too high an evaluation on public performance with its frequent emphasis on a few star performers. What appears to be a wide ranging series of activities may in reality influence only a minority of the students, while others are inactive members or nonparticipants. We should always bear in mind the importance of the process, for if the process is wrong, the product will be wrong. It is imperative that the activities program offer opportunities to each and every individual student. No compulsion should be placed on any student, and yet there should be opportunities for the developing of interests on the part of the students.

A proper evaluation of student activities cannot be made unless the program is thought of as an integral part of the total instructional task of the school. If the activity does not enrich the student's program of studies nor implement the student's growth toward his ultimate potentials, its value is subject to serious question.

[39] McKown, Harry C. *Extra Curricular Activities*. Third edition. New York: Macmillan Co., 1952. p. 631-55.

Community Support

Community support is essential to any school activity, but community influence may sometimes cause overemphasis on one or more student activities. The only way to overcome this hazard is thru more and better contact with the adults of the community. The school that keeps the community well informed of all programs and makes plans with the community usually has no lack of intelligent support. Schools have a responsibility for keeping parents and the general community aware of the educational possibilities of all student activities. Only with this community backing will the schools be able to provide the student activities that will contribute most to both the general and the specialized education of all students.

IV

community, a force in education

community, a force in education

HIGH SCHOOLS in many communities present only a stereotyped instructional program. All pupils are subjected to experiences in academic learning, originally designed as preparation for college entrance. The school is an island within the community. It cares little how the community functions or how it can improve the community. Available community resources are not used to enrich the curriculum nor does the community utilize the school's resources to improve its quality of living. The school building is closed at four o'clock; the staff does not participate actively in community organizations.

Contrast this school with the community-type high school which is vitally concerned with the community area that it serves. The school curriculum uses the available community resources to enrich and vitalize the instructional program. The community is a laboratory where the students learn how the community functions and how they can contribute to the goodness of living. The school in turn is a service agency for the community. By providing leadership, training, and counsel to the citizens, the school helps the community to identify its problems, to make plans for improvement, and to

125

set the plans into action. The lay people are encouraged to become involved in school and community affairs by serving on problem-study committees and thru other activities. There is always a close working relationship between the lay public and the school.

When a community tolerates a lifeless secondary-school program, it may do so in ignorance of what a broader community program would provide. Patterns of secondary education depend, as stated in Chapter I, upon controls exercised within communities. The decisions of the voters, the trends of urbanization, of industry, of shifting wealth, of type and mobility of population—all these help to mold the school. National and international forces likewise work thru local circumstances and affect the ways of living in the community and in turn bring pressures on the school.

If those responsible for local secondary education are sensitive to these trends and forces, the school will adapt its program to meet the needs. It may then itself have a reciprocal effect on the life and development of the area it serves. Thru the forces the school sets in motion, a still larger community may feel its influence.

For a secondary school to provide a program that in any practical way will meet the individual educational needs of each of its students, those responsible for school policies must be aware of shifts in community life and undertake to respond to them. But the secondary school is part of a total program of public education. A community-type high school can exist only when the school system of which it is a part is sympathetic to the community-school idea.

The secondary-school administrator who seeks to operate at this level needs a deep understanding of community problems, as well as professional insight into the school's part in their solution.

Citizens Are Seeking Help

Because the modern community has grown so rapidly in size and complexity, people have lost the sense of unity with their neighbors. They do not know how to work effectively with large groups of people; they do not know the new processes and technics of social interaction in modern community living. Many of them would welcome leadership that would show them how to work effectively with other people.

Communities still fail to meet people's needs. They criticize:

> The city smoke dirties my curtains.
> Our aged have nothing to do.
> Many teen-agers are getting into trouble.
> Our schools are overcrowded.
> Most high-school graduates leave town.

Comments such as these are signals for help. People want to understand the causes, and they want to find solutions.

The final test of society is not only the material things it produces, but also the sorts of personalities it nurtures. Atomic power may bring world destruction, or it may revolutionize man's way of living, depending on the wisdom of the human decisions about its use. The people in our many local communities, conditioned by their public schools and by community influences, will decide the fate of our nation.

The Community Must Be Understood

School district and community boundaries are not always identical. In many instances school districts constitute only a part of a community or parts of several communities. The school administrator must know and understand the real community even tho he may serve in only a part. The administrator must ask himself five basic questions in trying to define and understand the community:

1. What are the distinctive population characteristics?
2. What are the basic economic characteristics?
3. What is its ecological pattern?
4. What is the character of the social differentiation?
5. How adequate is the institutional structure? [1]

---

[1] Wayland, Sloan, R.; Brunner, Edmund deS.; and Hallenbeck, Wilbur C. *Aids to Community Analysis for the School Administrator.* New York: Columbia University, 1956. p. 6.

One would need to measure the spirit and tone of the community as well as the provision made for the educational, recreational, cultural, and spiritual interests of children and adults to determine its strengths and weaknesses. Edmonson developed a Community Score Card that describes the best type of community as one which is characterized by: A cooperative spirit; civic pride; an emphasis on providing for good music, wholesome entertainment, and good reading; an active concern for individual health and well-being; provision of adequate recreational facilities; high standards in its educational program; a religious program that exercises a constructive influence in the community; opportunities for workers to maintain a comfortable standard of living; leadership by outstanding citizens whose lives meet high standards of conduct; one or more organizations that assume real responsibility for cooperative planning and action in all matters pertaining to community welfare; and an efficient and honest local government, genuinely concerned with community betterment.[2]

The school, as the center of community life, must assume some responsibility for leadership. When most effective, this leadership is widely shared. Great skill is required to enlist constructively the abilities, interests, and drives of persons from every walk of life in the community. But sound community educational leadership can do this, bringing together in a common effort the contributions born of the special abilities and unique experiences of many people. Long-range planning and skilful social engineering are needed.[3]

School Has Major Responsibility

The public school is one of the community's major institutions for guidance of the educational experiences of youth and adults. It is not necessarily *the* major educational institution

[2] Edmonson, J. B., and Fisher, Charles A. *A Community Score Card.* Ann Arbor: University of Michigan, June 1942. 2 p.

[3] American Association of School Administrators. *Community Leadership.* Washington, D. C.: the Association, a department of the National Education Association, 1950. p. 9.

in the community, but it has the major responsibility for promoting education for all. Since a child's learning takes place thru all his associations in the community, the school must work with all agencies to provide for the child a well-rounded program of education. The school should work with other community agencies and organizations without duplicating the functions of any.

The Metropolitan School Study Council has developed a charter for school-community cooperation and planning which has had general acceptance:

> We believe that educational planning is a high type of social engineering.
> We believe that the educational program maintained by a community is the concern of all its citizens.
> We believe that channels must be established and kept clear so that the people may express their wishes and opinions to their representatives, the Board of Education.
> We believe that the Board of Education and the school staff should make full use of the expert knowledge existing in the community.
> We believe that the staff of the schools should be available at all times to advise and assist lay persons in their study of the educational program.
> We believe that the participation of lay persons in educational planning should be kept as direct and informal as possible.
> We believe that the Board of Education and the school staff should give full value to opinions of lay individuals.
> We believe that the extent and nature of the participation of each individual will be determined by his interest in the program and his competence to make a contribution.
> We believe that the lay participants in educational planning should recognize the authority and responsibility of the Board of Education to make final decisions.[4]

The School Has a Role in Community Betterment

The traditional secondary school has been a dispenser of the organized cultural heritage of the world, but the efficient high school of the future must fill a much broader role. The

---

[4] Metropolitan School Study Council, Committee of 14. *Public Action for Powerful Schools*. Research Studies, No. 3. New York: Teachers College, Columbia University Press, 1949. p. 77.

school should assist youth and adults to meet the current problems of living, and in doing this should serve as a coordinating agency for community betterment. Clearly the school cannot impose a program of community improvement on the people but it may lead and assist them to do the job. "A local school system, well organized, well led, well supported, and working in co-operation with other agencies can by means of its services and executive energies contribute significantly to the goodness of living in the community." [5]

Pioneer schools were the concern of all. Altho limited in program they served well as a unifying force in the early development of our country. Everybody took part in building the school, in adopting operational policies, and in financing the school program.

Today we need a renewal of the old spirit of identity of school and community. Also we need a new spirit of responsibility for the community as a whole, on the part of the school board, administrators, teachers, other staff, and students. This new spirit is taking form in the work of the *community school*.

The Community School Provides a Challenge

The community school concept is still young. Because it is emerging in many different forms, it tends to elude definition. But its reality and vitality are shown in the quotations that follow. Each reveals a different facet of the total picture.

The Role of the Community School

The role of the school is, therefore, twofold: (1) to provide educational experiences through which young and old are enabled to live effectively and happily with themselves and with others, and (2) to continually stimulate and help develop and refine the community processes through which the people continue to live, grow and improve.[6]

[5] Seay, Maurice F., and Crawford, Ferris N. *The Community School and Community Self Improvement*. Lansing: Michigan State Department of Public Instruction, 1954. p. 15.

[6] Henzlik, F. E. "Our Role in Improving Communities." *School Executive* 76: 21; May 1957.

When asked "What does a community school do?" Clapp gave the following answer:

> First of all, it meets as best it can, and with everyone's help, the urgent needs of the people, for it holds that everything that affects the welfare of the children and their families is its concern. Where does school end and life outside begin? There is no distinction between them. A community school is a used place, a place used freely and informally for all the needs of living and learning. It is, in effect, that place where learning and living converge.[7]

Masters, when serving as educational director of the W. K. Kellogg Foundation, expressed his viewpoint of the community-school concept as follows:

> The school becomes vitally concerned with the economy, productivity and social development of the community. It seeks to know something about the occupational patterns of the community and to use that "know-how" in vesting skills and understanding in the people of the community so that they can become more effective and desirable members of the community itself.[8]

A definition published by the National Society for the Study of Education emphasizes these attributes of the community school: concerns beyond its basic education task for its students, conscious use of the school by the citizens, a curriculum adapted to unique community needs, a school plant made available for adult use in community advancement, and a direct concern in efforts for improving all aspects of living in the community.[9]

Criteria for the Community School

The ultimate community school is yet to evolve. Much experimental work has been completed and much more remains

---

[7] Clapp, Elsie Ripley. *Community Schools in Action.* New York: Viking Press, 1939. p. 89.

[8] Masters, Hugh B. "The CPEA in 1953." *School Executive* 73: 64; January 1954.

[9] Hanna, Paul R., and Maslund, Robert A. "The Community School Defined." *The Community School.* Fifty-Second Yearbook, Part II, National Society for the Study of Education. Chicago: University of Chicago Press, 1953. Chapter 4, p. 49-63.

to be done. The Michigan Curriculum Program listed nine criteria by which one might judge a community school: [10]

1. *The community school surveys community needs and resources.* Some of the activities which would be appropriate are: (a) a sociological survey to determine unmet health needs, (b) a survey to determine if school program is satisfying community needs, (c) a survey of business places, (d) a survey of public opinion on issues, and (e) a survey to determine natural community.

2. *The community school gives initial leadership to constructive community improvement projects.* Schools here can cooperate with the community to initiate or assist with (a) community drives, (b) bond issues for community purposes, (c) a community recreation plan, (d) a "community festival," (e) a rat eradication program, (f) street beautification and landscaping, and the like.

3. *The community school helps to develop a sense of community in both children and adults.* Appropriate activities might be: (a) organization of a community council with youth as members, (b) organization of an advisory committee to seek citizen participation and thinking, (c) organization of a community festival, such as a "tulip festival," which includes school and community, (d) planning a community Fourth-of-July celebration by involving many agencies, and (e) organizing a Community Development Corporation for the purpose of economic or social improvement.

4. *The community school expands and diffuses leadership thruout the community.* Among suitable activities might be: (a) organization of a Community Council which would have many leaders serving as heads of study committees, and (b) organization of temporary advisory committees to assist in solution of community problems.

5. *The community school practices and promotes democratic procedures.* Many activities fall in this category. Any activity that diffuses leadership and involves citizens in a democratic

---

[10] Taylor, Clair L. *Community School Criteria of the Michigan Curriculum Program.* Lansing: Michigan Department of Public Instruction, September 1955. 3 p.

way would satisfy this criterion. Democratic procedures may be exemplified in the classroom and in community projects.

6. *The community school coordinates all constructive efforts to improve community living.* This criterion is well illustrated in projects that raise the economic level of the people. It may be industrial expansion, a new money crop, a library, a community college, or a new health center. Art exhibits, publication of a tourist guide, and tree planting are all good examples.

7. *The community school uses human and material resources in the instructional program.* A Business-Education Day would exemplify this criterion. A conference on the value of soils sponsored by school and farm leaders makes use of human and material resources. Groups studying vocations may be helped by talks given by representatives of various occupations. School trips to community historical sites, observations of court procedures, and other community contacts are of educative value.

8. *The community school involves all persons concerned in planning and appraising the school program.* Adults and youth gather to discuss common problems. Citizens work with teachers to enrich and vitalize the curriculum. Parents and teachers study the reporting system.

9. *The community school is genuinely life-centered as a social institution.* Activities include work experience programs, core classes, and an approach to agriculture and homemaking classes which involves citizens in the planning. A community placement bureau, follow-up studies of graduates and dropouts, an area speech correction program, and a noon-hour program for school children are other examples.

The secondary-school program outlined in the "Random Falls" proposal would be a true community school—a program which removes the barriers that separate most high schools from their communities.[11] This program would offer a solid curriculum of common and special learnings, would provide the students with purposeful experiences in the contemporary

¹¹ Shaw, Archibald B., and Reid, John Lyon. "The Random Falls Idea." *School Executive* 75: 47-86; March 1956.

world of work and service, and would also open the doors of
the school to the citizens of the community who could enter
either to help instruct or to learn.

The Random Falls idea is thus a program of apprenticeship,
partnership, and achievement in citizenship whereby all youth
can attain maximum development in an atmosphere of participating in efforts toward a betterment of self and of community.

Schools Are Building Better Communities

Rural communities as well as the large urban areas need the
community school. When people have been enabled thru
educational leadership to share in the solution of their community problems, the economy and the welfare of all the
people have been greatly improved.

Many areas are capitalizing on the community-school concept. Strub examined 22 communities that present a wide range
of variations in size, climate, tradition, type of economy,
geography, race, and religion.[12] These districts are improving
their community living, recreation, business and industry,
agriculture and conservation, education and culture, and
citizenship. School personnel and other citizens share in the
planning and effort that make these advances possible.

A high school in a rural area handicapped by eroded soil of
low fertility demonstrated what could be done thru the work
of its agriculture classes in landscaping the school grounds and
later the students' lawns. In cooperation with the county
agent, the students were a task force for a major reforestation
project. Over the years a million trees have been planted;
they have not only reduced soil erosion but are providing a new
source of local income.

A community development council is often the channel for
school-community cooperation. One council studied the inadequate medical facilities, worked toward the construction of a
needed clinic, and succeeded in having 300 children provided

---

[12] Strub, Grace F. "Building Better Communities." *School Executive* 76:
83-111; September 1956.

with needed glasses. In another community the council set up seven study committees, which in less than a decade undertook over 100 projects. Thru the committee on farm and land use, the high-school science laboratory was used to make soil tests, until school facilities were outgrown and a separate laboratory was opened. The community services committee has made many recommendations for economic improvement; one led to a profitable venture in the manufacture of fencing from locally-grown cedar. In another area, a consolidated school district lacked cohesion until the school leaders stimulated a development program which resulted in such projects as a community newspaper, an improved water supply, and progress toward local zoning. These and many other examples show how the school helps in building better communities, and that interagency cooperation usually leads to the broadest type of community program.

Role of the Lay Citizen

Many citizens are willing to give their time and effort for community welfare thru proper encouragement and leadership. These people are the custodians of our democratic heritage. They want to cooperate with the schools and to work jointly and cooperatively with the youth and the staff. They expect professional leadership in organization.

School administrators must recognize the citizens' controlling role in school and community affairs. The school should not try to superimpose a program of activities upon the community, but rather should serve as a catalyst. It should help as the community itself discovers its problems and needs, determines what is best for it in terms of need and available resources, and then puts the approved plans into action.

Citizens committees in more than 12,000 communities in all 48 states are organized for school and community development and are increasing in number. There is no set pattern or blueprint for any one type of organization for all communities. The organization must fit community needs. Citizens committees vary in size and plan of organization, objectives, and procedures. Some are temporary organizations that dissolve when a specific problem is solved; others are more permanent and carry on for years. All organizations serve in an advisory capacity to the established authority. Their objective is to help the authorities do the job that the majority of people want and can afford. The National Citizens Council for Better Schools (9 East 40th Street, New York 16, N.Y.) is actively engaged in assisting local citizens committees to take an active part in school and community affairs.

Coordinating community councils that have a wider scope of concern than schools alone are of special significance where the community-school idea is developed.[13] Such groups, usually made up of representatives from a variety of organizations and agencies, may serve a large area, such as a city, or a neighborhood within a city or county. They usually raise questions and propose plans, leaving actual operation to new or existing agencies. Often they establish new patterns of contacts and working relationships among individuals and agencies. They tend to focus on specific local and neighborhood interests.

Role of the Teacher

The teacher must become a worthy and active member of the community in which he lives. He must understand the functions of community living and know how he can involve his boys and girls in community processes.

All teachers have opportunities that should be recognized and used to interpret every subject of the curriculum as an accepted and understandable part of community life.

Specifically, teachers can make their students more community conscious if they bring information about the community and its problems into the classroom. Students can assist in making and analyzing community surveys of such problems as water supply, health needs, fire hazards, and safety problems. Students can visit adults in the community and interview

---

[13] Hillman, Arthur. *Community Organization and Planning.* New York: Macmillan Co., 1950. Chapter 8, "Community Councils," p. 157-79.

them to secure opinions and information. Adults may be invited to the school to show pictures and souvenirs of travel. Excursions and field trips in the community can supplement classroom experiences. Libraries, museums, art galleries are sometimes unused by the schools. Citizens can contribute to various phases of the school curriculum if requested to do so. The Citizens Council for Better Schools has reported more than a score of specific ways in which local industries have cooperated in the school program, ranging from providing personnel for career conferences to making contributions toward the cost of school surveys.[14]

The potentialities for educational experiences are many times as great in the total community as they are in a schoolroom. The community is usually ready to cooperate with the school to make these potentialities a reality. By modifying its curriculum content and developing an attitude of cooperation, these community resources may be used to enrich and vitalize the school program. They need to be inventoried and catalogued for better use. A handbook of community resources may be developed in cooperation with community agencies, indicating places that might be visited thru school excursions, agencies that will provide guest speakers, agencies that will give demonstrations of their work, and those that will lend or donate visual materials. Explorations of local history prove valuable to many social studies classes. A listing of the skills and hobbies of parents may often lead to sources of curriculum enrichment.

The schools, in turn, have many resources, little known to the public, that can and should improve the life of the community—school buildings, equipment, and personnel. Teachers may encourage their students to participate in solving community problems. Citizens should find in the school an institution which can provide some assistance in working on any community problem.

---

[14] National Citizens Council for Better Schools. "Industry and Schools—Team for Future?" *Better Schools* 3: 5; June 1957.

Role of Youth

Student participation in community life should be recognized as a joint responsibility of the community agencies and the school. New methods are needed for incorporating programs in the school curriculums to help boys and girls participate more fully in community life. Students should have the opportunity to work on problems that are of concern to them. They might well serve on problem-study committees in the community council. They can be encouraged by their teachers to take part in youth organizations in the community. They can assist in community drives and projects.

Students must learn to understand what makes a community function. When the school acquaints youth with the processes which govern a community, they become better prepared to assume their responsibilities as citizens. Schools must share the responsibility for providing students with firsthand experiences in rural, suburban, and urban living. In some places the high-school students accept assignments to give voluntary service after school to selected organizations and social agencies. Careful planning and scheduling is, of course, required. The school curriculums must reflect broad community experiences and can do so by having students share in conducting factual investigations and surveys of community problems and needs, making outlines of possibilities for improvement, making detailed plans for action, helping the adults put plans into action, and participating in the evaluation of results.

Role of the School Administrator

The school administrator in the twentieth century is in a highly specialized occupation which requires specific training and talent. The position requires competence as a leader of a community service designed to improve individual and group welfare. The school administrator in a community school must have an adequate knowledge of:

> (a) The values, mores, traditions of the community and important groups within it, and especially significant deviations

from the norms of the Great Society. These affect, and may condition or dictate, the expectancies of the community regarding its school.

(b) The composition of the population of the community, its economic base, the pattern of social organization, the status and power structure. These affect, and may condition or dictate, the amount of support for the school and the type of program it develops.

(c) The means, on the basis of analysis of *a* and *b*, whereby full use can be made of all community resources in operating the school system and of operating effectively with all community agencies and forces in programs of community betterment and school improvement.[15]

The school administrator must know people and how to work with them. He must understand the community's history and its potentialities and must understand the processes of social interaction for community progress. He should:

- Know methods that can be used to determine problems and needs of the school and the community
- Understand and practice the democratic processes
- Like people and be able to inspire in them a faith in his willingness to help them solve their problems
- Have patience, persistence, and tact
- Know how to discover and train leaders
- Give credit for achievements to the groups involved
- Be tolerant and respectful of the opinions and views of others
- Be enthusiastic and sincere
- Be an outstanding community citizen in every respect.

The Line of Progress

Schools of both the types mentioned in the opening paragraphs of this chapter exist today. Some educational leaders would hesitate to see a universal effort to apply the community-school principle in all high schools, but a growing development of community awareness and participation seems to be essential to the high school of the future. There are varying degrees

---

[15] Wayland, Sloan R.; Brunner, Edmund deS.; and Hallenbeck, Wilbur C., *op. cit.*, p. 3.

of community involvement, depending in part upon the resources within the school and in part upon the community in which the school operates.

The school may use the community as a laboratory for learning, making full use of human resources and institutional agencies which may supplement the learning experiences provided in the school itself. The school may cooperate with community agencies thru helping those agencies carry their programs forward. The school may in effect become a service agency for the community. Or there may be a give-and-take in the control and operation of both school and community activities. At this latter degree of cooperation, the community-school idea becomes fully effective.

Those responsible for the program in each secondary school have the obligation to study the total setting of the school and to decide at what level of community identification the school should seek to operate. The closer the school can come to helping the community realize its full potential, the more effective will be the service of the school to the youth it is dedicated to serve.

5

extending the common school

V

DURING THE PAST FEW YEARS, in more than one-third of the states, studies have been made of the needs of public education beyond the twelfth grade. The reports of these studies are in remarkably close agreement on the place of the local public junior or community college in the American educational system. A typical statement appears in the report made by the Board of Regents of the University of the State of New York:

> Two-year *comprehensive* community colleges, characterized by low cost to the student, geographical availability and direct responsiveness to community needs, offering both transfer and technical-terminal programs, are considered to be the best single means of (*a*) accommodating future demands for higher education; (*b*) embracing the increasing heterogeneity of abilities represented in the students graduating from the secondary schools and (*c*) providing the education necessary for an emerging group of semi-professional occupations.[1]

Because of the importance of the junior college and its responsiveness to community needs thru local control, further

[1] University of the State of New York. *Statement and Recommendations by the Board of Regents for Meeting the Needs in Higher Education in New York State.* Albany: New York State Education Department, 1957. p. 13.

143

development of the junior college is given first priority in meeting state needs for higher education in California. A recent report in that state includes this sentence:

> The assumption that *adequate junior college facilities will be provided through local initiative and state assistance prior* to the establishment of new state college or University campuses is basic to the priorities developed in this report.[2]

Characteristic of the nationwide demand for an upward extension of the common educational program is this statement by the President of the United States:

> I firmly believe that more extensive education than that obtainable in high schools must be brought to every community and every locality in such a way that every young person regardless of his means, or his lack of means, can go to school for a minimum of two additional years.[3]

Social Forces That Create the Demand

The wide agreement in recommendations in all parts of the nation portends a continued rapid growth of two-year community and junior colleges, in both number of institutions and enrolments. The community junior college now stands about where the American high school stood in 1900. Its basic character has been developed and its purposes clarified. America at mid-century needs its services.

Educational institutions persist in a democratic society only if they serve the needs of the society. New educational institutions emerge only as new needs arise or as existing needs remain unmet by existing institutions. The recent rapid growth and impending expansion of the junior college are but a reflection of new forces and new needs in American life.

The first and most apparent change which has stimulated interest in junior-college development is the increasing number of students who must be educated in the immediate future.

<hr />

[2] California State Board of Education and the Regents of the University of California, Liaison Committee. *A Study of the Need for Additional Centers of Public Higher Education in California.* Sacramento: California State Department of Education, 1957. p. 103.

[3] Eisenhower, Dwight D. At cornerstone laying ceremonies, Anthony Wayne Library of American Study, Defiance College, Defiance, Ohio, October 15, 1953.

With the number of births in the 1950's roughly twice that of the 1930's it is clear that the number of individuals seeking post-high-school training will at least double by 1970. In addition, the maturity of the high school and its ready availability to all youth has increased the *proportion* of the age group prepared for and seeking education beyond high school.

> This great expansion of capable young people seeking education beyond high school represents an enormous opportunity and challenge for our society. But our institutions of higher learning, despite their remarkable achievements in the past, are in no shape today to meet the challenge. Their resources are already strained; their quality standards are even now in jeopardy, and their projected plans fall far short of the indicated needs.[4]

A second force creating the need and demand for the junior college is the profound belief of the American people in the efficacy of education and their commitment to the provision of equality of educational opportunity. Arthur S. Adams, addressing the California Junior College Association in 1956, spoke of the dedication of the American people to the principle that its welfare depends upon the individual and that the fortunes of the individual and of society rise and fall together. He said:

> It was dedication to this belief that led to the development of publicly supported elementary and secondary education. . . . It is this belief and public concern that educational opportunity should be provided for every individual, insofar as he is capable of profiting from it, that has led to the development of numerous types of institutions designed to serve new constituencies and to meet emerging social needs. Teachers colleges, engineering colleges, schools of commerce and business, junior colleges—all had their beginnings in the closing years of the Nineteenth Century. All of these developments mean that the people of our country have an abiding devotion to the ideal that each individual shall have the chance for education in accordance with the kind and degree of his talent.[5]

---

[4] The President's Committee on Education Beyond the High School. *Second Report to the President.* Washington, D. C.: Superintendent of Documents, Government Printing Office, 1957. p. 3.

[5] Adams, Arthur S. *The Place of Junior College Education in the Future of Our Country.* An address before the California Junior College Association, Yosemite, California, October 30, 1956.

A third force stimulating in particular the diversified vocational programs of the community colleges is the increase in the amount of skill required in a majority of occupations. At the turn of the century, unskilled labor constituted a significant majority of the labor force; today it is a minority. The demand for the worker with subprofessional training—the trained, skilled technician—has mounted with each new technical development:

> Under the stimulus of the technological advance, many new semi-professional occupations are emerging. . . . Such occupations require more than a trade training and something less than full professional training. Many of them have not yet been defined to the point where educational programs can be readily set up for them.[6]

The local community college is ideally located to analyze the subprofessional occupations which appear in the community and, in cooperation with advisory committees, to define appropriate training programs for them. Thus, these institutions can at once serve the needs of the individual and of the growing technical economy. The rapid increase in demand for the technically trained worker has stimulated the demand for local community colleges. Equal in force is the need for retraining and upgrading workers thru evening, extension, and extended-day programs of the local institution.

A fourth and perhaps corollary stimulus to the development of local junior colleges is the recognition of the necessity for training a greater portion of the available ability of each generation. It has been demonstrated repeatedly that a significant portion of the able people of each generation have not made their potential contribution because of lack of training. This is a waste that can no longer be tolerated.

Frequently it has been demonstrated that *accessibility* is a significant factor in each person's decision regarding advanced training. Analysis of enrolments in various types of higher institutions in different parts of the nation has shown

[6] National Education Association and American Association of School Administrators, Educational Policies Commission. *Manpower and Education.* Washington, D. C.: the Commission, 1956. p. 29.

that a significantly larger percentage of high-school graduates attend college when the higher institution is close to the district of graduation than do when the district of graduation is remote from a college. The development of the *local* two-year program brings the training institution to the students.

Why the Concern of Secondary Education?

It may well be asked why this present and impending growth of the junior college is of concern to secondary education. The mere fact that the junior college appears in cities and communities of varied size and character makes it of concern to those in charge of the high school. Both institutions serve the same people. Those concerned with the development and administration of a community's program of secondary education can scarcely fail to have vital concern with the nature and program of the community or junior college regardless of the type of control of the college.

It is most likely also that those responsible for the development and control of secondary education in a community will have similar responsibility for the public junior or community college serving the area. Four fairly distinct patterns of community college have developed:

1. An upward extension of the local public-school system with responsibility for government and administration placed with those responsible for the control of the local elementary and secondary schools.

2. A local public institution with a board and administration separate from those controlling the public schools for younger students. This organization is in the form of an overriding district which may include several local public-school systems, or it may include a territory that covers one or more counties.

3. An independent state institution, with primary control residing in state rather than local officers.

4. A branch of the existing state university. This is the primary organizational plan in Indiana, Pennsylvania, and Wisconsin, and to a lesser degree in New York and Ohio.

Plans that allow local organization and control are now most common. At least 26 states have statutes which authorize local governmental units to organize and operate community or junior colleges. Of 344 public junior colleges existing in 1956, 258 were operating under some form of local control; 33 were organized as state junior colleges; and 53 were outlying centers of state universities. Of the 258 institutions under local control, 163 were operated by districts which also controlled schools for lower grades.[7]

There is general agreement among authorities that the junior college should be a local institution, locally controlled. The effective equalization of educational opportunities, the elimination of the barriers that restrict the most effective development of our nation's talent, appears to demand further decentralization or localization of the freshman and sophomore years of college. The expanding need for post-high-school centers of technical-vocational education and adult education demands an institution which is locally controlled and is responsive to local needs. For administrative and legal purposes it seems essential that the institution be developed within the established framework of public education in each state and be coordinated with the existing secondary-school system as well as with the statewide program of higher education.

Those now in charge of programs of local secondary education need be concerned with the growing community college movement because it is most likely that, in the future, community colleges will appear as an upward extension of the local school system. Many existing institutions of this type began as postgraduate or integrated branches of existing high schools. While rocketing enrolments have resulted in many separate plants, with their own administrative officers, many successful

[7] Martorana, S. V. *New Mexico's Needs for Further Post-High-School Educational Programs.* Santa Fe: State Board of Educational Finance, 1956. p. V-5.

Bogue, Jesse P., editor. *American Junior Colleges.* Fourth edition. Washington, D. C.: American Council on Education, 1956. p. 18.

junior colleges still share the facilities of high schools. It is only reasonable to assume that both patterns will continue to appear as new schools are founded.

High School or College?

It is also pertinent to ask whether this new institution is an upward extension of the American high school or a localization of the first two years of the college program. The most nearly accurate answer would be *both*—and neither.

Thru this discussion the terms *junior college* and *community college* have deliberately been used interchangeably. This dual designation is characteristic of current practice. The term *junior college* was first applied to the freshman and sophomore program of a university. The program of the early junior colleges, and many present institutions, was limited to the presentation at a local level of a two-year liberal arts or preprofessional program. A majority of students enrolled with the intention of transferring to a four-year college or a degree-granting professional school. Institutions so limited have usually been called junior colleges, and it is probable that the term will continue to be applied to those schools which serve primarily to bridge the gap between the high school and the third year of college or university.

Junior colleges once established began to assume other functions and offer other curriculums responsive to community needs. Many vocational, technical, business, and subprofessional curriculums were added in which training for a vocational skill was combined with general education for civic and personal competence. Two-year general-education curriculums were developed for students who did not contemplate transfer to the four-year colleges. Adult education courses in great variety were developed for citizens seeking personal development or vocational upgrading. Broad areas of service to the community were attempted. Guidance became a major emphasis. While the college transfer program remains one of the functions of these comprehensive institutions, the term *junior college* became too narrow and the term *community college* came into use. In this characteristic adaptation to the needs of the community the institution is more akin to the high school than to the standard college or university.

A distinction between the meaning of the terms *junior college* and *community college* would certainly add clarity to much of the professional literature. Actually, no such differential definition as attempted here has either wide agreement or acceptance.

Out of a half century of growth and development, however, is emerging an institution which has its own unique dimension and character. It is neither an upward extension of the high school nor a localization of the lower division of a college. It finds its varied functions in the needs of the community it serves, and its major characteristic is its ability to adapt readily to meet community needs and maintain the required diversity of program. It is becoming truly the "People's College." Three essential characteristics of the emerging local post-high-school institution are apparent:

It is closely identified with community affairs. The offerings grow out of and are directly related to local demands, to needs of individuals and of the community. Since attendance is voluntary, the number, size, and duration of classes depend primarily upon public need and demand, upon the appropriateness of content, and upon the effectiveness of instruction. Programs are altered in conformity with changing socioeconomic patterns within the community. The direct advice of representatives of business and industry and of other lay leaders in the community is systematically secured and applied in planning, developing, evaluating, and revising the educational programs.

It has great diversity. It provides a wide range of opportunities. Programs are flexible, adaptable to the specific needs of individuals with varying goals, interests, and abilities. Courses range from a few weeks of instruction to recover a lost skill to two years of study in preparation for a semiprofessional career.

It emphasizes immediate as well as long-range educational goals. While post-high-school education includes lower-division college courses in preparation for further college work, the content for a majority of the courses is selected on the basis of use immediately upon completion of the instruction.

Purposes of the Community College

Many attempts have been made to state the purposes of the emerging community college. Perhaps the most nearly complete is that accepted by a study in California:

(1) *Occupational Education:* Complete training should be given to those students who will finish their period of formal education in the junior college. This training should be designed to achieve occupational competence . . . and personal adequacy for living.

(2) *General Education:* Every junior-college student should be given that training which will prepare him to function effectively as a member of his family, and as a citizen of his community, his state, his nation, and the world.

(3) *College Education (Lower Division):* Each junior college should provide lower division or the first two years of college work for those students who plan to transfer to a four-year college or university after completing two years in a junior college. This training should be broad enough to include the lower-division requirements in the liberal arts and in the scientific, engineering, and other professional fields.

(4) *Guidance:* The junior college will help each student to help himself in the choice of an occupation adjusted to his interests, aptitudes, and abilities. A program of training and guidance should be provided, so that every student may discover his aptitudes, choose a life work, and prepare for the successful pursuit of such work.

(5) *Community Service:* Every junior college should cooperate with other public educational institutions in providing instruction to meet the needs of all people living in the region. The program of training should include occupational and general education.[8]

---

[8] Regents of the University of California and the California State Board of Education, Liaison Committee. *A Restudy of the Needs of California in Higher Education.* Sacramento: California State Department of Education, 1955. p. 52.

The Role of Leadership

It is becoming increasingly clear that the American people are committed to the principle that every student qualified to pursue education beyond the twelfth grade should have the opportunity to do so. The companion principle is that educational opportunity should fit the special capabilities of the individual student. The length of the course should vary with the objective; and in modern America the list of possible objectives, in terms of knowledge, intellectual development, and skills, is constantly growing. Hence, junior colleges are integral and essential parts of a well-rounded system of higher education in the United States.[9]

The community junior college has no single pattern—no standard curriculum. If it fulfils its true destiny, it will emerge in as many forms and with as many programs as there are distinct characteristics and needs in the various cities and communities of America.

Heavy indeed is the responsibility of the local educational leaders who must guide this institution and shape it to meet the complex and unique needs of each community. Theirs is the opportunity and duty:

• To develop community understanding of the need for post-high-school education and of the function it must perform

• To direct the discovery and analysis of community needs

• To define and develop the educational programs which will serve these needs.

The junior college is at the growing edge of both secondary and higher education. The role of the leaders responsible for its development will be that of blending the contributions of each in the formation of institutions that will serve the diverse needs of each community.

---

[9] Bogue, Jesse P., editor, *op. cit.*, p. v.

high schools and higher education

VI

high schools and higher education

HENRY ADAMS, observing the deficiencies of his own formal education, states the classic dilemma of education:

> The attempt of the American of 1800 to educate the American of 1900 had not often been surpassed for folly; and since 1800 the forces and their complications had increased a thousand times or more. The attempt of the American of 1900 to educate the American of 2000, must be even blinder than that of the Congressman of 1800, except so far as he had learned his ignorance. During a million or two of years, every generation in turn had toiled with endless agony to attain and apply power, all the while betraying the deepest alarm and horror at the power they created. The teacher of 1900, if foolhardy, might stimulate; if foolish, might resist; if intelligent, might balance, as wise and foolish have often tried to do from the beginning; but the forces would continue to educate and the mind would continue to react. All the teacher could hope was to teach it reaction.[1]

Shall the educator stand on the safe ground of the past, transmit its values, state its problems, and rationalize its solutions; or shall he brave the future and accept the risk of failure in

[1] Adams, Henry. *The Education of Henry Adams.* Boston: Houghton Mifflin Co., 1918. p. 497.

the establishment of any values, or the definition of any problems, or the presentation of any method of reaching solutions?

It is this dilemma that has brought about the repeated formal
reviews of our total system of American education that have
changed its purpose and its direction without ever affecting
for so much as a moment the forces which have driven it in-
exorably to expansion and incredible complication. Three solutions of the dilemma have been presented during this century,
each enduring for about 20 years. Each solution has been in
terms of a change in relationship between secondary school
and college, and each in turn has been altered by forces
partly within and partly without the educational system. Today we are approaching still another solution.

In broad terms, the relationship between secondary education and higher education has come full cycle in 60 years. As
the century began, it was marked by approximate unity of
purpose and curriculum, combined with a high degree (approximately 33 percent) of pupil retention.[2] Subsequently,
there developed a separation as to both purpose and curriculum
while pupil continuity declined, reaching at one point a low
of less than 20 percent. Today, we are again approaching a
unity of purpose and curriculum, but on a basis completely
different from that of 1900, while the percent of student continuity is at an all-time high of 42 percent, with every indica-
tion that it will continue to rise.

This chapter discusses the evolution of this relationship,
notes the changes that have taken place, and indicates lines
along which the relationship may be expected to develop. The

---

[2] In 1900 the total enrolment in secondary education was approximately
700,000; in undergraduate higher education it was 232,000; thus there were
33.1 percent as many pupils in colleges as in the high schools. (Secondary
enrolments here and thruout this chapter refer only to Grades IX thru XII.)

When the school and the college enrolments are taken as percents of
the population aged 14 thru 17 years and 18 thru 21 years, respectively—
11.4 percent and 3.9 percent—it is seen that the service of the college to its
age group is 34.2 percent that of the high school to its age group. In neither
case, however, were enrolments and age groups matched exactly.

Either of the foregoing rough measures of pupil retention from high school
to college gives about the same results.

The above and similar comparisons in this chapter are based on the biennial statistical reports of the U. S. Office of Education.

chapter is in four sections, the first dealing with the relationship between secondary and higher education in 1900; the next two sections dealing respectively with changes in those relationships, 1900-1920, 1920-1940; and the final section dealing with present and immediately foreseeable relations.

In 1900

The relationship between secondary education and higher education in 1900 was marked, as noted above, by a high degree of unity and of purpose. There is, however, an important qualification to this statement. At the turn of the century, there were essentially two systems of education. One system was long established, well developed, self-perpetuating, and dominant in the sense of exercising substantial control over the higher reaches of American intellectual and professional life. The other system was still in the early stages of development; it lacked the strength and resources for self-perpetuation, and exercised relatively little control over American intellectual and professional life.

The Old Pattern

The first system was composed of four segments:

1. A small group of historically strong private colleges centered, for the most part, in the Northeast. These institutions still retained their classical programs, operated on a largely prescribed curriculum, and admitted their students in terms of rigidly prescribed entrance requirements which had, thru a series of conferences and agreements, become fairly uniform about 10 years earlier. A few of these institutions—Harvard, Columbia, Pennsylvania—were well along in process of development into universities; others had barely begun to so develop. Hopkins, Clark, and Chicago, recent foundations modeled on German universities, were, at that time, exerting important influences on the development of the older institutions.

2. A relatively small number of state universities, founded in the time of the classical dominance of higher education, closely allied in tradition to the dominant colleges, and interchangeable with them as to personnel and standards.

3. A sizable group of small church-related institutions, widely distributed thruout the country. Most of these had been founded during the 30-year period preceding the Civil War (and relatively few have been founded since). These institutions were modeled upon the older private colleges and had, in fact, been established in their educational tradition by graduates of those colleges. These institutions, with limited resources, were serving small constituencies, but serving them well, and within their tiny budgets, were prospering educationally.

4. A group of private secondary schools, attached so closely to the private institutions of higher education that the secondary-education activity was often an inseparable part of the college.[3] But, whether attached physically or not, the schools and colleges were always integral in a curriculum sense. A student prepared for entrance to this system of higher education by entering this system of secondary education. This was not a matter of snobbishness but of necessity; there was no other way to obtain college preparation, except in urban centers. Some public high schools, such as Boston Latin, Classical High in Springfield, Central High in Philadelphia, and Erasmus Hall in Brooklyn, were modeled on the private schools and offered equivalent preparation.

Within this system of education there was, as noted above, a high degree of unity, of agreement as to purpose, of pupil continuity, and of curriculum similarity. There were several reasons why this was so.

The total system was an American adaptation of the European and English concept that higher education was essential only for those members of the middle and higher classes re-

---

[3] One of the early problems encountered by the Carnegie Foundation in establishing its pension plan was the separation of secondary and higher education as carried on simultaneously by the same institution, a task necessary in order to identify the college teachers eligible for pension.

quired to carry on the four important professions of the time: clergyman, lawyer, physician, teacher.

Like the systems from which it was derived, this system was closed and self-perpetuating. It operated on standards that were recognizably comparable because all those who taught, administered, and applied the standards were products of the system, a situation prevailing even today in most European countries and in parts of the English system.

The system was relatively immune to change from internal pressures because it dealt with little that was controversial. The newer disciplines, specialties, and professions had not yet entered the ken of the older institutions. When they did, they would exert their pressures from the outside, not the inside.

Admission to the system was based largely on economic selection. A few able students hurdled the economic barriers thru enduring hardship, but by and large the basic entrance requirement was financial. Once within the system, individuals tended to carry on. Pupil continuity was high since there was little purpose in entering the system except to complete it.

The New Pattern

In contrast to the older system of education—with its stable program, its classical tradition, and its well-established relationship to the major professions, and with its support assured from endowments, private benefactions, and church groups— the second American educational system was still new and unproven in 1900.

The new system was based primarily upon tax support, altho important segments of it were supported by private benefactions. Its program was flexible, its educational traditions were still unformed. To the extent that it was concerned with professions, it dealt with new applications of method and knowledge that had still to be recognized as professions—and it was deficient in the facilities, the resources, and the human materials that it required for its growth. Its purpose was not the education of a privileged class but the extension of educational opportunity to all who could profit therefrom.

Public high schools—The public high schools, enrolling about 520,000 students and graduating approximately 60,000, were already considerably larger numerically than the private college-preparatory schools which, counting secondary courses given in colleges, enrolled about 180,000 students. The public high schools were relatively new. The definitive legal decision which established the right to expend public funds in support of secondary education was barely 30 years old, and most of the development of the schools had taken place after that decision.

Because of their newness and scarcity, they were unevenly distributed and difficult of access for the rural population. Because, lacking any other model, they had used the private-school curriculum as a starting point, their instruction often had little apparent value for noncollege-bound students. Because of shortages of both teachers and money, they were notably variable as to standards. These internal factors, combined with the job opportunities available and the climate of opinion that work was to be begun at an early age, caused a high drop-out rate.[4] Altho many left early, a large proportion (estimated at two-thirds) of those who actually graduated from high school went on to college.

Teacher education—Because of the rapid growth of the public high schools, their demands for teachers were enormous. And, because the private colleges were not producing enough teachers to supply the needs of the older system and to staff the public high schools also, it was necessary to produce teachers from other sources. State normal schools, training schools, a few pioneering teachers colleges (public and private), and state universities all shared in supplying our public grammar schools and high schools with teachers.

Privately supported technical schools—Much of the early work in the development of technological education and sub-professional programs was carried on by low-cost or free institutions conceived as a form of workingman's college and supported by private benefaction. It is probably not inaccurate

---

[4] In 1900, out of 9,000,000 youth aged 15 thru 20 years, only 2,443,000 were in school and college.

to say that such institutions were relatively more important in technological education in 1900 than they are today when they have either disappeared or become complex degree-granting institutions. The number of such institutions was not large, but they were the first to offer night-school courses, to offer programs for the part-time student, and to offer low-cost or free technological education to urban students.

Closely related to these schools, but on a professional level, were a few scattered technical and engineering schools. These were highly professionalized engineering schools which were important mainly because of their control of professional standards in engineering, which meant at least partial control of the development of any new engineering programs.

Land-grant colleges—The land-grant colleges, still relatively small and, insofar as higher education was concerned, unimportant, were first authorized during the Civil War. Their objectives reflected the needs of the times—agriculture and the mechanic arts to meet the demands for better trained farmers, the engineering skills needed in opening up the new lands, and the rudiments of military science to provide for the national defense.

Their development had been slow, for, just as the public high schools had represented a new idea in large-scale secondary education, so the land-grant colleges represented new ideas in higher education—increasing the opportunities for higher education, and providing a "practical" form of higher education.

State universities—Altho a few of the older state universities held to the pattern of the classical tradition, most of the newer ones were building new traditions, experimenting with the curriculum, and establishing more liberal entrance requirements in receiving high-school graduates. Most of the state universities had departments for the preparation of teachers; some of them included the land-grant projects as integral parts of the university; others had developed parallel university departments in agriculture and the familiar branches of engineering, as well as strong liberal arts departments.

As the components of this system are described, it becomes clear that the contrast with the older system was a sharp one. In the new system there was little unity, or pupil continuity, or curriculum similarity. There was, however, a broad agreement as to purpose—generally accepted as the extension of educational opportunity.

It was not in fact a system, but a number of separate, largely unrelated expressions of the same idea, carrying within them, however, the openings and even the requirements of major change that would in time weld them into a single dynamic force.

Higher Education in Control

To conclude this review of the factors determining the relationship between secondary education and higher education at the beginning of this century, it may be noted again that the relationship was a simple one. Secondary education was under the control and dominance of higher education. Its purpose was to prepare for higher education. Its effectiveness, measured in terms of the products of secondary education entering college, was high—higher, in fact, than it has been at any subsequent date.

However, within the factors controlling the relationship, there were forces which would produce tremendous changes. The review of the next 20-year period will be concerned with those changes.

1900-1920

The extent of the change in the relationship between secondary education and higher education during these 20 years can be indicated by a single set of figures—that during this period the enrolments in secondary education increased from 11 percent of the number aged 14 thru 17 years in 1900 to 32 percent of that age group in 1920, while enrolments in higher education were increasing from 4 percent to 8 percent of the group aged 18 to 21.

This tremendous growth—an approximate tripling of the drawing and holding power of secondary education, a doubling of this power for higher education—was a product of the rapid industrialization of the nation, the acceleration of urbanization as a result of industrialization, and an increase in the per-capita productivity of American workers.

Secondary Schools

Several related sets of events took place with respect to secondary education during this period.

The requirements of industrialization tended to raise the requirements for employment. Industrialization cannot be based on unskilled, undereducated labor; the requirements for skill and education could best be met thru the public high schools and the technical institutes. The demand for education forced a change in the nature of the public high school. The education required for early employment, as contrasted with the requirements for college admission, tended to be "practical." Commercial and technical subjects were given greater emphasis; mathematics, science, and foreign language were modified to make room for the new subjects.

With the changing curriculum, problems began to arise with respect to able students who had taken high-school courses which were not acceptable for college entrance. Little could be done, except for the student to spend additional time in high school, but the problem was identified.

The changing high-school curriculum opened the doors to new groups of students, or made it possible to hold old students for longer periods, resulting directly in increasing enrolments.

Employers began to realize that high-school graduates outperformed nonhigh-school graduates, on the average, and started setting employment requirements accordingly.

Increasing urbanization, better roads, and better transportation brought larger numbers of potential high-school students into contact with the schools. High schools continued to be built and reached the point of reasonable accessibility, tho standards remained variable.

Higher Education

While industrialization and urbanization were changing the nature of the secondary schools, they were also having their effect upon the colleges and universities. These effects were not as dramatic as the effects upon secondary education, but they were the forerunners of important changes.

A number of new professional fields appeared in substantial numbers within higher education. Education, business and commerce, agriculture, home economics, journalism all rose in relative importance. Degrees in engineering accounted for only 4 percent of the degrees granted in 1900 but for 9 percent in 1920.

The established colleges of the older system continued more or less unchanged, except for four moves: (a) They increased their graduate programs; (b) they began to develop preprofessional programs to strengthen the established professions of law, medicine, and theology; (c) they expanded their undergraduate programs which did not require the classics, altho continuing to denote those programs as of inferior category; (d) they modified entrance requirements for students not entering the classical course.

Because the colleges of the older system remained essentially unreceptive to changes in entrance requirements and to admission of professional programs into the curriculum, the pressure that came upon tax-supported institutions to accommodate themselves to the new condition resulted in rapid development of those institutions in contrast to the stability of the older institutions.

Because the secondary schools grew more rapidly than the colleges, college preparation began to be a matter of decreasing concern to secondary schools and a smaller fraction of their programs.

Colleges that had maintained preparatory departments or offered secondary-school courses as part of their curriculum began to divest themselves of all secondary-school work. Such divestment was now possible because of increasing accessibility of public high schools.

Effects on Relationship and Function

From these descriptions of the effects of social and economic development upon secondary and higher education in the first two decades of the century, two central facts emerge:

First, the growth of secondary education at a rate far exceeding the growth of higher education indicated its acceptance of two distinct and separate tasks: one, the time-honored task of college preparation; the other, the newer task of direct and specific preparation for immediate employment.

Second, the rate and nature of the change in higher education indicated that the older system referred to in the first section of this chapter had successfully resisted change, but had not increased its enrolments as rapidly as had the new system of secondary and college education.

Altho in hindsight it is possible to see that the years 1900 to 1920 were setting a pattern of change in our educational system, it must be said that at the time these patterns must have been only barely discernible. Certainly, so far as the older colleges were concerned, the changes up to that time had been relatively unimportant. And the relations between secondary and higher education must have appeared firmly established on the basis of continued dominance of the secondary schools by the colleges. On the other side of the coin, it must have seemed to the leaders of the new movement in secondary education as tho the control of older concepts of education over their developing enterprises was of a restrictive, not to say stifling, nature.

In other words, the relationship between secondary and higher education, as late as 1920, remained at least superficially stable. The development of secondary education as the instrument of general education was well under way, but had not gained sufficient strength to overturn the controls of higher education. The most that had been accomplished in this direction was the acceptance of the fact that a certain amount of the program of secondary education was set aside for work which was not of college-preparatory grade and was regarded by many as inferior.

However, all of this was to change, and shortly.

1920-1940

As has been noted, the tremendous rate of growth in secondary education during the first 20 years of the century had been the result of social and economic changes and requirements, rather than the product of any plan based on analysis of those changes and requirements. The period 1920-1940 saw the introduction of programs based on such analysis and a change in the secondary-higher education relationship as a result.

During these years the drawing and holding power of secondary education more than doubled. Whereas in 1920 high-school enrolments equalled 32 percent of the 14-17-year age group, by 1940 the enrolments had risen to 73 percent. (Enrolment figures for both years are for Grades IX thru XII.) During the same period undergraduate college enrolments as a percent of the population aged 18 thru 21 years increased from only 7.9 percent of the age group to 14.2 percent. Undergraduate college enrolments as a whole were only 19.3 percent of high-school enrolments, as compared with 33.1 percent in 1900, and 24.5 percent in 1920.

The percent of high-school graduates who went on to college dropped from a little more than half in 1920 (it had been more than two-thirds in 1900) to only about a third in 1940.

These trends meant that for two successive 20-year periods college preparation had affected *relatively* fewer high-school students, tho the actual numbers were larger. This did not necessarily mean any lower standard of college preparation or of opportunities to obtain college preparation. What it did mean was a full recognition of a change in the nature and purpose of secondary education and acceptance by secondary education of the responsibility for developing a general-purpose curriculum for students not headed for college.

Changes in Secondary Education

In the process of accepting this responsibility and devising such a curriculum, a number of things happened in secondary education.

Since the schools were now drawing over half of the eligible age group, the mean ability level of their students, no longer self-selected in terms of college ambitions, was dropping steadily and with noticeable effect upon performance in the standard courses of secondary schools. If these students were to be retained and graduated—and social philosophy called for them to be so retained—new courses had to be devised to meet their educational needs.

Two steps were involved: (a) The schools began to slough off responsibility for certain forms of education that were tied to college preparation. The principal casualties were certain courses in foreign languages, advanced mathematics, English composition, sciences, and political and social history, which came to be considered the province of the college rather than the secondary schools. They continued to be taught but they were not taught with the same urgency as before. (b) The schools began to accept responsibility for general education, recognizing that for the majority of their students the high schools represented all the formal education that would be available. In so doing, they changed the nature of many of the older subjects given as required courses and added new ones.

As a result of these changes, the standards of secondary schools, no longer tied to rigid curriculum patterns, began to be tied to achievement patterns. Students came to be judged in terms of their performance *in* whatever curriculum they were enrolled rather than *by* the curriculum in which they were enrolled.

Because of the drastic curriculum changes in secondary schools, there arose between school and college a strong difference of opinion as to what schools should teach. Colleges, insisting that the old college-entrance curriculum was the only true gospel, were challenged by the schools to join in research and experiment. They did so and, in the end, accepted the finding that it was student ability and achievement rather than curriculum pattern that controlled success in college, and that insistence on curriculum pattern could not be justified.

With this finding and its implementation, the secondary schools assumed a greater degree of control over their entire curriculum, and colleges began to shift their entrance patterns to accommodate the new emphasis upon achievement as measured by objective means.

This action had a side effect of tremendous tho temporary importance with respect to the private college-preparatory schools that had for so long been a central feature of the system of privately supported education. Apparently they lost much of their reason for existence when the curriculum which was the main prop of their existence became optional. If all students prepared for all colleges, then the private schools were not necessary. Eventually, they were to work out of this trouble, but for a time their difficulties were serious.

Changes in Higher Education

While the secondary schools were undergoing their changes, major changes were also taking place in higher education. The causes were complex and could scarcely be catalogued in full. But a central cause with demonstrable effects was the rapid development in American life of various lines of specialization, which were identified and developed as professions. This development, within the period of the 20 years under review, brought major changes in higher education and set the stage for even more important changes to come.

The older professions of the ministry, law, and medicine changed their requirements and their mode of admission to professional status. The ministry had entered upon a period of difficulty in drawing new recruits. It is arguable that some of its loss of appeal was due to the drawing off of some ministerial functions into secular channels. The community of interest that the church had once represented was replaced by other foci of community enterprise. Law and medicine became more difficult of access. Professional schools were improved in quality and reduced in numbers. Selection for these professions was based upon college work followed by competitive examinations. Furthermore, the professions subdivided, introducing specialities in professional practice and turning some of their functions over to new professions, such as accountancy, public administration, public health, or hospital administration, or to semiprofessions such as nursing and medical technology.

While this was going on in the colleges which were the strongholds of the older professions, the tax-supported institutions were also changing. The land-grant colleges, having accepted at their founding the function of specific and practical preparation, continued to fulfil their function by developing new professional programs and were joined in this function by the state universities. Hence, new professions emerged: social work, public administration, librarianship, home economics, accountancy, journalism, nursing, medical technology, hotel administration, as well as hybrid professions such as agricultural engineering and hospital administration.

Preparation for teaching, once handled on very different bases by the two systems of education began to be merged into one inclusive operation and to be recognized as part of professional education. It was in 1932 that the U. S. Office of Education for the first time included the statistics of teachers colleges and normal schools with the statistics of higher education; it was a change that reflected new trends in teacher education. The former normal schools were becoming degree-granting colleges and acquiring some of the characteristics of liberal arts institutions. At the same time, some liberal arts colleges were shifting their teacher-preparation functions to the graduate level, in professional programs designed for that purpose.

While these changes were taking place in the older institutions, both private and tax-supported, two other essentially new types of institutions were emerging. One was the urban service institution usually, tho not necessarily, under private auspices, offering a wide variety of courses, providing both four-year and shorter courses, enforcing minimal entrance requirements (and for noncredit students, none at all), and supporting itself meagerly but sufficiently on student fees. These institutions, in response to the demands of urban populations, developed primarily along professional lines; they supported a remarkable number of pre-professional and professional schools and programs and, except for some of the professional areas, offered them in both day and evening sessions. The other new institution was the public junior college, discussed in Chapter V.

As the demand for professional training developed, the new professions, like the old, began to subdivide and specialize, which required increasing amounts of advanced training. Much of this advanced training was provided by the established graduate schools of the older private institutions and the state universities, which found their offerings in education, business, and technology proliferating in unexpected directions.

The colleges, particularly the older colleges, having to accept the fact that they could no longer prescribe the college entrance curriculum, began to modify their own programs to free themselves from dependence upon secondary schools. This modification took two forms:

1. The application of standardized tests to measure student achievement provided a basis for placement of students in courses, and at the same time led to the discovery that colleges would have to give "remedial" instruction, in reality a review of high-school studies, if they were to salvage their investment in a considerable number of their incoming freshmen. This use of tests was to lead later to the establishment of present selective admission practices, but at a time when no college had a supply of applicants large enough to permit selective admission, its effects were felt only within the college.

2. The curriculum was modified to introduce courses that were not tied directly to secondary-school preparation.

These changes in college testing, placement, and program developed slowly, but in their development they established procedures that a few years later were to be of great importance. Among the private institutions, Columbia and Chicago early developed large-scale programs of testing and placement and at the same time introduced programs of study in what were then called survey courses, but were later to be renamed under the more acceptable title of "general education." Among the public institutions the University of Minnesota pioneered by setting up an entire division of the university as a General College, for students not ready for work in the established college patterns.

Resulting Developments

From these developments in both secondary and higher education, several different sets of results emerged.

The secondary schools, partially freed from curriculum controls imposed by college entrance requirements, had assumed greater control of their own programs and were continuing to expand. From the standpoint of relations with colleges, it might be said that all secondary schools were now in a position to prepare for all colleges.

The increasing requirements for specialists in American commercial, industrial, and professional life had forced the creation of a long series of new professions, the training for them being controlled thru college and university programs. These creations in turn had brought about a new unity of function within the entire community of higher education.

Since all schools could now prepare for all colleges, the colleges in turn were now able to draw on all schools in implementing their desire for national rather than regional student bodies. In this they were aided by the shift from emphasis on curriculum patterns to emphasis on performance, which made it possible to substitute simple objective tests of ability and achievement (widely and probably permanently misnamed as aptitude tests) for cumbersome subjectmatter examinations.

With quick and useful "aptitude" measures at hand, both schools and colleges began to realize the extent of the loss of superior-ability students between the tenth grade of secondary school and college entrance and to pay increasing attention to measures for minimizing this loss.

Thus, while this period from 1920 to 1940 had seen the struggle for control of the secondary-school curriculum decided in favor of the secondary school and for a time had witnessed a widening gulf between secondary school and college, it had also established patterns which promised to open the way to a new unity between these two segments of our educational system. The results of this were to become apparent before very long.

1940-1960

As we approach the end of the mid-century readjustment of American education to the mid-century scale of economic, cultural, and social values, our concerns naturally move to the years ahead. We know that our educational system must be expanded because our population is increasing. We know that our educational system must assume new tasks because our culture and our economy create new problems in their growth. We know that the segments of our educational system must move closer together because we cannot afford the wastages that come from the loss of time, the duplication of effort, and the failure to use our resources, human and material, to their full potential.

Knowing these things and knowing, too, where the wastages are most likely to occur, we can cast ahead, using present trends and present needs as guidelines, to explore speculatively some possible developments. These developments which *may* occur are considered under five heads:

Curriculum

The secondary-school curriculum, after a long period of relative independence from the requirements of higher education, appears to be entering upon a period in which it must necessarily draw closer to college requirements if it is to serve the needs of a school population in which a large percent will be college oriented. As the proportion of college-bound students increases, colleges, in response to pressures for admission, will increase their present expectations as to the specific preparation their students will bring to college classes, and may be expected to differentiate among students in terms of both quantity and quality of preparation.

In terms of quantity of preparation, it must be anticipated that entrance requirements will become more specific. This specificity will be felt particularly in the sciences and mathematics, fields where the secondary schools must bear the major responsibility for identifying and motivating those who are to become our doctors, engineers, scientists, and teachers. However, the restatement of entrance requirements cannot be expected to stop with science and mathematics. Foreign languages, the social studies, and English must come in for their share of renewed attention and revision.

Adjustments in high schools—Much of the effect of the revision of college entrance requirements can be turned to advantage by the secondary schools if they will give their attention to qualitative improvements in their offerings. It is a common and justified complaint that many students entering our colleges in any given year have not been pushed to their full intellectual capacity by their school and that their readjustment to college work must therefore include acceptance of demands that they henceforth work up to their capacity.

The changes that high schools will make to recognize these trends will doubtless include the following, already being tried by some schools:

1. The introduction of advanced courses for individually identified students, as early as the beginning of junior high school. Such courses, in their simplest forms, can be a telescoping of three years of work into two so that superior students in seventh-grade English, social studies, mathematics, or science can finish their ninth-grade work a year ahead of time and be prepared to move directly into tenth-grade subjects. In the foreign languages, this concept requires adjustment since these offerings which do not ordinarily begin until the ninth grade would have to be pushed forward in time and fitted into a schedule which ordinarily is not designed to accommodate them.

The early introduction of advanced courses would permit increased flexibility in the later high-school years and the introduction of specialized courses in the eleventh and twelfth grades. Such courses might or might not be of college level, but they would represent an achievement beyond the standard secondary curriculum.

2. The introduction of college instructional methods in the higher grades of high schools. An important part of the ad-

justment to college comes in the shift from secondary-school instructional methods, often based upon single texts and at a pace geared to the mean ability of the class, to college instructional methods emphasizing extensive reading assignments, problem solving, and written reports, and to a college pace which is ordinarily more rapid than in secondary schools. Secondary-school adaptation of these methods in college-preparatory classes would be an important step in acceptance of the secondary school's increasing responsibility for their graduates' success in college. (It is also true that colleges, with profit to the students, might well adopt methods more consistent with the psychology of learning.)

Adjustments in college—Changes in the secondary-school curriculum such as those mentioned above would go far toward adapting that curriculum to present and foreseeable trends in the enforcement of entrance requirements by the colleges. These are:

1. Higher qualitative admission requirements. A substantial number of colleges are today enforcing admission requirements based upon achievement far above the minimum requirements for high-school graduation. It is foreseeable that the colleges now practicing selective admissions will, within a decade, be selecting freshmen whose mean achievement in their high-school courses would prepare them for the second semester of the present freshman year.

2. Closer relation of admission requirements to the college curriculum. It will become increasingly necessary to state them in terms of the workings of the college curriculum. It may soon be necessary for a student who wishes to complete an engineering course in four years to be prepared to begin calculus in the first semester of his freshman year and to move directly into a freshman chemistry course which will include the elements of qualitative and quantitative analysis. Tho not now necessary, it is conceivable that a student in the liberal arts curriculum will enter a freshman foreign-language course based on a reading, writing, and speaking knowledge of the language; and a

freshman course in the humanities which is essentially a course in comparative literature. These and similar curriculum features now exist to some degree in our leading colleges, and all of them represent demands for preparation not reflected in current statements of entrance requirements. The rewording of entrance requirements to conform to these curriculum demands will be a difficult technical process, but it is a process which the colleges are likely to undertake.

3. More liberal transfer arrangements. Colleges have become relatively restrictive in their arrangements for recognition of achievement in secondary schools and in other colleges; they must face the necessity of lifting some of their restrictions if they wish to attract superior students. This liberalizing process is slowly gathering momentum with respect to advanced achievement in secondary schools, but it has far to go with respect to the transfer of students from other colleges and from such upward extensions of secondary education as technical institutes and community colleges. It may even be necessary to adapt a testing mechanism in order to accomplish this liberalization, but by some means this must be accomplished.

Both schools and colleges, in developing curriculum changes, must recognize that our school system is responsible for an increasing span of the student's life. The *quantity* of education now required to fit an individual to take his place in society is greater than ever before, and schools and colleges must accept and adjust to this fact. In process of adjustment they must give increasing attention to individual differences and must be prepared to offer greater opportunities for specialization. Specialization in its turn demands specific preparation, a demand which must necessarily be reflected in more specific and more rigorous college entrance requirements, more carefully adjusted to actual programs of study.

Guidance

Guidance, which has required many years to achieve recognition as a standard part of a college entrance program, may be expected to assume major importance in the years immediately ahead. This development may be expected to involve several steps:

1. Appraisal of student ability and the formulation by the student of educational and occupational plans in terms of those abilities, which is now often delayed until the later years of secondary school, may be expected to become a standard part of the secondary-school program of counseling in all its grades.

2. Student guidance will be expanded to include parent orientation and guidance as a part of the planning program. This broadening of the guidance counseling program will present a serious problem of staffing for the schools and probably will lead to a considerable increase in guidance staffs. It will, however, prove a most helpful step in resolving the difficulties in guidance now being encountered by college students.

3. College admissions offices will add staff members whose primary responsibility will be that of assisting secondary schools in planning their guidance programs. This is already a significant part of the load of many admissions offices and will become so important that it will have to be handled as a separate admissions specialty and staffed accordingly.

4. Guidance materials, written in nontechnical language and addressed to parents, students, and teachers, will be published and may be expected to ease some of the less difficult, but most common, guidance problems.

5. Colleges, which have been slow to adopt in their own programs the guidance activities they urge on the secondary schools, will, in time, add such programs to their present student personnel activities. In some colleges this will mean only a formalization of work that is already being done, but for many it will involve a new dimension in personnel activities that is now largely centered on student life, health services, and the provision of a placement office.

6. Training programs for guidance counselors and admissions officers will be developed, both qualitatively and quantitatively, far beyond their present level. The serious shortage of trained workers in these fields calls for early cooperative efforts toward expanded programs of training.

In summary, both high schools and colleges will find it necessary to expand their guidance activities to cover a period of work with each student which will extend from the beginning of junior high school until well into the college years and will go deeply into individual abilities and problems.

Administration

Many of the problems of school-college relationships will necessarily be solved administratively. Some of the areas in which administrative action can ameliorate present difficulties are:

Application and selection—Present difficulties, including multiple applications by students, poor timing of application and admission procedures, and poor communication between schools, colleges, and applicants can be dealt with, altho perhaps not completely solved, by joint school-and-college planning and scheduling. Areas in which such joint activity can be effective are:

> Agreement on common forms for records and applications.
> Agreement on time limits for the period of application, of testing, of selection, and of admission.
> Possible agreement on the use of central clerical services at certain points in the application and admissions operations. This is listed only as possible because of inevitable objections to the creation of any central agency, as well as because of the technical problems involved. If these difficulties can be overcome, such agencies would prove useful in expediting the handling of applications and of notifications of admission.

More liberal transfer arrangements—This development already referred to under the heading of curriculum is essential if the colleges are to deal equitably with the increasing numbers of community-college and other students seeking to enter with advanced standing. It is specifically referred to here because some leading colleges have become, in recent years, less rather than more liberal in their handling of transfer cases.

Referral of candidates—All colleges and many schools know that the present workings of the admission system result in the failure of able candidates to be enrolled in colleges suited to their abilities and interests. A referral system would reduce this misplacement. Such a system would require a considerable amount of education of schools, candidates, and colleges before it could be accepted. Granted such acceptance, there are no serious technical difficulties involved.

Much can be done administratively to reduce the present problems of movement from school to college, but only if schools and colleges will accept the fact that effective joint administrative action involves more give and take on matters of sovereignty than either party now seems willing to grant.

Instruction

As both schools and colleges commit themselves to an ever-widening range of programs, designed to accommodate students having a wide spectrum of abilities, the problems of instructional relationships will increase.

Both schools and colleges must continue their search for more effective and more economical methods of instruction. Both must seek ways of making better use of specialized teachers; each must seek information on what the other does. Limited experiment and experience have shown that schools and colleges can establish communication on this problem of instruction, but to be effective it must be direct contact between teachers, not indirect contact thru administrators, publications, or the reported experiences of students.

It must be recognized that the devisement of methods for direct contacts between school and college teachers will involve considerable time and money. However, the improvements in college preparation, the instructional gains on both sides of the line between Grade XII and the freshman year, and the economies in teacher time would certainly justify the expenditure. The possibility that efforts will be made to draw schools and colleges together instructionally is admittedly highly speculative. It can only be said that it needs to be done.

Testing

As already mentioned in this chapter, testing has become an important tool for both school and college in the evaluation of individual differences and also in the measurement of educational achievement. It may be expected that the use of tests will increase over the years ahead, but if they are to be used effectively, several further developments are needed.

Secondary-school testing programs must be reviewed to eliminate duplicating tests and tests that produce unimportant or irrelevant information. Unfortunately, tests are often administered rather than used, and many testing programs now fail to meet the criterion of full usefulness.

College entrance tests must be based firmly on joint school-and-college study of the characteristics and use of such tests and on joint participation in test development.

There must be a continuation of research for effective measures of motivation and personality. Many of the instruments now in use in these areas are inadequate, and some are based on highly speculative hypotheses. Improved measures can and will be devised, but the process will be a lengthy one, and even the best solutions will remain incomplete.

The training of guidance counselors and admissions officers in the understanding and use of tests must be improved. At present, too many of the practitioners in this field are using tests in a purely mechanical fashion. This situation is improving, but it still has far to go.

In summary, with respect to the use and development of tests we must recognize that we are working with a tool which is far from perfect and that our present use of that tool is also far from perfect. We do not know whether the decades ahead will produce another set of intellectual breakthrus such as those which form the basis of our present testing programs. If they do, we will gain tremendously in our ability to analyze and understand the individual and his development thru education. But even if they do not, we have much that we can do within the framework of our present knowledge. The important thing is to be sure that we do it.

Conclusion

The 20 years that lie ahead of us will be a time of educational effort which when measured in terms of dollars spent will be greater than the total educational effort that all Americans together expended from the founding of the republic until the outbreak of World War II. The conduct of this effort will control the future of our country for an incalculable period of years. The management of this effort will be in the hands of thousands of individuals; the expression of their management will determine the shape and the actions of our institutions.

Such, in essence, is the recurrent theme of every chapter of this book. The purpose of this chapter is to describe the evolving relationships between secondary education and higher education and to emphasize these constantly changing relationships.

organization of the secondary school

VII

the organization of the secondary school

A CONSIDERATION of the organization of any institution calls for constant reference to the purposes to be achieved by that institution. For organization is a means rather than an end, and its analysis must never blind us to this fact. Yet, with increasing size and complexity, the organization of any enterprise may be an effective stimulant to achievement of its goals or an inefficient vehicle which defers or blocks their realization.

The organization of the American secondary school can be neither simple nor uniform. That one common pattern should exist has never been deemed desirable except by those who seek comparable statistics or favor a centrally controlled system of education. Thus it is impossible to know just how many schools of different organizational patterns exist or to know the specific educational programs in progress in these schools.

Nevertheless, certain common trends are discernible. The first is that for some years the pattern of organization has been in a state of flux. The factors which force such change include availability of space and staff, purposes to be achieved, and increased knowledge of the nature of those to be taught, and how to teach them. Recently, too, proposals have been made for greater emphasis on multiple and separate provisions for specialized schooling beyond the elementary years. This latter trend has been stimulated largely by a national concern for the development of technical and professional manpower, particularly in reference to the academically able student, and is often championed by those who question the purposes and effectiveness of the comprehensive high school as discussed in Chapter III.

The new relations between the school and its community, the dilemma of more students and apparently fewer teachers, the trend toward larger schools, the requirements of fiscal prudence, and basic dissatisfactions with inherited organizational patterns all seem to have prompted experimentation.

Major Aspects of School Organization

Three aspects of the organization of our schools deserve special attention. The means of clustering together into some organizational groups the young people who are our clients, the structuring of the teaching staff into workable relationships, and the arrangement of administrative and other non-teaching personnel to increase the effectiveness of the work of the teacher and the taught are all critical conditioners of the effectiveness of the school in accomplishing its tasks.

Groupings of Students by Grades

Consistent with the consecutive years of education, we have grouped students by grades. How we arrange these grades into larger groups for administrative purposes, however, has varied significantly. One simple solution, which is found in many thousands of schools thruout America, is to group the 12 consecutive grades into one school. Thus we find six-year-old children and 17-year-old youth as members of one student body, sharing many of the same facilities under the guidance of the same school staff. This type of school is not passing from the American scene, but continues to flourish, particularly under the stimulus of consolidation of school districts.

This grade grouping, however, is not typical and is relatively new in American education. The eight-year grammar school, long a symbol of the typical common school, followed in turn by the separate four-year high school, representing somewhat selective secondary education for favored youth, is the traditional pattern.

In the final decade of the nineteenth century, however, there began a series of studies on the need for reorganization of secondary education. With increased knowledge of how young people grow and learn, and in the face of changing demands upon the secondary school, these studies have continued to seek better means of structuring secondary education.

In 1893, the Committee of Ten recommended the introduction in Grades VII and VIII of certain subjects which had previously been limited to the high-school years.[1] The Commission on the Reorganization of Secondary Education, which developed the Seven Cardinal Principles, subsequently proposed that the secondary school include Grades VII and VIII, bracketing them into a three-year sequence with the ninth grade, as had already been done in a number of school districts.[2] This constituted a recognition of the junior high school as a legitimate phase of secondary education and no doubt contributed to its mushrooming during the next decade.

The early functions of this new unit of secondary education included important terminal education for the impressive numbers of youth who left school before reaching traditional high-school age. They were readily employable because the national economy demanded much unskilled and semiskilled manpower and the dominant social philosophy was still tolerant of such child labor. In the intervening years, this terminal function has largely disappeared and a consequent re-examination of the junior high school has logically followed. Other functions have persisted and emerged as our understanding of early adoles-

---

[1] National Education Association, Committee of Ten on Secondary School Studies. *Report*. New York: American Book Co., 1894. 249 p.

[2] National Education Association, Commission on the Reorganization of Secondary Education. *Cardinal Principles of Secondary Education*. U. S. Department of the Interior, Bureau of Education, Bulletin 1918, No. 35. Washington, D. C.: Superintendent of Documents, Government Printing Office, 1918. 32 p

cent development.has increased so that the junior high school has flourished in numbers and importance.

The early downward extension of secondary education in the 1920's was matched by its upward extension in the local public junior college. Thus, as is indicated in Chapter V, there emerged for many youth a program of individualized education at a local center, extending into Grades XIII and XIV.

Since their establishment, both the junior college and the junior high school have been the subject of much study and speculation. Changing circumstances as felt in a variety of communities have stimulated interest in these organizations for youth education. Recent professional literature supports the claim that both are an established part of our program for youth education in America.

Secondary schools, then, tend to include those years involving young people from early adolescence to early adulthood. They are formed of a variety of grade arrangements, depending on local requirements, state recommendations, legal provisions, available space, and increasing knowledge about the nature of young people and their needs.

A national study reported in 1957 showed the grade organization of the schools in which secondary-school teachers were teaching, as follows: [3]

Grades Within the School	Percent of Secondary-School Teachers
Four-year high schools	33.3%
Elementary-thru-senior-high-school combinations	19.5%
Three-year senior high schools	16.8%
Five-year or six-year junior-senior high schools	15.0%
Two-year or three-year junior high schools	11.1%
Elementary-thru-junior-high-school combinations	4.3%
Total	100.0%

[3] National Education Association, Research Division. "The Status of the American Public-School Teacher." *Research Bulletin* 35: 43; February 1957.

The traditional four-year high school was in the minority—only 33.3 percent—but no other single type accounted for as many teachers. Nearly a fifth of the secondary-school teachers (more than half of those in rural schools) were in consolidated all-grade schools. When junior high schools, senior high schools, and junior-senior high schools were combined, their teachers represented 42.9 percent of the total.

On the basis of apparent further evidence concerning later childhood, a few districts are including the sixth grade in the junior high school, and moving the ninth grade "back" to the high-school unit, thus creating a 5-3-4 pattern.[4] In some cities, due to the desire to avoid excessively large high schools and to increase the number of locally centered community secondary schools, five-year units housing Grades VIII thru XII have been provided.

Frequently the plan for grade grouping has been based upon the space available rather than upon a design justified by the maturity of the students or the curriculum organization. With the explosive growth in enrolments in recent years, many local decisions on grade organization have been limited to the critical necessity for housing and the best use of existing structures.

Finally grade groupings are often the result of legal statutes based on the older concept of the four-year high school as covering secondary education. These may require a separate district organization, board of education, and taxing base for the high school, beginning with the ninth grade. The disadvantages of such legal restrictions are obvious and fortunately are disappearing with improvement of public understanding of the nature of secondary education and its goals.

Whatever may be the grouping of grades and subjects, we have established a ratio of teachers to students which has come to be commonly accepted in practice if not in theory. This type of empirical knowledge leads us to frown upon classes in which more than 25 or 30 young people are taught at one time by one teacher. This upper limit has been balanced by financial

---

[4] For example, Pearl River and Scarsdale, New York.

restrictions which force us to avoid classes with fewer than 15 students. When it has been necessary to offer specialized subjects to fewer students, we have used various devices to compensate this imbalance. The large groups of young people assigned to one teacher in a so-called study hall and the enrolments in the hundreds in physical education classes are dubious practices fortunately vanishing from our better schools.

Conversely, there is reason to believe that programs in activities where large numbers may possibly increase the effectiveness of learning, such as in choral groups, need not be restricted to the same student-teacher ratio as most classroom subjects require. The obviously small ratio involved in driver instruction, the advent of more flexible plant facilities described in Chapter X, and various types of lecture-demonstration learning do not negate the present evidence that for most teaching, the grouping of approximately 25 students with one teacher is the best that we know.

Program and Faculty Organization

How knowledge and understanding can best be learned, which knowledge is of the greatest worth, and the degree to which that knowledge should be useful (and for what purposes) are matters upon which agreement is not readily realized. In any group of students, parents, or teachers, there will be sharp differences of honest opinion on each of these issues and the continuing study of them constitutes a major task of the educational profession.

Such study and such differences are likely to be reflected in the organization of our secondary schools. Altho we may group young people by grades, roughly related to the number of years spent in school, there is marked disagreement relative to the bases upon which young people should be moved from one grade to another. There is frequent controversy as to "standards" and "achievement" in faculty meetings, parent discussions, and board of education sessions. As a common practice we continue to group by grades and by subject achievement.

Separate courses that present organized bodies of subject content are a part of our scholastic inheritance; they have been basic elements in the structure of the secondary school. The earlier schools, from which our program for youth has evolved, were concerned with the transmission of only a few specific fields of knowledge. These remain as the most important function of the school in the minds of many, as part of the classical tradition, especially to those who conceive of learning for the sake of learning, who believe in transfer of training, and who equate the acquisition of certain subject content with education.

That subjectmatter is of critical importance is agreed. Without consensus as to specific details of its content, how it is best to be learned, and for what purposes, it is safest and simplest to employ the familiar discrete subject fields as the organizational building blocks for our educational program for youth.

There is comfort in such a plan. We can quantify certain items as they are memorized. We can divide areas of knowledge into somewhat comparable units to use as educational currency in the transfer of students between institutions. We can give assurance of a type of accomplishment to our students, their parents, and all who have an interest in our schools.

Of course, much more difficult to discuss with parents and students are the behavioral outcomes of such learning. With increased acceptance of the organization of the program into general education and specialized education in the secondary school (as described in Chapter III) and with clearer and more specific definition of the purposes and tasks of the schools, there is reason to devote serious study to certain proposals concerning the structuring of the school program in line with these changes, in programs that cut across subject boundaries.[5]

As the offering of subjects has expanded with the growth and functional changes of our high schools, choices about them have been required. Such choices are related to the immediate interests, life goals, and educational aspirations of the in-

---

[5] See Chapter III, p. 93-94.

dividual student. Listing parallel "curriculums" to help young
people make these choices is a well-known practice. The college-preparatory and the commercial curriculums are examples.
For others a general curriculum will usually be found available.
These are patterns of requirements and suggestions based upon
subjects offered, things to be "taken," and credits to be earned.
Such a plan of program organization is nearly universal in the
three-year senior and regular four-year high schools.

Junior high schools, on the other hand, range from a similar
subject-based program to one which is primarily concerned
with a core of common learnings and persistent life problems
of young people. The seventh and eighth grades, in particular,
are frequently scheduled so that a given group of students
and one teacher are in the same room for two or more consecutive periods to study two or more general areas. The importance
of helping young people change from the one-teacher relationship of the elementary school to the eventual complete
subject departmentalization of the traditional high school
justified such a plan.

Such terms as *social living* and *language arts* are commonly
used in describing the program of the junior high school, lend-
ing additional emphasis to the avowed purposes of the school.
Such organization of the school program is not limited to specific subject fields. The organizational framework for the accomplishment of such purposes seems reasonable.

Program organization needs a built-in plan for evaluation;
lack of such a plan has been a stumbling block to changes in
organization. On the high-school level we may be limited to the
totally inadequate assessment of the school in terms of success
in college admissions by the graduating class. Pursuing such
students further into higher education, we may be able to
assess their preparation for *success* in college as a more legitimate measure of the work of the school than mere *admission*.
The sad plight of the superintendent whose tenure of office
hinges upon admissions of students to prestige colleges and
universities merits the sympathy of all who conceive of the
high school as more than a college-preparatory institution.
Other administrators suffer from the results when the least

able young people from the high schools go into local employment and naturally fail to impress the employer with the quality of their high-school training. Criticism occurs despite protest of school counselors and administrators that such is not an adequate basis for measuring the success of the school.

The recent cooperative study of the behavioral outcomes of general education in the secondary school may lead to further revisions in the organization of our common learnings program as definite, specific appraisal of the ultimate success of the schools becomes possible.[6]

The professional study of internal organization of the secondary school must always draw heavily upon the relationship between what we seek to accomplish within these schools and the degree of success which we discover. The complex and varied cause-and-effect factors must be reviewed as we draw upon our experience and on the studies of organization in noneducational fields. Our most logically developed hypotheses concerning structure must be tested and retested in a host of instances.

When the school is of such size as to require formal coordination of the work within certain subject fields, it is common practice to group faculty members into a departmental type of organization. The designation of a chairman or department head usually follows. Such a person is often charged with the responsibility for calling meetings, checking textbooks, and coordinating plans within the subject field. The balance between the advantages and evils of such an arrangement is not clearly established, but the legitimate need for such coordination is obvious. To achieve coordination without creating individual departmental pressure groups whose enthusiasm for their own fields may blind them to the real purposes of the total school is a constant challenge.

In many larger schools, permanently assigned department heads are relieved of some teaching responsibilities, in order for them to supervise instruction and guide and "rate" new teachers; they draw additional compensation for such duties.

---

[6] French, Will, and associates. *Behavioral Goals of General Education in High School.* New York: Russell Sage Foundation, 1957. 247 p.

Because such permanent assignments may lead to departmental isolation and interference with a balanced school program, some faculties have elected to use a rotating chair-
manship which carries no stipend and little prestige and which
is limited largely to duties of clerical and housekeeping caliber.
Still other schools, seeking to build on the advantages of subject-field loyalties without the hazards of separate departmental
organization, have designated chairmen or coordinators, each
with leadership responsibility for two or more subject fields.
Examples are such logical combinations as mathematics and
the sciences, English and the other language arts, fine and industrial arts. In such cases, as few as four or five such positions
may be adequate, with each of the responsible persons making a major contribution to the coordination of the entire instructional program in terms of the goals of the school.

Altho the organization of the faculty by subject-field departments is traditional and altho certain functions can be performed best thru this means, the controlling considerations
should be the most effective plan for accomplishing the ultimate
purposes of the school. If departmentalization is the dominant
basis of organization of the faculty, it may actually retard the
realization of the ultimate purposes of the schools. There is an
increasing awareness of the conflict between strong faculty
departmentalization and a balanced educational program.

How can provisions for coordinated activity of all teachers
in a given subject field be assured within the complexities of
a large high school and, at the same time, the interest of departmental teachers be maintained in what goes on in the rest of
the school? This problem demands the honest efforts of all.
Thru various modifications in traditional faculty-meeting plans,
such as small conference groups during nonteaching periods
and thru preschool and inschool work conferences, teachers
from all subject fields are being encouraged to study matters
of schoolwide curriculum concern. Special committees and commissions within a faculty to deal with plans and problems relative to the stated purposes of the school can cut across the
various departmental organizations. The assignment of teachers
to more than one subject field, and the pairing or teaming of

teachers with a common group of students also reduces the tendency toward isolation within subject departments.

In his "Notes on the Theory of Organization," Gulick suggests that there are four basic systems of organization, each of which is present to some degree in any complex enterprise, and one of which is dominant in any plan for organization of that enterprise. These four are defined as: organization by major purpose, organization by major process, organization by clientele or *materiel,* and organization by place.[7] Commenting on the balance among these bases of organization he says:

> The major purpose of organization is co-ordination. . . . It should therefore be noted that each of the four principles of departmentalization plays a different role in co-ordination. In each case the highest degree of co-ordination takes place within the departments set up, and the greatest lack of co-ordination and danger of friction occurs between the departments, or at the points where they overlap.[8]

If the purposes of the school are neither exclusively nor primarily the acquisition of knowledge in discrete subject fields, and if the best coordination is achieved within the framework of a department organization, it would seem time to constitute the faculty organization of the secondary school so that the basis of departmentalization is consistent with the school's stated purposes and functions. Coordination relative to the purposes of the school should and can take precedence over the relationships based upon mutuality of interest in subject areas. A break with tradition will lead to discomfort and concern lest knowledge and its attainment be overlooked. The personal and social relationships among teachers may be confused by such a shift, and the misunderstanding on the part of many people both within and without the profession may provoke charges of anti-intellectualism and downgrading of standards. The fact remains that the alternative, which is the preservation of sharp subject-field departmentalization as the dominant basis

---

[7] Gulick, Luther H. "Notes on the Theory of Organization." *Papers on the Science of Organization.* (Edited by Luther H. Gulick and Lyndall Urwick.) New York: Institute of Public Administration of Columbia University, 1937. p. 21-30.

[8] *Ibid.,* p. 33.

for organization of the faculty, cannot be justified on the simple basis of commonly accepted purposes of the secondary school, no matter how common and deep-rooted the practice may be.

Administrative Organization

Changing concepts of the role of the building principal have stimulated numerous reassessments of the internal administrative and supervisory organization of the secondary school. Increasingly the top of the principal's desk is being cleared, as competent clerical and administrative assistants handle requisitions and routines, in order that the principal may devote more attention to the program of instruction. Thus, there is provision for his leadership in working with staff, parents, students, and other members of the school community in actual study of the program, its effectiveness, and its improvement. (This point is discussed further in Chapter XI.)

To accomplish all the tasks, the administrative organization must reconcile responsibility with authority, provide time and personnel, and make all the resources of the school and community readily available so that the program of instruction may be rich, meaningful, and productive. For these reasons, as secondary schools increase in size and complexity, there must be ample provision for administrative and clerical help. The modern school is adequately staffed only when reasonable tasks are performed by all in harmony with the skill and potential of each.

The plant and equipment must be maintained as safe, healthy, and efficient instruments which contribute to the best possible learning for all young people. This means that a competently trained and supervised staff of devoted workers must be deployed most efficiently to accomplish this important service. Each must understand and accept his role in contributing to the educational program of the school under the leadership of a head custodian who will be responsible directly to a member of the administrative staff of the school.

Records must be accurately maintained and readily available thru the clerical section. Many schools waste the time of professional staff by assigning them clerical tasks that a nonprofessional may do as well or better. Funds must be handled prudently and plans for their collection and disbursement intelligently developed and executed. Correspondence must be prepared and transmitted, instructional supplies stored and distributed, telephone calls handled, heat and light provided, and students transported. These are but a few of the many important tasks which make possible the work of those who teach and of those who learn.

In schools with more than 200 or 300 students enrolled, part-time or full-time administrative personnel are usually assigned. The staff members relieve the principal of specific tasks to free him for his major role as leader in the development and coordination of the total school program. Assistant principals, deans, and directors work with him on teacher and student problems but at the same time must avoid the temptation to "protect" him from the faculty, students, and parents. The specificity of areas of responsibility and authority must be clear to all but subject to review and modification as changing circumstances may require. It means that an unusually high level of mutual respect must exist among all on the administrative team. It means that each one must be concerned with the school's success in the accomplishment of its total task.

Many schools now have one full-time director of student activities and another assigned for late afternoon and evening activities of the school; resource persons in various aspects of the curriculum are on call; and counselors and guidance specialists are reducing the necessity for the principal to be constantly available for parent conferences or for passing final judgment on cases of extreme misconduct.

Personnel relationships within the school have changed, and the role of the principal demands skill in working with people to an increasing degree. First and foremost is his responsibility to help each teacher realize his greatest effectiveness as a teacher working with young people. The distance between the principal and the classroom has been reduced since the day his private office was the center of the school's professional activity. Now the principal's office is the school as a whole,

and, altho he should possess a special competence in the coordination of the talent and skill of the staff, he is no longer
the expert in every phase of school life. The pyramid of authority has been flattened, and, altho the legal and moral authority remains with the principal, the accomplishments of the
school are more closely related to his effectiveness in working
with people in a cooperative and supportive role than to his
ability to make decisions concerning the teaching of French,
the purchase of furniture, or the conservation of fuel.[9]

The relationship between the building principal and the
superintendent is likewise undergoing change. The modern
school system, like the individual school, must draw upon the
contributions and counsel of all who are qualified to add to the
development of policy and practice. Thus the principals and
teachers of every school will in turn serve on committees, commissions, and councils thru which major improvements on a
systemwide basis will be realized. Members of the central office
staff are on call as resource persons and as helping teachers
who, as part of an instructional team, have cast off the threatening garments of authoritative power and donned the uniform
of a fellow worker in a common and vital enterprise. Within the
local school building, team approaches to many problems are
producing better teaching by utilizing talent where it is needed
and when it is available.

Problems of Size

Because of our concern for the individual student and his
welfare and because of our awareness of the necessary close
relationship which we seek to foster between teacher and
learner, large schools are viewed with distrust by parents, teachers, and administrators. Pressure of population and limitations
of funds, however, force many school systems into the maintenance of units far beyond a normally desirable size.[10] Many
unique advantages of the really small school are lost in schools

---

[9] Prestwood, Elwood L. *High School Principal and Staff Work Together.*
New York: Teachers College, Columbia University, 1957. 96 p.

[10] See Chapter X, p. 272-75.

of over 200 or 300 students, unless these schools are organized so as to retain those advantages. In a few isolated instances as early as the 1930's, the grouping of students into smaller school units within larger schools was practiced. Today, many modifications and variations of this arrangement are to be found.

Schools Within Schools

Thru careful planning with architects for separation of groups of rooms and facilities and thru staffing these separate units with parallel teaching groups, small schools can in a sense be achieved within the operating framework of an extremely large institution. In some cases this is done on the basis of grade-level organization; in others, on the basis of curriculum patterns and life goals; in still others, groupings are adjusted on friendship patterns or on the basis of random choices.

Administrative personnel are designated as principals or deans of such divisions, while the building principal serves as a coordinator of all the smaller units. Each school-within-a-school has its own identity, for purposes of group guidance activities, program development, and parent relationships with the school. By combining such smaller units for purposes of sharing many common and relatively expensive facilities, reasonable economy can be assured altho rich and varied program offerings and equipment are available.

Specialized Secondary Education

Large cities have often found it desirable to provide specialized high schools, usually organized in terms of life goals (technical and vocational) or educational goals (college preparation) and have assigned students to these schools on the basis of such goals or unusual endowments of talent and skill. That most schools are of the more comprehensive type is due not only to the relative sparsity of population, but also to the belief that values essential to secondary education may be lost thru attendance at specialized schools. This issue is discussed within Chapter III.

Departures from the Traditional

In view of changing demands upon the secondary school of today and despite unusual problems of growth and lack of funds, certain tentative trends in organization are clear. Other approaches to the adaptation of the structure to the purposes and functions are becoming well established, and altho subject to mild modifications, will no doubt persist as an integral part of the organization of modern secondary education.

Student Grouping

As indicated above, there are many varieties in the arrangement of grades within schools. Altho a study of the opinions of 66 recognized authorities in secondary education clearly established a preference for the 6-3-3 plan of organization,[11] and we have seen that the 6-3-3 or 6-6 plan is much used, communities continue to experiment, seeking a reclustering of grades more consonant with the identified characteristics of their youth in early adolescence. There is a further compelling question as to the degree to which young people should be held to rigid assignments to grades. Wide ranges of interests and needs, so typical of the junior-high-school years, have prompted a more flexible assignment of students and permitted variations in the length of their experience in that school. A more dependable basis for grouping students in terms of interests and maturity is needed. Rather than a specified sequence of grade programing in science, for instance, the intensity of interest and the degree of intellectual maturity may justify an abandonment of traditional practice. Thru careful advance planning, chaos in schoolwide programing can be avoided with little sacrifice to flexibility and fluidity of student progress thru the school.[12] For such flexibility, that cuts across the traditional grade groupings, the wide span of grades of the junior-senior high school is clearly an advantage.

[11] Wood, William C. *Structural Organization of Public Schools in the United States.* Doctor's thesis. Boulder: University of Colorado, 1951.
[12] Examples of such practices are found at the Battle Hills School in White Plains, New York, and at Bloomfield, New Jersey, Junior High School.

A challenging proposal, reminiscent of some of the pleas for economy of time in education which were current 50 years ago, has recently attracted much public and professional interest. This is a scheme for increased flexibility in the admission and promotion of children and youth to different levels of the educational "ladder" with the result that the average college-entrance age would be 16 instead of 18. The plan is based more on readiness for acquisition of subject content than on the length of time in school or the social and emotional maturity of the student.[13]

The experimental early admission of gifted students to higher education, with the consequent shortening of their time in secondary schools, has long been controversial. First formally attempted at the University of Chicago, and subsequently supported and expanded in a significant number of colleges, the program has largely been successful when judged by the appraisals of college and university officers. On the other hand, the complete realization of the specific purposes of secondary education for such students may not have been achieved. It is significant that the National Association of Secondary-School Principals has officially expressed dissatisfaction with the plan.[14]

Curriculum Organization

Altho "tracking" of students into curriculum patterns has long been a common practice in many high schools, increasing numbers are seeking to avoid rigidity in such practices. Thru effective guidance they are helping students to develop programs of a high degree of individuality in terms of a variety of goals and interests. An example of individualized programing is found in the enrolment instructions to students at Pascack Valley Regional High School, Hillsdale, New Jersey:

> The Pascack Valley Regional High School does not divide its program of studies into course patterns such as an academic,

---

[13] Woodring, Paul. *A Fourth of a Nation.* New York: McGraw-Hill Book Co., 1957. 255 p.

[14] National Association of Secondary-School Principals. "The Nine Point Program." *Bulletin of the National Association of Secondary-School Principals* 38: 446-48; April 1954.

business, or general curriculum. Each student is expected,
through Guidance, to develop a program of studies which
relates to his abilities, interests and life work plans. . . . While
it is not possible for all freshmen to have a clearly defined
future goal, it is important that they give careful consideration
to the probable directions in which their abilities and interests
will take them and enroll for courses which will best aid them
attain such goals. The Guidance Department is geared to help
parents and pupils interpret talents and interests. Pupils are
urged to not wait until the senior year before selecting a
definite post-high school goal.

Such a statement is not only typical of modern practice in
an increasing number of high schools but also reflects an awareness of the fact that the early commitment to life goals is not
always desirable or practical. Loss of time and talent which may
be forced by required early decisions concerning a program
track can be avoided thru more flexible programing. Such
early decisions in a complex industrial society with its increasing
demands for general education for all competent citizens can
lead to a waste of human resources. Young people normally do
change their minds and make mistakes. This constitutes one
additional argument for the extension of the comprehensive
high school into even our most complex metropolitan centers.

The expansion of earlier developments of the school-within-
a-school organization gives recognition to the importance of the
individualization of the school's responsibility to the student.
Evidence is mounting that in one form or another many
schools are experimenting with such organization. At the
Andrew Warde High School, Fairfield, Connecticut, assignments of personnel are made to four "houses"; each such unit
numbers approximately 300 students. The Syosset Junior-Senior
High School on Long Island arranges "project areas" sur-
rounded by 10 classrooms each, within which the general
educational program of some 250 students, their social activities,
counseling, and similar services are programed. The interpretation of such school organization by the architect is referred
to in Chapter X, and it is significant that much of the current
periodical literature in this respect is found in journals with

which this profession is familiar. A list of such references is appended.[15]

Modifications of the homeroom program to include an organization of several multiples of classroom grouping is a promising step. The coordination of this type of grouping with occasional large-group activities as part of the planned instructional program, such as is found at Newton, Massachusetts, and at Syosset is still another aspect of this organizational experimentation. A recent study of the unusual homeroom organization at Evanston Township High School, Evanston, Illinois, led to the current plan of organizing students into four "divisions" of some 800 students each, including all four grades in each division, rather than the units of some 220 pupils each which had been the Evanston plan for over 20 years.[16] In all such reorganizations there is great concern that the face-to-face relationship between each student and a counselor-friend shall not be jeopardized, regardless of the size of student grouping or the type of unit established.

---

[15] Architectural Forum. "Six High Schools." *Architectural Forum* 106: 127-31; February 1957.

Architectural Record. *Schools for the New Needs: Educational, Social, Economic.* New York: F. W. Dodge Corp., 1956. 312 p.

Architectural Record. "Educational Concepts: Hagerstown, Maryland." *Architectural Record* 120: 161-72; July 1956.

Beach, Karen, and Donald, Eleanor. "Let's Take a Walk Through New Schools." *School Executive* 76: 71-85; June 1957.

Engelhardt, N. L., Jr. "Laboratories for Learning." *School Executive* 74: 63-66; November 1954.

Essex, Don L. "Trends in School Design." *American School Board Journal* 134: 37-40; January 1957.

Gribben, Helen W. "School Within a School." *High Points* 25: 54-58; May 1943.

Koopman, G. Robert. "Changing Secondary School Programs and Their Implications for Design." *American School and University.* New York: American School Publishing Corp., 1955. p. 199-204.

Leggett, Stanton. "Schools Within Schools." *American School and University.* New York: American School Publishing Corp., 1956. p. 111-18.

Obata, Gyo. "Four Little Schools + Special Areas = Riverview Gardens High School." *American School and University.* New York: American School Publishing Corp., 1956. p. 249-52.

Reid, John Lyon. "Architectural Design of Schools." *School Executive* 74: 92-95; January 1955.

[16] Evanston Township High School. *Annual Report, 1956-57.* Evanston, Ill.: Board of Education, 1957. p. 37.

Scheduling Problems

As adjustments have been made in program organization and as we have encompassed a richer variety of learning experiences within the respected limits of the curriculum, the scheduling of student activities has continually challenged the ingenuity of school administrators. Two trends clearly emerge. The first is the recognition and acceptance of more and more activities within the program; the scheduling of glee club and journalism as regular classes, granting credit toward graduation, are examples. The second, found particularly in schools where the length of the day is sharply defined by transportation and work experience, is the assignment of a period within the day or week for such activities as student government, interest clubs, intramural sports, and assemblies. In at least one school a longer period of time, articulated with the lunch hour, schedules all major activities (including practice of interscholastic sports) before noon each day.[17]

The organization of teachers, students, and teaching space, when related to the clock and calendar, constitutes what is generally known as the "master schedule." Changes in organizational plans call for parallel changes in the schedule. Altho any good textbook in secondary-school administration lists principles, and various periodical references reveal a host of practices, the actual process of preparing the schedule is finally the product of local conditions, ingenuity of the staff, and the philosophy to which the school is committed and to which the community subscribes. Several trends in scheduling are worthy of note:

> • The development of the schedule is no longer an esoteric matter, practiced in seclusion by an administrator. The judgment and experience of all members of the staff are sought and used.
> • The comfortable and traditional practice of scheduling each class and subject to meet five times per week is frequently abandoned. The floating period, the two-week cycle, and the five-by-five plan, the latter allowing for "freezing" a period into an all-day session and thus allowing for longer consecutive

---

[17] Alexander Ramsey Junior-Senior High School, St. Paul, Minn.

study of one project, or participation in a lengthy field trip, are examples of this trend.

• The creation of block periods, in which two or more periods of time are held for a given teaching situation, is common practice in junior high schools and is apparently used increasingly in many senior high schools.

• The increased length of the class period, allowing for more study time with a given teacher, or more laboratory time adjusted to the learning situation, has generally been accepted as desirable. This tends to reduce the number of student contacts for each teacher each day, but also reduces the elective choices for each student because of the fewer number of total periods a day. Summer programs may allow students to take these electives. The staggered school day, in which all the students are present only during a few periods in the middle of the day, some coming and leaving early, others on the late shift (with the faculty likewise assigned) is a device for increasing building ultilization.

• The assignment of the "floating" teacher permits the use of otherwise unscheduled classrooms and is recommended as a temporary expedient for further increasing building utilization.

• The persistent problem of feeding many mouths in a short period of time has stimulated much lunch-hour experimentation. One increasing practice involves the "calling" of successive groups of classes to the service area as facilities become vacant, so that instead of several distinct lunch periods, there is a constant flow of students and teachers, thus keeping the facilities continually in use and reducing the total length of time devoted to the lunch period.

• In larger high schools, the departmental program schedule is made thru the leadership of department chairmen and then related to the total school program in the school office in order to avoid conflicts.

• The large amount of clerical tabulation and recording involved in the preparation of a schedule, whether decentralized or not, is being simplified thru the use of marginal punch cards or by utilization of electronic equipment.

Again, it is wise to note that the modern high school cannot and certainly should not employ an annual repetition of an established schedule. Altho last year's worksheet will be of inestimable value in guiding the development of this year's, any sensitivity to varying circumstances within the school or community will require appreciable changes from year to year.

Teacher Utilization

Efforts to improve organization so as to use teacher talent more effectively have been made on several fronts and for many years. The twilight zone of study, however, has long since passed. We are no longer concerned merely with providing teachers with tools such as textbooks, Bunsen burners, and film-strips. Rather, we have made bold thrusts into various demonstrations of using new materials and mediums, employing various means of relieving the teacher of noninstructional duties, manipulating class sizes, and examining afresh the role of the teacher in the total program of the school.

What is a reasonable working assignment for a teacher? In facing critical problems of manpower shortages in many fields, the attraction of teaching has been diluted for many young people by fear of unreasonable tasks. Attempts to find the answer to the basic question have at best been disappointing, largely because of the great variety of skills of individuals, the range of tasks, and the actual as well as imagined demands to which the conscientious teacher must respond to fulfil his assignment regardless of published descriptions of the position. Teacher load can, in a sense, be judged on a comparative basis. Probably the best instrument now available for this purpose is the Douglass formula. The various factors included and weighted in this instrument will help in arriving at some balance of work assignments within most high schools.[18]

No experimental studies in education have received more attention in the public press than the recent ones related to utilization of various persons and technical devices to spare the teacher from noninstructional tasks and enhance his effectiveness thru supplementary instructional devices. The spotlight is on the master teacher, performing before a television camera and thru it before many multiples of the usual class. Regrouping of students for special presentations by the individual superior teacher who has been relieved of at least part of his regular

---

[18] Douglass, Harl R. "The 1950 Revision of the Douglass High School Teaching Load Formula." *Bulletin of the National Association of Secondary-School Principals* 35: 13-24; May 1951.

responsibilities to prepare for major lecture-demonstrations has been introduced as another facet of this same program. Support of each teacher's contribution to the educational program has been strengthened thru the availability of a range of kinescopes and live telecasts in subjects where no one teacher may be competent. The use of adult helpers for teachers on the high-school level, similar to the Bay City program on the elementary level, is being explored.

How effective these devices and projects may be in achieving the purposes of modern secondary education has not yet clearly been proven. Critics of some of these studies challenge the proposed methods of evaluation as well as the apparent motivation behind them. The National Association of Secondary-School Principals is supporting and endorsing a series of projects from which it is hoped that more definitive answers may be obtained.[19]

It is significant that none of the present plans now operative in the study or demonstration of teacher utilization will suffer the persistence of traditional organizational patterns; each involves a change in the pupil-teacher ratio, the recognition of different levels of identifiable skill on the part of teachers, or the creation of situations in which the student plays a role as a passive learner among other passive learners. There is much attendant professional controversy, and more time will be required before convincing proof of the value of many of the utilization projects will be available.

Less popularly recognized, but of at least equal significance, is the availability to teachers of various resource persons. Many urban and suburban school systems now include shared-staff personnel who as cooperating teachers lack administrative status but strengthen the teaching skills thru team-teaching, distribution of unusual materials, and discussion of professional problems from varied vantage points. The transformation of the traditional supervisor into this new role is effectively increasing the meaningful contribution of the regular classroom

---

[19] Trump, J. Lloyd. "Our Experimental Studies on Utilization of Staff." *Bulletin of the National Association of Secondary-School Principals* 41: 306-11; April 1957.

teacher. Shared advice-plans, intermediate administrative units, and other administrative organizational patterns are similarly providing such services for the rural school.

Relief of the burden of clerical duties on professional workers has been initiated thru the employment of systems of marginal punch cards or machine punch-card operations. Such equipment has been specifically adapted for school use by certain large corporations. An example of the reduction in the clerical load of teachers is found in the recording and reporting of students' grades. Using an electronic machine punch card, the teacher marks one brief line on the master card. From that point on, the permanent record of the grade, the teacher's class grade sheet, and the student's individual report card will be quickly and accurately completed thru the modern magic of electronics.

Problems for Study

What principles should underlie the organization of a high school? This is but one of many related questions inviting continued study in this area of professional concern. Older schools have often tailored the assignment of personnel to the individual interests and strengths of those available. How does one select, organize, and assign the staff of a newly created school?

Selection as well as preparation of the principal, too, deserves more study. The position too often has been considered in the past as a reward for faithful service or a steppingstone to the superintendency, rather than an important position of professional status in its own right. Fortunately the break from such traditional practice, stimulated by the unhappy results which such practice often induced, has led to a high degree of professionalization for secondary-school administration.

The grouping of students in relation to their own social interests, the redeployment of staff, the reconstitution of departments with the faculty, the employment of machines for clerical work—these are some of the specific invitations to creative experimentation and critical analysis.

long-range district planning

VIII

long-range district planning

THE PATTERN of school districts is changing to meet better the needs of people in the new types of communities that are now developing. The number of districts is fast diminishing, thus securing better instruction and more economical operation. However, secondary education still is blocked from progress in many communities because of the ways school districts are organized. Many districts are too small; many districts have no logical relationship to the boundaries of presentday communities; and districts in some states can organize only elementary schools or only secondary schools. Secondary education suffers when any one of these handicaps is present.

Professional and lay leaders in education are urging a major revision of the entire structure of school-district organization. This revision must be based upon an appraisal of the role, functions, and relationships of the state, the counties, and local communities in the various states, for public schools cannot be effective if the district structure is unsound. Educational leaders need to agree on basic principles for reorganizing school districts and for clarifying the functions and relationships of the three administrative units—the state, the county or other intermediate district, and the local school district.

Citizens are waking to the fact that many school systems are operating inefficiently because of a faulty district organization. A movement is under way which is involving lay people in study and research into the potential power of school-district reorganization to improve the physical and instructional facilities of their schools. Citizens understand some of the social and economic changes that are reshaping their neighborhoods into new and larger emerging communities, but the total development needs study. On the basis of these trends, school authorities should do long-range planning to meet the educational needs of the school service area, to forestall inefficient, costly, emergency planning. The planning must involve the elementary, secondary, and post-secondary needs of youth.

In the last decade many school districts have modified their organization because of sociological pressures. Ten years ago there were 100,000 local school districts in the United States. We now have fewer than 50,000. The efforts of many districts have been in the right direction, but the efforts of others have lacked a well-defined and integrated plan. Ever-increasing socioeconomic change makes it imperative that evaluations of our educational system be made often to learn where we are and how effective we are. Comprehensive long-range planning is needed for organizing larger units of administration.

What Is Happening

For about the first hundred years of our history as a nation, our people were encouraged to move to undeveloped areas to start life as pioneers of a new era. Horace Greeley's "Go West, young man, and grow up with the country" reflected a national policy. Thousands of people accepted the challenge, and by the 1890's, nearly all areas were occupied.

Communities Are Changing Fast

The American standard of living, the economy, population, industry, agriculture, transportation, communication, and education changed profoundly as the country grew. The early community structure, both in the newly settled West and in the much older East and South, began to shift and even to dissolve. Rural neighborhoods and communities were no longer isolated. Small rural centers of population lost significance. The cities and the surrounding country areas came to understand each other better.

Many people now want to live in the country near a city. For instance, Michigan's population increased by 21 percent in the ten years between 1940 and 1950. In the same period the farm areas lost 19 percent of their population while the cities gained 19 percent. However, the nonfarm rural areas, between the cities and the open country, gained 67 percent. This trend will continue for several reasons: (a) There is a housing shortage in most of our cities. (b) Few areas are available within cities for new homes. (c) Families have more leisure time and want more space and a freer way of life. (d) Transportation facilities now make suburban living practical for city workers. (e) Families want the more intimate community life found in the suburbs. (f) People feel that the threat of bombing is less in the country area. (g) Some families want to supplement their income by gardening. (h) Families feel that the country atmosphere is healthier and safer for their children.

This flight of city residents to the country is creating problems of great magnitude for all civic and educational planners. Opportunities are created also. Suburban people tend to be intelligent and progressive. They want better community services and better public schools. They want a share in improving the educational program, and they are demanding the kind of program that modern conditions have shown to be essential.

It is evident that any plan for reorganizing school districts must involve the rural people, the suburbanites, and the city dwellers. In recent decades people have been moving from one area to another more than they have at any other time in the history of our country. This migration represents more than just a movement and redistribution of people. It includes a transplanting of personal attachments, wealth, social values, ideals of local and other governments, community organizations, education, religions, modes and means of communication, and economic production.[1]

Many School Districts Are Being Reorganized

School districts are being organized and reorganized at an alarming pace without adequate research and planning. The number of one-teacher schools and the number of school districts in the United States are declining rapidly. No fewer than 20,000 neighborhoods and communities were concerned with problems of school reorganization in the two years from 1954-55 to 1956-57, recognizing that usually more than two districts are involved in each reorganization. Over 7000 fewer school districts were in existence at the close of the two years than at the beginning. The reorganization trend is shown in the figures below:[2]

Year	Number of School Districts in the United States
1931-32	127,530
1947-48	100,946
1952-53	67,045
1954-55	59,270
1956-57	51,941

Year	Number of One-Teacher Schools in the United States
1929-30	148,711
1947-48	77,832
1952-53	47,114
1954-55	39,061

[1] Jehlik, Paul J., and Wakeley, Ray E. *Population Change and Net Migration in the North Central States, 1940-50.* Research Bulletin No. 430. Ames: Iowa Agricultural Experiment Station, Iowa State College, July 1955. p. 487.

[2] Figures for 1931-32 to 1954-55, inclusive: Committee for the White House Conference on Education. *A Statistical Survey of School District Organization in the United States, 1954-55.* Washington, D. C.: Superintendent of Documents, Government Printing Office, January 1956. p. 3. Figures for 1956-57: National Education Association, Research Division. *Advance Estimates of Public Elementary and Secondary Schools for the School Year 1956-57.* Washington, D. C.: the Association, November 1956. p. 10.

(Preliminary figures show that in 1957-58 the number of school districts will be approximately 49,500.)

There is no reason to believe that the reorganization trend will not continue. The change in the size and the number of school districts is exerting a tremendous influence on what the secondary schools of tomorrow will be and can be. Illogical organization of administrative units can increase the cost and lower the quality of the educational program in schools; sound organization is basic to the performance of the functions of a good secondary education.

Short-Sighted Reorganization Should Be Prevented

Physical facilities and the school program are sometimes expanded without adequate consideration for either present or future educational needs of a potential school service area. Too often, things begin to happen only when the pupils overflow a school building. At this stage the administrator and the board become alarmed. They may call in an "educational expert" or a survey team to help them with their immediate dilemma. A few facts on impressive charts are presented to groups of citizens at a mass meeting, and thru high-powered salesman-ship, citizens are persuaded to finance a building program for the district. Little attention is given to the logical school service area or the natural community area to be served by a school district. Recent sociological changes in the related rural and urban areas are not studied objectively. Too often, citizens are not involved in any study of the problems. In the absence of the study needed for an over-all plan, school buildings are built and programs are expanded. Many of these projects may become monuments to poor planning. A school district working only on its own educational needs may lose sight of the fact that the primary need may be one of reorganization involving several school districts.

Three Levels of Organization Exist

The original pattern of school-district organization was not thought out in advance. One-teacher school districts grew up

where population centers started. A school became identified
with a neighborhood and soon represented an attendance area
and also a school district. These one-teacher districts have all
but disappeared from the American scene. It is now generally
agreed that the larger administrative districts with more pupils
and teachers in one system can provide a broader and more
efficient program of education. The one-teacher schools that
still remain are more and more likely to be logical parts of
larger school districts.

Students of the subject agree that the present status of local
school district organization in the United States is far from
satisfactory, even tho there has been much consolidation in recent years.[3] Districts that exist today include too many that
overlap identical areas, that lack the power to meet their responsibilities, and far too many that are still too small to be educationally effective.

Three general types of school administrative levels are recognized; namely, the state, the intermediate or regional, and the
local district's school service area.

The State

The state is concerned with the performance of statutory
requirements for supervision of instruction and the use of
public monies. Recently many states have increased their staffs
and have become more concerned with leadership and consultative services.

The state educational agency is responsible for five major
functions: (a) It develops policies thru which it defines minimum standards of practice, establishes teacher personnel
standards and procedures, clarifies relationships and duties of
the state agency and other school units, and gives leadership
in standardized financing of the state school system. (b) It
plans, conducts, and authorizes research. (c) It recommends
changes in school statutes for the improvement of education.

---

[3] McLure, William P. *The Intermediate Administrative School District in the
United States.* Urbana: University of Illinois, College of Education, Bureau of
Educational Research, February 1956. p. 8.

(d) It provides informational services. (e) It coordinates and provides leadership of education in the entire state.[4]

Altho separate from the state department of education, another source of state leadership in district reorganization should be recognized; namely, the state supported colleges and universities. Many of them, thru their research studies and thru staff consultative service, have developed principles of district organization and have helped in showing how these principles may be applied in local communities.

The Intermediate District

The intermediate or regional district functions between the state and a number of separate local districts. It has been defined as an administrative organization for "an area comprising the territory of two or more basic administrative units and having a board, or officer, or both, responsible for performing stipulated services for the basic administrative units or for supervising their fiscal, administrative, or educational functions."[5] Thirty-four states have some type of intermediate school administrative units, most of them based on the geographical areas of the counties.

The functions of the intermediate district have been stated as coordination and leadership, provision of transitory or emergency services, provision of advisory and consultant services, certification of the local district's compliance with minimum standards established by the state, limited review of specified district action, and the internal organization of the intermediate unit itself.[6]

[4] California Commission on Public School Administration. *School Administration in California: A Pattern for the Future.* San Diego: the Commission (Chairman: Cecil D. Hardesty, Superintendent of San Diego County Schools), 1956. p. 52.

[5] National Commission on School District Reorganization. *Your School District.* Washington, D. C.: Department of Rural Education, National Education Association, 1948. p. 52.

[6] California Commission on Public School Administration, *op. cit.*, p. 46-47. See also: National Education Association, Department of Rural Education, National Commission on the Intermediate Administrative Unit. *Effective Intermediate Units—A Guide for Development.* Washington, D. C.: the Department, 1955. 16 p.

The kinds of services rendered by intermediate units were illustrated by the 1954 Yearbook of the NEA Department of Rural Education.[7] County superintendents of schools and superintendents of other types of intermediate districts provided the information, which told of services to local districts focused on the needs of pupils, services to help teachers meet the needs of pupils, and administrative and business services. Such specifics were mentioned as library services; instruction in specialized fields, including classes for atypical pupils, thru cooperative employment of teachers; guidance, counseling, testing, and attendance services; health services; instructional supervision; instructional materials centers; curriculum leadership; inservice education for teachers; financial services; school building planning and maintenance; centralized purchasing; pupil transportation; securing and placing teachers; research services; coordination of educational programs; and leadership in school-district reorganization.

The Local District

The local school district is an administrative unit which is governed by a lay board of education with responsibility and authority to maintain the minimum program of education guaranteed by the state and with authority to exceed the minimum program in accordance with its means and the desires of the citizens. In practice, its geographic area may include only a one-room elementary school or it may include hundreds of schools, from elementary thru college level, all under the authority of one board of education.

The natural community is an area where people trade, do their banking, attend church, secure medical services, and satisfy other wants. It is a strategic area for organizing a local school program for kindergarten thru Grade XII because there is a definite relationship between the socioeconomic interests of people and their educational interests. In large cities these

---

[7] National Education Association, Department of Rural Education. *The Community School and the Intermediate Unit.* Yearbook 1954. Washington, D. C.: the Department, 1954. p. 57-133.

several interests may be met in different overlapping areas that vary in size.

Views vary on what is the ideal size for a local administrative unit. The Educational Policies Commission of the NEA recommended that one should strive to have 10,000 to 12,000 pupils in one district for economical operation.[8] The National Commission on School District Reorganization stated that a local district should have a minimum of 1500 to 1800 pupils.[9] Minnesota and South Dakota recommended a minimum of 100 pupils for a 4-year high school and 150 for a 6-year high school; Illinois and Wisconsin, a minimum of 300.[10] These wide variations suggest that definite standards to apply to all situations may not be possible. Differences in topography, density of population, occupational patterns, and related factors must be given weight.

The school administrator must have the vision to be on the alert for the pattern of school organization for his area that will be consistent with the goals of education. Changes are needed only if they will result in the improvement of educational opportunity for the youth of the area served.

The lay board of control of the local administrative unit has wide authority in providing the kind of public school system it desires. Its broad functions have been stated as follows:

1. The adoption of policies not inconsistent with the laws of the state for the internal organization, development, and improvement of the local instructional program.

2. The adoption of policies not inconsistent with the laws of the state for the selection, assignment, and supervision of professional personnel.

3. The adoption of policies not inconsistent with the laws of the state for financing of the total program.

4. The development of a master plan of information and communication.

---

[8] National Education Association and American Association of School Administrators, Educational Policies Commission. *The Structure of Administration of Education in American Democracy.* Washington, D. C.: the Commission, 1938. p. 38.

[9] National Commission on School District Reorganization, *op. cit.,* p. 87.

[10] Fitzwater, C. O. *School District Reorganization Policies and Procedures.* U. S. Department of Health, Education, and Welfare, Office of Education. Special Series, No. 5. Washington, D. C.: Superintendent of Documents, Government Printing Office, 1957. p. 54.

5. The adoption of rules and regulations governing the conduct of its own affairs.[11]

What Should Be Done

Both lay and professional people need to understand better the sociological and technological changes that have occurred and are occurring and their impact on education. Hence, school administrators and lay citizens should work together in research and study to plan a long-term course of action on school-district organization.

No magic formula can be prescribed to assure the solution of the problems. But every community that contemplates an expansion or a study of its school needs, requires an answer to certain key questions, namely:

1. Does the existing school district organization permit a complete and efficient educational program for all of the children (grades K-12) in the service area?

2. Do school district lines follow logical service, geographical, and community boundaries?

3. Are there sufficient local financial resources to support a sound educational program? [12]

Unless the answers to all three questions are affirmative, the primary problem is school-district organization. The decision on reorganization must be made *before* school plant studies can be launched wisely.

Leadership Is Necessary

Public education is recognized as a state function. The local school district is a subdivision of the state and the state legislatures prescribe the powers and duties of the local unit. School-district reorganization is therefore a joint responsibility of the state and the local district. However, the local administrator

---

[11] California Commission on Public School Administration, *op. cit.*, p. 21-22.
[12] Leu, Donald J., and Forbes, John L. *What Is Involved in Conducting a School Plant Study?* Professional Series Bulletin No. 9. East Lansing: Michigan State University, 1956. p. 2.

should assume responsibility for encouraging the lay and professional people in his district to take a look at their educational needs and for helping them gain a better understanding of the advantages or the disadvantages of school-district reorganization. He must help the public to realize that the number of students in public schools will continue to increase, that the demands on the schools for a wider program and for a high quality of teaching are steadily rising, and that one inevitable result is that education will cost more.

The local administrator will need to know where he can secure technical advice and assistance in problems relating to school-district reorganization. Help is usually available from the state department or the public colleges and universities of the state. Where the intermediate unit is well organized and staffed the leadership provided thru that unit is helpful on problems of district reorganization and on subsequent administrative adaptations.

Criteria of a Good School District

Reorganization of a potential school service area should take place only if the newly defined district can serve the needs of local youth and adults better than the existing districts. To provide a well-rounded educational program for all, a good school district would measure up to the following requirements:

1. A comprehensive program of elementary education, high-school education, post-high-school education, and adult education.
2. A competent staff of teachers, administrators, supervisors, and other workers.
3. Schools properly located to:
    a. Meet community needs
    b. Be convenient to children, and
    c. Bring together enough pupils for good instruction at reasonable cost.
4. A sound way of financing and administering its program.[13]

---

[13] National Commission on School District Reorganization. *A Key to Better Education.* Washington, D. C.: the Commission (Department of Rural Education, National Education Association), 1947. p. 8.

Consultants Can Help

School administrators do not always make the best use of the valuable resources at their command for working on district organization. Most state education departments and many colleges are prepared to provide guidance in using effective social processes for involving lay people in the solution of their own problems. The administrator must provide leadership that will help the people to study, plan, and act. He will need aid in finding answers to questions such as these: What rural and urban sociological and technological changes are taking place in the community, and what impact do they have on the educational system? What is the trend in school enrolments in the school service area? What changes are necessary to meet the educational needs of all of the youth and the adults? What size of district or what physical facilities will be required for the new program? Are the financial resources of the school service area adequate to support a good program?

Lay People Must Be Involved

Citizens must be organized for action. Once the people know and understand what is needed for their schools, they seldom fail to provide the necessary efforts and funds to make improvements. Informed citizens become interested citizens who demand better school buildings and instructional programs. The educational system will be as good as our citizens want it to be.

Special temporary advisory committees and community councils are increasing in number. Advisory committees, which help the board of education with a specific problem and are then dissolved, may exist only a short time. Community councils usually continue research and study for a number of years and make recommendations over a long-term basis.

What Some Communities Are Doing

Many school districts have developed master plans as a guide for the future development of their educational systems. The steps taken in the development of the master plan generally follow a pattern such as this:

1. The school administrator looks ahead and informs his board of education of things to come.

2. The board of education studies the suggestions made by the administrator and agrees to make an objective study of its future needs.

3. A consultant or a survey team is enlisted to assist the administrator and the board of education in agreeing upon a plan of attack.

4. Citizens are involved in collecting the necessary data.

5. Consultants analyze and help to interpret the data collected.

6. Citizens study the data and the interpretations and make recommendations to the board of education. A master plan is suggested.

7. The board of education reviews the recommendations of the citizens and agrees on a plan for the development of the educational system.

8. The board of education takes legal action to bring the master plan into reality.

Many states are enacting legislation to encourage lay people and educators to study their needs. The Michigan Area Study Project has involved thousands of citizens and professional people in over 30 counties in grass-roots studies of their educational needs.[14] Master guides developed in each county suggest the direction that school reorganization should take. The movement represents a uniquely democratic approach in attacking educational problems on a long-term basis.

A school district may employ many methods to initiate and develop a long-range plan for the improvement of education. Since no one method can be used as a blueprint for all school

---

[14] Michigan Department of Public Instruction. *Guide for Area Studies.* Bulletin No. 1020. Lansing: the Department, 1949.

University of Michigan and Michigan Department of Public Instruction. *Making an Area Study.* Ann Arbor: University of Michigan, School of Education, 1950. 32 p.

systems, the administrator will want to study the various methods used successfully by other schools and then devise one to fit his local system.

Below are a few examples of various practices in developing master plans for educational improvement.

Use of Self-Survey

The Menominee County (Michigan) Area Study is one example of how the lay and professional people worked jointly to survey their educational needs and to give direction to the future development of the school systems in the area. Menominee County had in 1950 a population of approximately 25,000 persons. The largest city (Menominee) had a population of 11,000. Approximately 60 lay and professional persons met monthly for over two years. Study and research committees were organized to evaluate every phase of education and many surveys were made by the lay people under educational leadership. Recommendations were agreed upon for the future improvement of the area. The project was completed by the lay people under the leadership of the educators of the area and with the aid of consultants from the Michigan Department of Public Instruction and the various colleges.[15]

Use of a College Survey Team

In the Grand Ledge (Michigan) Community School Area project, a college, the boards of education and some of the staff members jointly and cooperatively studied the community area and population, the school service area, the school population, the school program, the school plant, and finance.[16] Imminent overcrowding of the union school building in Grand Ledge, in which both elementary- and secondary-school pupils

---

[15] For a discussion of the state program of which the Menominee project was one example, see Strolle, Roland S. "Educating Citizens for Reorganization." *Nation's Schools* 58: 48-49; December 1956.

[16] Roe, William H., and others. *A Survey of the Grand Ledge Community School Area.* East Lansing: Michigan State College, School of Education, 1954. 89 p.

were housed, was one factor that led to the survey. The Grand Ledge school authorities took the lead in starting the study and paid the bills; however, the 40 rural districts concerned were invited to cooperate in the study, and their support was assured before the study got under way.

A college survey team provided leadership in the study. The report was comprehensive and objective, of the type that should prove helpful to citizens and boards of education in formulating policies for action. It presented information for the Grand Ledge school district and for surrounding rural districts in three counties. It outlined seven possible courses of action, ranging from a continuation of present practices, with the understanding that the instructional program would suffer, to a complete district reorganization of the school service area. On the assumption that the most likely outcome would be either (a) the annexation of rural districts by the city district, or (b) complete reorganization into a new district, the advantages and disadvantages of each plan were set forth. (A letter from the superintendent of the Grand Ledge schools in April 1957 stated that 19 rural districts had chosen to be annexed to the city district and that 10 more annexations were anticipated within a year.)

Use of Study Council

Schools for Atlanta's Future[17] illustrates another method of evaluating and suggesting the future development of a school system. The Atlanta School Study Council, composed of outstanding educators from many sections of the country, recruited by local school authorities, focused its efforts on the development of a sound plan for the future operation of Atlanta's schools, evaluating present operations as a basis for determining what the future of the school system should be. The council realized that the ultimate development of the school system would be achieved only with the full participation and backing of the entire community.

---

[17] Atlanta School Study Council. *Schools for Atlanta's Future*. Atlanta, Ga.: the Council, December 1955. 51 p.

The study council began its work on the assumption that a study of the organization, administration, and financing of the Atlanta school system should involve members of the board of education, school personnel, and citizens of the community in various phases of the inquiry and in the development of the recommendations. A citizens committee was appointed to work with the council, to examine the conclusions reached by the council, and to reach its own conclusions as to the adequacy of the study and the soundness of the recommendations.

The completed study was approved by the board of education. The recommendations are being implemented at a rapid pace—thanks to the master plan.

A Plan for Joint and Continuous Evaluation

Milwaukee's long-term educational planning has been in effect for more than 30 years.[18] The planning function is continuous and is delegated to a commission appointed by the superintendent of schools. Commission membership includes board members, assistant superintendents, school architects, and representatives of both the city and county planning divisions. A representative of the city real estate department, which purchases the desired sites, serves as a consultant on matters of site locations and cost. At times the membership has also included representatives of civic groups. One outcome of the plan is to keep the citizenry continuously informed about the educational needs of the schools.

On the basis of data gathered by staff members, a tentative listing of anticipated building needs for the next five years is made. At the same time, a tentative list of needed future sites is also prepared. Field trips are made for on-the-spot checking as to the desirability of the proposed locations of new schools and the need for enlarging, modernizing, or replacing old schools and for enlarging present sites. The tentative list of projects is then revised or approved, and arranged in order of recommended priority, and estimated costs and proposed

[18] Theisen, W. W. "Long-Range Planning for School Plant." *Nation's Schools* 58: 64-67; July 1956.

sources of revenue are outlined. The report is then submitted to the superintendent, and by the superintendent, after study and approval, to the board of education.

From 1923 to 1953 the building and sites program was restudied 13 times and in 1956 was in the process of a fourteenth study. But during the 30-year period the superintendent and the board have at no time been without a future building and sites program. Many thousands of dollars have been saved by early purchase of sites, and changes in the educational program have been integrated with the building program.

Help in Planning from a Private Firm of Educational Consultants

One city school system employed a firm of educational consultants to survey needs, make recommendations, and assist in the details of carrying them thru. The survey recommendations went beyond forecasts of pupil loads, site selections, and similar major practical responsibilities; they included consultation on such fundamentals as the nature of the educational program itself and the possibilities inherent in sound school-community relationships. Educational needs were discussed with teachers and staffs, and on occasion superintendents and specialists from other parts of the nation were called in for group consultations. The studies were completed, and the physical plants of the city and the suburbs were greatly improved. The city has a tradition of long-range educational planning so that the school administration seldom has been caught napping. A unique feature of the current program is that both the city and the surrounding county school system have retained the same firm of consultants, so that integrated planning can go forward to meet the urban, suburban, and rural educational needs of the area on a continuing basis from year to year.

The Challenge

The population of the United States is expected to reach 200 million by 1970. Sociological factors will bring new pressures on communities and will modify our way of life. Secondary education will need to conform to sociological and technological changes. School districts will require reorganization. State and local efforts will need to be coordinated in a plan of long-term development. School administrators will need to assume the responsibility for motivating citizens to carry on research, to study the findings, to formulate a plan of development, and then to plan an action program.

the staffing problem

teacher

teacher

TEACHER

teacher

ADMINISTRATOR

9

people and purposes:
the staffing problem

THE CRITICAL ROLE of the classroom teacher and those others who are to staff our secondary schools is fundamental to the secondary school's response to the new demands upon it. However, the problems concerning teacher shortages, salaries, and utilization are abundantly reported elsewhere and will receive no extended treatment here. The discussion turns rather on the needed qualifications, as related to the new duties, of high-school classroom teachers and the other workers needed to man a modern high school.

Effective teaching in the modern secondary school requires certain qualities which may have been of little moment a generation ago. The changing world and the changing place of the school in that world bring a new series of tasks for the school and ultimately for those who teach in it. Thus the persons whom we seek for future assignments and those who are now employed must be prepared and stimulated to do things, to know things, and to seek results which may not have weighed heavily in earlier assessments of the school and its products.

On the other hand, we can agree upon certain assumptions that have long guided us as we have recruited teachers for

229

secondary schools. As always, we will see people of honesty, integrity, and good health who are interested in young people and their growth. We continue to expect our teachers to have intellectual curiosity and a good background in general education. We further expect them to know their own profession, its foundations as derived from the many disciplines which contribute to its status, the bases upon which learning is stimulated and guided, the nature of young people and the dynamics of their growth, the considerable body of knowledge of one or more of the several fields which are commonly taught in our secondary schools, and an intelligent awareness of the relationship among these fields in developing curriculums for youth. These skills and knowledge have long been assumed as part of the competence of teaching.

There remain, however, additional qualifications for competence in harmony with new expectations for the schools of today and tomorrow. Further, there is increasing evidence that the classroom teacher must be supported by other staff members whose importance is seen in a new light. The clerical staff, the custodial staff, the special professionals in guidance, health, administration, and other services—all these individuals must be specifically trained and committed to the ultimate goal of making the work of the teacher increasingly effective.

The Teachers We Seek

In addition to the competencies which have long been part of the professional equipment of good secondary-school teachers, four other major classifications of ability and concern on the part of teachers may well be specified. Teachers who can meet the new tasks of the secondary schools will increasingly serve as intelligent and responsible citizens; they will have a humane perceptiveness of the relations between youth and the adult world; they will see clearly the role of the emerging school in the emerging world; and they will have both a pride in and a realistic understanding of the teaching profession itself.

Teachers as Citizens

Altho high intelligence and intellectual curiosity have always been essential assets for high-school teaching, their application to the personal life of the teacher has often been overlooked. The teacher's own interests—his use of leisure as well as his participation in civic life, travel, and social pursuits of all kinds —will inevitably shape his feelings, thoughts, and actions within the classroom.

The teacher who is a voting citizen, and who is high-minded enough to act on the knowledge that the rough-and-tumble of politics is not something to be left to the self-interested but is a responsibility of the educated citizen, can bring to his classes an adult understanding and appreciation of community life and progress. The teacher who is willing to share his talents and training in the promotion of a local volunteer project for the welfare of youth or for other community service will grow in realism as well as idealism and will be that much better equipped for the classroom.

As always, the enthusiasms of the teacher whose life is full will enrich his teaching. The traveler who values the cultures of many lands, the hobby enthusiast, the member of a harmonious household, the leader in church and youth-serving groups, the student of international affairs and responsibilities —any one of these who is also a teacher is likely to be a better teacher thereby. There is great need for the school in the years ahead to so lighten and distribute its teaching load as to make it possible for the teacher to live the normal life of the cultivated, socially responsible adult.

It is from such adults, with a clearly defined sense of values and ability to act thoughtfully upon these values, that we can expect the superior teaching which alone will accomplish the tasks of the modern secondary school.

Youth and the Adult World

The teacher of today and tomorrow is called upon to help youth understand and rationalize his relationship with the world about him. The confusions forced upon the young man or woman by confused adults in a world racked with tensions and foreboding are not easy to resolve. The qualified teacher must draw from sound knowledge of the role of youth and from sound concepts of world events and enduring values if the relationships of youth to their world are to be clarified. This responsibility is great, and the preparation for it is neither simple nor static. The difficulties of changing from responsible youth status to responsible adult status are aggravated by international rivalries, the probable requirement of military service, challenges to moral certainties, "easy money," popularity of early marriage, expectations of longer commitments to formal education, and other blocks.

The age-old charge of elders concerning the shortcomings of youth has again won headlines. Some young people engage in retaliatory corroboration of the charges. Or they may withdraw into a shell of cynicism. Yet with helpful guidance and opportunities for participation in community life, they refute these reckless criticisms. The demand for such guidance and opportunity falls largely on the school and its teachers. An understanding teacher who, with sympathy for youth and knowledge of the world, can assist youth thru this transition with poise and dignity is fulfilling the highest duty of teaching.

Changing Schools

Former concepts of what constitutes a broad program of general education as a background for teaching may be seriously inadequate for today's world. Present concepts may be inadequate tomorrow. The quality of spirit and the knowledges and attitudes that mark the free man—aware of tradition but untrammeled by it, able to meet new occasions and responsibilities without fear—these are needed today as never before by the teacher who is to be more than a pedant. Any program of general education which hides its deficiencies behind the title of liberal arts and claims respectability because of highly specialized erudition on the part of a few of its graduates is not only inadequate, it is dangerously deceptive.

What is required as a background for professional preparation of today's teacher is a program of breadth and integrity which helps prepare the student to understand his world and his place in that world. It is to be found in many splendid institutions and lacking in many others. The awareness of this need is manifest in the reorganization of a few top-ranking institutions preparing students for such professions as medicine and engineering. To quote James R. Killian, Jr., President of M.I.T.:

> The Massachusetts Institute of Technology is a professional school in which professional standards of conduct, performance, and unselfish public service are controlling. Within the framework of these professional ideals, we at M.I.T. seek to educate men and women who have the competence of specialists plus a sense of the human values which extend far beyond specialized interests. We believe that this combination of professional and general education has exceptional relevance and power in preparing young people for careers of action and effective citizenship. . . . In the Faculty, in the student body, and throughout the Institute we are preoccupied with a basic concern for the individual, his responsibility, his growth, his freedom, and his dignity. We can thus exemplify the liberal arts as well as teach them.[1]

Certainly teaching, even more than medicine or engineering, demands a similar breadth of educational background.

It is with such a background that the qualified teacher can best maintain a balance between school and society, between concern for the welfare of the individual and concern for the welfare of the group. Those qualities of intellect and sensibility which represent the best of our liberal arts as they affect man will also affect man as a teacher in the world of responsible free men. How these qualities are to be acquired is the basis for much study among thoughtful workers in higher education. That they must be part of the equipment of the competent teacher is a certainty.

The concern of such teachers will embrace careful study of the role of the school in our modern world. No longer can the

---

[1] Killian, James R. "We are Preoccupied with a Basic Concern for the Individual." This Is M.I.T.; The Undergraduate Catalogue for 1958-59. *Bulletin* 92: 2-3; May 1957.

teacher be indifferent to such matters and remain in the isolation of subject and classroom, trusting others to administer the school, determine the curriculum, assess its effectiveness, and report to the patrons. The qualified teacher must be intimately involved in the study of that community relationship of the school which has increased in importance by virtue of the changing circumstances of the community the school purports to serve. The reciprocal flow of influence between school and community must be studied as a constant element in the work of the effective teacher. The knowledge and skills for such study are among the necessary tools of the professional worker.

The Professional Person

Such knowledge and skill is not enough, however, without the willingness to accept the obligations they imply. The attitude of the modern teacher toward the responsibilities of the profession of teaching is more critical than ever before. No effective school faculty can be composed of isolated individuals who lack teamwork abilities, no matter how well prepared they may be in subject content and classroom method.

This teamwork has many aspects and each is of major importance. The work of the teacher is not limited to contacts with young people; it calls for constant collaboration with fellow teachers. It requires team study of youth, of the community, of the curriculum, and of the art and science of teaching. Further, as reported in Chapter III, there is emerging a practice of teamwork in teaching itself, not only in the sense of the program of general education and the interrelationships of the various subject fields, but also in the utilization of special competencies and interests on the part of the individual teacher, enhanced and employed by fellow teachers in subsequent teaching in all classrooms thruout the school.

There is, therefore, ample demand for high levels of individual excellence on the part of teachers in all fields of study and interest; but there is the parallel requirement of skill in working with others to the end that the program of education resulting from use of such excellence in working with young people will have balance, integrity, and meaning. Solo and team teaching are both required.

The professional teacher will also recognize his obligation to his profession beyond the limits of his own school and school system. As recently stated by the Educational Policies Commission:

> To those who have become members of professional organizations is entrusted the ultimate welfare of the profession. The progress of the profession, its solidarity, and its public support all derive from organized activities. Thus mere membership in professional organizations, even if they have been wisely selected, does not satisfy the obligations of membership in a profession. Participation in the program of selected organizations is essential if full value is to be received, either by the individual or by the profession, from the investment in membership.[2]

Teachers We Now Have

The major task of educating secondary-school youth in the immediate future falls largely on the shoulders of teachers now in the classroom. This group, averaging approximately 41 years of age, is experienced, legally qualified, and already on the job. Typically, they have completed some work beyond the bachelor's degree, and over 40 percent hold advanced degrees. They are committed to their profession and despite numerous frustrations and disappointments find satisfaction in their work. They will form the solid core of the faculties of our secondary schools for some years ahead.

We expect much from these teachers. The attitudes toward the profession of teaching developed by young people now in school will in no small degree depend upon their teachers. By precept and example, by emotional climate, by physical appearance, and effectiveness as friends of youth these teachers will affect the reactions of today's youth toward teaching tomorrow. Despite public confusion and private consternation con-

---

[2] National Education Association and American Association of School Administrators, Educational Policies Commission. *Professional Organizations in American Education.* Washington, D. C.: the Commission, 1957. p. 61.

cerning the behavior of some young people, these teachers must constantly work with youth to help them develop an understanding of themselves and their world. The remuneration for such work is not commensurate with the effort required and the importance of the task. The tempting attractions of outside employment are well known to all.

Further, there is the critical problem of finding in teaching a constant challenge to growth. The school atmosphere should stimulate the teacher continually to add to his intellectual capital and to experiment with new and better solutions to problems of teaching. The routine of repetitive recitations and unimaginative assignments can depress the intellect, the physical demands of a host of unimportant details can weaken the strongest, and the overload of meaningless clerical tasks can discourage the most courageous. In the face of such influence, many potentially superior teachers may become routine and mechanical manipulators of textbooks, tests, and names in the roll book. Administrative service to teachers has failed when these conditions prevail.

The responsibility of the present teacher for the effective induction of new teachers to the staffs of our schools is certainly greater than ever before. This relationship is often unofficial and informal, but if accepted as a professional service, can be dramatically effective. Informal reports by first-year and other probationary teachers frequently reveal that the person to whom they turn for help and counsel is most commonly the neighboring and experienced teacher. This information may undermine the self-confidence of many conscientious principals and supervisors, but the logic of such reports is inescapable.

With increased and changing tasks of the school, this responsibility of the experienced teacher to help the beginner takes on new meaning. Knowledge of individual students, teaching materials, and procedural practices has long been associated with such guidance and counsel by older teachers. Methods of working with other teachers, of contributing to the program development of the school, of relating teaching within one subject to other fields, of teaching specifically toward the ultimate goals of the school, of drawing upon the talents and resources of other members of the school staff, and of understanding the community and its relationship to the school are all areas in which the successful, experienced teacher can guide the new teacher in the modern secondary-school faculty.

As the skilful administrator recognizes the intelligence and ability within the faculty and seeks counsel concerning school policies, the professional teacher has the opportunity to aid in shaping the work of the school to the new demands and tasks which society and our times impose.

Where We Find New Teachers

As earlier suggested, there is no need to restate the current problems of salary and teacher shortages within the context of this chapter, altho they do have a bearing upon recruitment. It is pertinent, however, to review sources of supply and certain qualities and characteristics which we must seek in tomorrow's teachers for tomorrow's secondary schools. The quality factor is less pressing in the minds of many harassed governing boards than quantity; yet the final effect upon youth and the world about them leaves no question as to the primacy of quality in the long view of education.

There are two directions toward which we must look for the teachers and other workers in our secondary schools in the immediate as well as long-range future. Young people finishing undergraduate programs of general and professional education have made, or will soon make, decisions concerning professional careers. This is the long-term program, and one which must constantly be studied both as to recruitment and professional preparation. The second source, and one which promises an increasing richness of talent, has been drawn upon recently thru "crash" programs of recruitment combined with studies of available teaching talent in our adult population. It involves the preparation of mature adults to return to the teaching profession or the conversion of persons withdrawn from another career to competent performers in the field of teaching.

The New Young Teacher

Those who follow a long-range plan for teacher preparation, based upon an early decision to enter that profession, will face changing programs of study and experience in the years just ahead. Teacher education is undergoing constant appraisal and improvement. Despite hastily developed emergency plans to staff classrooms, there is no substantial evidence to deny the necessity of graduate-level professional work augmented by observation, practice teaching, and other field work before certification with full professional status. The increasing tasks of the secondary school require that those who enter its classrooms as teachers must be better prepared in general education and professional orientation than many of their predecessors have been. Not only must there be a stronger program of general education in the pre-professional background, but the knowledge and skills of teaching must be developed to a degree which yesterday's school might have considered desirable but not mandatory. The responsibilities of teaching, like those of the school, are greater than ever before. There is no short cut to excellence.

The Mature Candidate

During the past decade two groups of older people have entered secondary-school teaching, and their valuable services have proved their future importance to staffing our secondary schools.

The first consists of former teachers, mostly women, who have ended one phase of an adult career as homemakers, and are now available for teaching. Two cautions are called for concerning this group.

Because a person once taught is no guarantee that he was a good teacher. In fact, many may have purposely left teaching for another career because of incompetence. It is therefore particularly important to weigh carefully all personal data concerning previous experience before seriously considering the employment of former teachers. Yet, there is no denying that many splendid ex-teachers, with maturity and experience in business or homemaking, have acquired qualities and understanding which will make them even more effective in subsequent classroom service. Schools have often recognized such men and women as among the strongest members of strong faculties.

The second caution deals with the necessity of orienting such older teachers to the changes which have taken place since they last served in a school. This calls for a period of careful study and observation if it is to be effective. It requires planned observation and study of the newer relationships between teacher and student as well as among teachers in the accomplishment of the tasks of the modern school. It demands professional restudy of the ways of learning, of curriculum development, and of the status of youth in our society. The support of fellow teachers and the administrative staff in this important phase of reintroduction to teaching can forestall many bewildering experiences which otherwise the returning teacher may suffer.

The conversion of the mature adult who has not taught youth and has not been professionally prepared for teaching into a successful teacher is also a challenging and rewarding practice. Such programs as that at San Francisco State College, where retired military officers are studying in preparation for secondary-school teaching, are most promising. Intelligent, richly experienced, and adaptable adults from many walks of life may find in teaching a satisfying second career. The evidence to date is strong in favor of expanding such programs, but the careful selection of candidates is of critical importance. The well intentioned who harbor the conviction that "anyone can teach," and are naively unaware of the scope of the teacher's role, are not likely candidates for such an assignment.

Those Who Also Serve

Tho fewer in number, those who serve in other categories of a professional caliber must be aware of the changing tasks of the secondary school. No longer can the guidance worker be content merely to administer tests and interpret them, and to give information on college opportunities and admissions. The breadth of understanding and trained skill needed by counselors is suggested in Chapter II, p. 70. Counselors must be prepared to supply teacher and students with specialized knowledge and understanding of youth as well as the usual materials of the older and more conventional services of former times. Methods of studying individuals and groups, recent findings from experimental and clinical psychology, community agency services, and a host of helps to better teaching can be supplied and interpreted by such a professional person.

No longer can health services be provided by rendering first aid and making routine examinations. Expert health guidance of many types is needed.

The school librarian has not only the mounting problem of selection, as printed materials multiply and student abilities and interests diversify. There is a further problem in many libraries of maintaining a working body of audio-visual aids to learning. If not the librarian, other professional personnel are needed to select and facilitate the use of a variety of such aids, which are constantly being improved.

The role of all these professional helpers is of necessity altered by the changing role of the school, and their professional preparation and personal qualities are consequently of a higher order. The major requirement of all these new roles is that skilful support be given to the classroom teacher.

Above all, the administration of the school can no longer be trusted to a manipulator of people and things, or to a benevolent despot. The continuing development of each teacher as a student of world affairs, of community life, of the nature of youth, and of the learning process is critical. Guidance of the teacher toward a richer personal life and consequent effective work with those who are to learn, must be a primary goal of the administrator. To do this well, he must acquire great skill in human relations. He must not only know his profession well but also be able to put that knowledge to use without patronizing the adults with whom he is to work.

Little is known about how much direct influence on the effectiveness of the educational program the work of the non-professional staff of the school may have, yet any experienced school employee will testify to the importance of highly quali-fied people in all positions. It is not a simple task to staff the school with competent men and women for this work. Their service, be it clerical, custodial, providing food or transporta-tion, or other useful occupation, is an integral part of the operation of the school. To find and select such people is a constant challenge to administrative skill; it is a further chal-lenge to recognize and efficiently use their talents to the end that the work of the teacher and the learning of the student may be enhanced.

The plea for more help of this type is a standard item in the principal's annual report; the search for loyal and competent workers in these fields is never ending. To enlist those so em-ployed in the common effort to provide the best possible educa-tional program for all youth is a fundamental responsibility of the administrative and teaching staff. All are co-workers in a difficult enterprise, and as each sees his role and its contribution to the goals sought, he will be to that degree more able to give efficient service.

Some Guideposts

To those who advise governing boards regarding school policy, certain recommendations are in order. The problems of effective staffing of the schools of today and tomorrow are neither simple nor static. Widely held traditional attitudes may be blocking their solution, and lack of information may lead to false conclusions. The wise administrator must encourage the governing board to take the long view and to help in assess-ing the trends and demands to which they must respond.

There must be recognition of the full-time professional teacher. Too many citizens still think of teaching as a tem-porary and part-time occupation. This attitude is encouraged by the employment of teachers for only part of the calendar year. An annual salary with the expectation of professional activities as a replacement of most of the traditional unpaid summer vacation is both reasonable and desirable if the salary is adjusted to the realities of our modern economy and if the school is to make maximum use of the limited supply of teaching talent.

This means in turn that teachers and all professional employees of the school must develop plans for continuing professional growth as a regular phase of their work. It means independent study, travel, and participation in professional conferences of many kinds and at many times. It means the sacrifice of some part-time employment and the economic advantages so realized, to the enhancement of the professional status in their own eyes as well as in the eyes of the community. It means seeking broader fields of study and deeper knowledge of those fields. It means that education of youth for our times and the future must be in the hands of stimulating, creative, and resourceful teachers whose personal and professional life is rich and attractive.

Within the life of the school there must be time for study, observation, and professional conferences. The teacher's involvement in community life as a professional worker is as important as his involvement as a responsible citizen. The role of the administrator and the governing board is clear; the teacher must be carefully selected, encouraged, and trusted if he is to be of the caliber to meet the requirements of modern effective schools.

housing the new high school

housing the new high school

PLANNING that makes it possible to translate programs of secondary education into school-plant facilities brings rich returns. In dealing with individual school projects, many questions arise that are unique to secondary schools. But in long-term planning the educational needs of a school district must be considered as a whole, with secondary education related to the elementary-school and post-high-school facilities of the entire community.

Planning—A Continuing Process

An organized process of schoolhouse planning must be carried on as a highly regarded and well-staffed part of the administrative branch of any school district. In small districts, such procedures may well be part of the chief administrator's personal duties. In a large school district, this function should be assigned to an educational housing department, with the head directly responsible to the superintendent. The degree to which planning is systematic, continuous, and comprehensive will determine in large measure the adequacy and cost of school-plant facilities.

Recognition of the need for continuous planning for the physical facilities of school districts has been long in coming about. School construction was almost at a standstill during the depression of the 1930's and the war years of the 1940's. After World War II, the question of providing schoolhouses for the great influx of war and postwar babies and of shifting populations became a major problem in many a community that had not had a new school building for years. Organized procedures were known to but a few. School districts were faced with a desperate need for housing, and the public clamored for action. The result—Topsy-like school-plant development that just "growed" in all directions without much attention.

Boards of education, administrators, and the lay public, in some communities, continue to act as if the exasperating problem of community growth and the need for school facilities will go away if they ignore it. Others, lacking a definite plan of action, salve their consciences by meeting immediate needs on an expediency basis, hoping for the best. Either of these attitudes in the housing of secondary education is disastrous. A high-school building represents a great community investment—if unwisely made, several generations suffer.

Many professional and lay people, however, are earnestly looking for any assistance they can get in making wise, policy-backed decisions for today's and tomorrow's school building needs. The best time for careful planning is when there is no immediate need for action. Those few extremely wise administrators and boards who took advantage of the depression and war years, when large-scale school building stopped, to study their most likely developmental patterns, are the ones who were ready with an organized plan.

Planning, to be valid, must be continuous. Procedures for collecting and interpreting pertinent data must be followed as faithfully as a baseball fan follows the sports columns if administrators are to stay in control of one of their most important educational problems.

If planning is to be effective, it must follow a procedural pattern. Competencies must be employed, information gathered and evaluated, decisions reached, action ordered in a sequence that brings an ultimate solution thru a series of organized steps. Bringing the proper competency to bear at the proper time is probably the most important single aspect of sound planning procedure.

This chapter does not explore fine points of planning procedure but rather discusses the major elements of sound planning which must be considered before intelligent action can be taken on specific school building problems, whether elementary or secondary.

A Study of the Community

School-plant problems can be studied intelligently only in relation to total community developmental problems and only by representatives of the total community. Responsible school officials must always make final decisions on school plants, but information on community development, evaluated by representatives of the community, should become an integral part of the background of school policy.

School officials must depend upon other than strictly educational sources for much information and help in planning a comprehensive schoolhousing program. Planning commissions, zoning boards, highway and street departments, chambers of commerce, utility companies, real estate organizations, bankers, farmers, businessmen, parents, students, and others can aid.

Careful analysis is needed of current information on such considerations as saturation land use and saturation enrolments, school district organization, grade-grouping policies, over-all needs for sites and facilities, a documented priority-of-development list, and financing programs.

Responsibilities and Relationships

Since a group of individuals and agencies should be involved in any school-plant program, it is important to identify these participants, their responsibilities, and their interrelationships. The administrator who does not make these responsibilities and interrelationships doubly clear may find himself in a lion's cage of planning without a whip, gun, or chair.

The American Institute of Architects and the National Council on Schoolhouse Construction, as major groups interested in school planning procedures, jointly prepared a statement covering the responsibilities and relationships of individuals and groups in the planning of a school-plant program (see Figure I) and defined their responsibilities as follows:

1. *The people of the community, through a representative cross section of the entire group.* They determine needs for school plant through study of community growth, size and condition of present plant, educational needs, financial ability, etc. The recommendations of this group are passed on to the school board for legal action. The action of the school board should be reviewed and finally approved by the people of the community.

2. *The school board.* Takes legal action, based upon consideration of facts and best judgment. Authorizes studies. Selects and appoints its staff, architects, and consultants. Reviews and approves recommendations, building drawings and specifications, bids for construction, and contract documents. Reviews and approves work of all employees. Selects and purchases sites. Accepts completed buildings. Authorizes and contracts and signs as employer and owner. Acts as legal agent for the community on all phases of the planning, designing and constructing of plants.

3. *The superintendent of schools.* The executive officer of the school board. Recommends policy, personnel and procedure, and advises the board on all phases of the building program. As the educational leader of the community, he suggests and takes responsibility for studies which need to be made showing plant needs. Collects and interprets data. Advises and assists school and community groups in cooperative planning. Acts as agent of the board on all phases of the program.

4. *The school staff.* Provide assistance and advice on educational program, facilities needed, operation and maintenance of such facilities. Assist in planning and carrying out studies. Aid in the interpretation of findings. Prepare educational specifications and space requirements of contemplated school plants.

FIGURE I—RELATIONSHIPS OF THE CHIEF PARTICIPANTS IN THE PLANNING, DESIGNING, AND BUILDING OF A SCHOOL PLANT

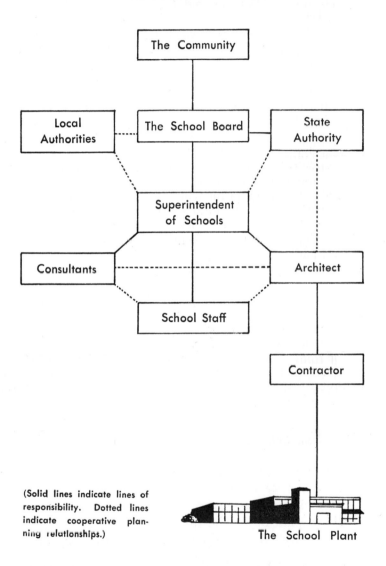

(Solid lines indicate lines of responsibility. Dotted lines indicate cooperative planning relationships.)

The School Plant

Adapted from: American Institute of Architects and National Council on Schoolhouse Construction. *Statement of Responsibilities and Relationships in the Planning, Design, and Building of the School Plant.* Washington, D. C.: the Institute, 1958.

5. *Educational consultants.* Assist in the school administration in the determination of need and in the development of a long-term plan for building. Assist in the preparation of educational specifications and the educational planning of a particular building.

6. *Local governmental groups.* Advise on matters for which they have legal responsibilities. Make sure that final program meets the local requirements for which they are responsible.

7. *The state department of education.* Advises the local groups on procedures, state regulations and other matters. Provides technical assistance and information to the local district. Assists in the planning process on request. Gives such formal supervision and approval of the building program and building plans as required by state law and regulations.

8. *Architects and their technical consultants as required.* Advise the school administration and the school board on phases of the program for which they have technical training and experience. Translate the educational program for which plant facilities are needed into building design and specifications. Advise on letting of contracts. Supervise or direct the supervision of construction. Recommend approval and acceptance of completed building. Supplement his services, when necessary, by consulting specialists such as landscape architects, heating, ventilating, electrical, structural or acoustical engineers.

9. *Contractors and builders.* Construct the plant in accordance with the approved plans and specifications. Accept responsibility for expert craftsmanship and skilled workmanship in executing the drawings and specifications under the supervision of the architect and the owner's designated representatives.[1]

A Realistic Time Schedule

School facilities being planned today will serve the educational needs of communities for 50 to 100 years. Much of the success of tomorrow's educational programs will depend upon how well we plan now. The quality of plans made now will depend to a large degree upon a realistic time schedule for

[1] From preliminary draft of: American Institute of Architects and National Council on Schoolhouse Construction. *Statement of Responsibilities and Relationships in the Planning, Design, and Building of the School Plant.* Washington, D. C.: the Institute. (Also to be available from the Council, George Peabody College for Teachers, Nashville, Tenn.)

planning. Educational adequacy, capital costs, and mainte-
nance-and-operation costs are all influenced greatly by the time
element in planning.

Often long-range master planning and the planning of a
specific building project will go on at the same time. The master
plan will determine the time sequence of individual projects.
The secret of having time enough to plan individual projects
well is to keep the master planning at least five years in advance
of immediate needs.

One of the best ways to provide a realistic time schedule
for a building project is to figure backwards from the date of
needed occupancy. For example, a new high-school project
schedule might work out as follows, assuming the site had been
chosen and the architect had been commissioned:

Time Schedule for a High-School Building Project

Date of occupancy, September 1, 1960

Construction and equipping . . . . 14 Months
    (Construction begins July 1959)
Bidding and preparation of construction
  contract . . . . 1 Month
    (Plans out to bid, June 1959)
Checking of final plans and specifications . . . . 2 Months
    (Final plans and specifications completed
    and ready for checking, April 1959)
Preparation of final plans and specifications . . 6 Months
    (Working drawings begin October 1958)
Preliminary plans and specifications . . . . 4 Months
    (Preliminary plans begin June 1958)
Preparation of educational specifications . . . . . 6 Months
    (Preparation of educational specifications
    begins December 1957)

Such a time schedule indicates that planning for a new high
school should begin at least two years and nine months before
it is needed for occupancy. A general rule-of-thumb is that the
planning time for a new school building should be at least
as long as the time needed to construct the building. Allowing
any less time inevitably results in an educationally less adequate plant and a premium paid for both the capital and main-

tenance-and-operation costs. Time taken for careful planning is one of the surest ways known to assure an educationally responsive school environment at the most favorable cost.

Site Selection

Probably more words have been written about the school site that any other one phase of the school plant. Much good material is readily available to anyone wishing to explore in detail the many facets of site selection. One authority states its significance as follows:

> The most important single act a board of education per-forms in relation to providing school facilities is the selection of the site for the school building. While initial cost may seem rather large and cause much discussion during board sessions it should be kept in mind that this single important investment is the least expensive part of the entire project. When one considers that the site will be used for over forty years—and in some cases over seventy-five years—and in rare cases over 100 years and that many hundreds and thousands of school children will utilize it, we can see that the first cost, even though large, is relatively small. Too often the most de-sirable site is rejected because it costs two or three times as much as an inferior one. This first decision, when it is wrong, is the most costly one made by the board of education.
>
> A site poorly located is costly. A site too small is even more costly. A site purchased too late can be highly costly. All these factors indicate the adequacy of the site to some degree. It is even more a truism that it indicates the foresight and the ability of the board of education.[2]

Each generation shows the need for larger school sites than formerly seemed acceptable. The National Council on School-house Construction continues to urge that school officials recognize this trend:

> Most school sites are too small. Modern schools require sites larger than were considered necessary a generation ago because of the continued expansion of educational programs, the greater use of schools by the entire community, and the neces-sity for sufficient space for present and future building needs.

---

[2] Thomas, Maurice J. "The Climate for Learning." *Climate for Learning.* Pittsburgh: University of Pittsburgh Press, 1953. p. 28.

The trend in some sections of the country toward campus plans and spread-out types of one-story buildings with single-loaded corridors, increases the amount of land area required for school sites.

The size of any school site should be determined largely by the nature and scope of the contemplated educational program. Actual layouts of the spaces needed by the various phases of the programs should be made.[3]

Recommended minimum areas for secondary-school sites as established by one state are as follows:

Junior High School—15 usable acres plus an additional acre for each 100 pupils of predicted ultimate maximum enrollment.

High School—30 usable acres plus an additional acre for each 100 pupils of predicted maximum enrollment.[4]

A summary of principles to consider in the selection of a school site follows, in outline form:

I. Basic Considerations

    A. The proper location, adequate size and shape, and favorable physical features of a school site are of paramount importance in the intelligent planning of a single school building project or the planning of a districtwide master plan of schools.

    B. The cost considerations for a site should not be made until all possible sites have been evaluated in terms of school service.

    C. The school district should acquire the highest ranking of these evaluated sites that it can possibly afford.

II. School Site Selection Factors

    A. Location

        1. Grade-grouping organization of school district, present and future

        2. School population, present and future

        3. Land use, present and future

        4. Natural attendance zones, present and future

---

[3] National Council on Schoolhouse Construction, Research and Publications Committee. *Guide for Planning School Plants.* Nashville, Tenn.: the Council (Secy.-Treas.: W. D. McClurkin, George Peabody College for Teachers), 1953. p. 26.

[4] *California Administrative Code.* Title 5, Education, Chapter 1, Subchapter 8.

5. Policy maximum enrolment to be assigned to site
6. Relationship to present and future sites
7. Access streets, walking distances, public transportation access hazards
8. Environmental factors—safety and health factors on the site and in the immediate neighborhood; noises from trucks, autos, railroads, airplanes; odors; esthetic features of surroundings
9. Relationship to public service facilities—availability of water, gas, electric power, sewers, fire protection.

B. Size, shape, and physical features
1. Number of acres available
2. Shape of site—relationship of length to width, etc.
3. Physical features—(a) Contours relative to building areas, possible flooding, drainage, sewage disposal, etc. (b) Soil relative to bearing qualities, drainage, topsoil quality, etc.

C. Cost.

Translating Program into Plant Facilities

A school building may be beautiful or ugly, large or small, traditional or contemporary in design, located on a city block or on a beautiful 100-acre site, but no one can tell by casual inspection whether it is good, bad, or mediocre as a school plant. The one real criterion of its value lies in the answer to the question, How well will it meet the needs of the educational program or programs it must house during its structural life? A factual answer can be given only after a painstaking evaluation of both the educational program and its relationship to the physical facilities in which it is housed.

Educational Specifications

Emphasis on the need for a comprehensive statement of the educational specifications for a new school plant gives the educator a real job in developing a school building. Before this need became a recognized part of school planning, the educator either did not participate in planning or he tried to advise on architectural design without the competence to do so. Now, however, he can participate in planning within his recognized sphere of competence, and his contribution, if skilfully done, will be indispensable. The educator has found his rightful, important place in the planning process.

Since the success of any educational program depends to a major degree upon the adequacy of the physical environment in which it must be carried on, the importance of a carefully and skilfully prepared statement of educational specifications becomes quite apparent. The statement should describe the program in detail; it should include these items:

1. A summary of the educational philosophy and program for a community and school
2. Possible future program changes
3. The location, size, and description of the site of the proposed project
4. The grade levels to be housed
5. Initial enrolment and policy on maximum enrolment
6. Policy on class sizes
7. A tentative time schedule
8. A summary of required teaching stations or classrooms (space-adequacy survey)
9. The desired relationships of these teaching stations
10. A description of each station in terms of the activities to be carried on, the furniture, equipment, and storage requirements
11. Proposed community use
12. Any special requirements.

Educational specifications also should include a description of such things relating to the general site as parking requirements, service facilities, after-school and summer community use, and possible future expansion.

A statement of educational specifications serves several major purposes. First, it represents the action point which makes necessary a thoro review and evaluation of the existing educational program. Educators responsible for that program must then decide whether or not the existing program is acceptable as a basis for a new educational plant. Second, it places educational considerations, instead of economic or architectural considerations, at the focal point of planning and design of the school plant. Third, such a statement forms a valid and objective instrument for the evaluation of plans and specifications as they develop. Fourth, it sets up an educationally defensible priority list of building features. If budget cuts become necessary, any reductions in scope or quality level will result in the least loss possible to educational program needs. Such a priority list tends to keep the program and facilities in better all-round balance than would be the case when such budget emergencies are not properly anticipated.

The Space-Adequacy Survey

Altho from the point of view of planning, the space-adequacy survey is only one part of the educational specifications, it is so important to sound and economical planning for secondary-school plants that it requires special discussion as a technical process.

One of several instruments developed in the past few years to assist in evaluating an existing secondary-school program and in planning a new high-school plant is the space-adequacy survey. This educational tool was developed by the California Bureau of School Planning, to take much of the guesswork out of the high-school planning process. It has been used in the evaluation of scores of secondary-school programs and in translating these programs into the number and types of teaching stations needed to house them. It assumes a continued organization in classes and subject fields such as is found in the typical comprehensive high school.

This device has the advantage of being as objective as basic mathematical processes can make it in the gathering of factual data about a given program for a specified number of students. It also has the highly desirable advantage of providing for the adjustment of mathematically correct data by conference so that desirable program changes can be reflected in new building plans. The space-adequacy survey is based on the following concepts:

> A working unit of measure of the need for teaching spaces in a high school is one student enrolled in a class for one period each day of the week (student-period enrolment). This unit multiplied by a desirable average class size for each subject and the product multiplied by the number of class periods per day available to all students for scheduling classes, gives a product that mathematically justifies one teaching space for *that type of school subject*. (Actually a school needs *more* than the mathematically computed teaching spaces in order to operate an acceptable class schedule, but necessary adjustments can best be made from the computed needs.)

Total teaching-space needs in a school plant can be controlled if the number of student-period enrolments assigned to a new course is offset by subtracting an equal number from some other subject previously offered.

The data forms grew out of the above-mentioned concept of measuring the needs for *teaching space* in a high school. In general or academic rooms, fractions resulting from computation are retained as such. In special-purpose rooms similar fractions are generally considered to require one additional room.

The sample charts (Figures II-IV) represent one sheet each from three forms, using information from the Union High School District, El Monte, Calif. The existing Rosemead High School was selected as the base on which the needs for a new North El Monte High School could be projected.

Figure II illustrates the recording of student-period data by department and subject. These forms are completed for each department and each teacher; the example shows the figures for mathematics classes.

Figure III illustrates one page from the school summary of student-period data for all departments and subjects; the mathematics totals are shown on this page.

Figure IV illustrates the projection of needs for the proposed new school, based on a predicted enrolment of 2000, as con-

FIGURE II—PUPIL-PERIOD ENROLMENT—DEPARTMENTAL RECORD FORM

FORM A—SPACE ADEQUACY SURVEY, SECONDARY SCHOOL

Clement Union High School District

Riverside School

Mathematics Department

(Use at least one line for each teacher. Separate sheet for each department.)

March 27, 1953 Date
Prepared by Chas. Gibson
Page 1 of 1 Pages

Teacher Name	Course Name	Enrolments by period								Pupil-Period Enrolment (Total of Col. 3)	No. classes reported each line	Average class size Col. 4 ÷ Col. 5
		1	2	3	4	5	6	7	8			
Mrs. E.P.	Geometry, Adv. Algebra, Trig.	28	17	13	DS	33	CP			61 / 17 / 13	2 / 1 / 1	31 / 17 / 13
Mr. M.L.H.	Inter. math			13	37					37	1	37
Mr. C.Q.	Basic math, Inter. math, Sec. math, Algebra	29	34	36	27	35	CP			29 / 69 / 36 / 27	1 / 2 / 1 / 1	29 / 35 / 36 / 27
Miss A.L.L.	Sec. math, Basic math	36	38	CP	26	31	17			105 / 43	3 / 2	35 / 22
Mr. R.M.	Inter. math			26						26	1	26
Mrs. H.R.	Algebra, Adv. Algebra, Sec. math	28	30	35	21	CP	24			93 / 21 / 24	3 / 1 / 1	31 / 21 / 24
Mr. B.I.	Algebra, Geometry	31	16	18	23	31	CP			62 / 57	2 / 3	31 / 19
Total Period Enrolments		152	135	128	134	130	41			720	26	28

(These totals should be transferred to Form B)

CP—Conference Period
DS—Department Supervision

California State Dept. Education, Office of School Planning 1/11/50. Revised 6/1/53

FIGURE III—PUPIL-PERIOD ENROLMENT—SCHOOL SUMMARY SHEET BY DEPARTMENTS

FORM B—SPACE ADEQUACY SURVEY, SECONDARY SCHOOL

El Monte Union High School District

Rosemead High School

Grand Total Period Enrolments, (Form A, Col. 4): 6828

PUPIL-PERIOD ENROLMENT CHART
School Summary Sheet by Departments

March 30, 1953 Date
Prepared by Chas. Gibson
Page 1 of 2 Pages

School Subjects	Total Department Enrolments (From Form A)								Total pupil-period enrolments Col. 4, Form A	% Col. 3 is of grand total enrolments	No. classes reported Col. 5, Form A	Average class size Col. 3 ÷ Col. 5
	1	2	3	4	5	6	7	8				
ENGLISH	290	336	268	229	230	129			1482	21.70	57	26
LANGUAGE	75	88	45	51	79	—			338	4.95	13	26
MATHEMATICS	152	135	128	134	130	41			720	10.54	26	28
SOCIAL SCIENCE	223	195	223	241	191	144			1217	17.82	40	30
AGRICULTURE—Totals	26	29	13	—	—	—			68	.99	3	23
Animal Agri.	—	29	13	—	—	—			42	.61	2	21
Horticulture	26	—	—	—	—	—			26	.38	1	26
ART—Totals	42	35	41	—	48	17			183	2.68	9	20
Art	20	18	24	—	25	—			87	1.27	4	22
Arts & Crafts	21	17	17	—	23	17			96	1.40	5	19
BUSINESS EDUCATION Totals	157	166	140	153	156	108			880	12.88	34	26
Bookkeeping	25	17	17	20	22	—			101	1.47	5	20
Bus. Arith	18	—	—	—	—	—			18	.26	1	18
Bus. Machines	25	16	—	—	17	22			80	1.17	4	20
Every Day Bus.	—	—	32	—	35	—			67	.98	2	34
Office Training	17	—	18	21	14	—			70	1.02	4	18
Sales & Pers. Law	—	17	—	15	—	—			32	.46	2	16
Shorthand	—	8	—	23	—	—			32	.46	2	16
Transcription	—	—	—	—	33	—			33	.48	1	33
Typing	72	107	73	74	35	86			447	6.54	13	34

California State Dept. Education, Office of School Planning 1/11/50. Revised 6/1/53

FIGURE IV—ESTIMATE OF TEACHING SPACES NEEDED

FORM C—SPACE ADEQUACY SURVEY, SECONDARY SCHOOL
El Monte Union High School District
North El Monte High School Date 1960
1. Predicted Enrolment 2,000
2. Present Enrolment 1,620
3. Predicted Increase 570
4. Working Factor (Line 1 ÷ Line 2) 1.21

* (Enrolment in Rosemead High School. Distribution of pupil-periods in Rosemead High, as recorded on Forms A & B, used as basis for computing estimated space needs for proposed new North El Monte High.)

April 1953 Date
Prepared by Chas. Gibson
Page 1 of 3 Pages

1	2	3	4	5	6	7	8	9
School Subjects	Current Pupil-Period Enrolments (Col. 3, Form B)	Average Class Size District Policy	Class Groups Required (Col. 2 ÷ Col. 3)	Class Groups Required for Predicted Enrol. (Col. 4 x Factor)	Teaching Space Needs Computed for Pred. Enrol. Col. 5 ÷ 6**	Teaching Space Needs Adjusted by Conference	No. Adeq. Teaching Spaces now avail.	No. Addl. Teaching Spaces Recommended
ENGLISH	1482	28	52.9	64.01	10.66	11	...	11
LANGUAGES	338	28	12.1	14.64	2.44	3	...	3
MATHEMATICS	720	28	29.3	35.45	5.91	6	...	6
SOCIAL SCIENCE	1217	28	43.5	52.64	8.77	9	...	9
AGRICULTURE Animal Agri. Horticulture	42 26	24 24	1.8 1.1	2.18 1.33	0.36 0.22	1	...	1
ART Art Arts & Crafts	81 96	24 24	3.6 4.0	4.36 4.84	0.73 0.31	1 1	... ...	1 1

**a Number of teaching periods in daily schedule 6.
California State Dept. Education, Office of School Planning 1/11/50. Revised 6/1/53

trasted with an enrolment of 1650 in the existing Rosemead
High School. Again the sample page includes mathematics.

Figure V illustrates a kind of "fringe benefit" that may be
derived from the space-adequacy survey. A chart of this
type, compiled and summarized from the kinds of data included
in the form shown in Figure III, can be a most useful administrative device. It presents in picture form the extent of student participation in the various subjectmatter areas. Such
information helps curriculum and guidance personnel to
evaluate the effectiveness of the program in light of the needs
of the students and community.

When a mathematical procedure is used to gather the basic
data about the space requirements for various subject fields,
administrators and architects are no longer required to depend
upon estimates from department heads. The space-adequacy
survey provides objective data against which to evaluate each
part of an educational program and detailed-to-the-fraction
needs of specific housing requirements. No longer is it necessary to use subjective judgment to determine the exact space
needs of a given educational program for a specified student
enrolment. The use of such an instrument results in a finer
balance of facilities, scheduling practices based on maximum
use of space, and real economy in costs.

Project Master Planning

School officials and their resource groups often do a fine job
of studying community needs and setting up comprehensive
developmental plans for long-range educational needs but then
overlook the necessity of going thru the same basic process
for each project. A master plan is necessary for each separate
school building project.

The first considerations in a project master plan should be
educational ones. The architectural planning that follows can
be good or bad only as it meets the needs of the outlined educational program. The educational information can be based
on the space-adequacy survey discussed previously. This survey requires that certain policies important to planning be

FIGURE V—ANALYSIS OF PUPIL PARTICIPATION
IN CURRENT EDUCATIONAL PROGRAM

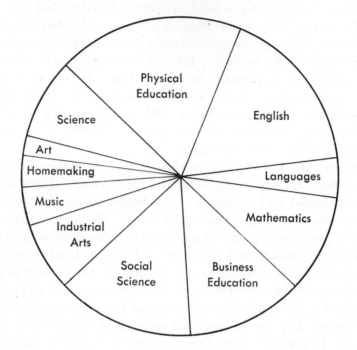

Subject	Pupil-Period Enrolment	Percent of Total Pupil-Period Enrolment
English	1454	17%
Languages	371	4
Mathematics	833	10
Social Science	1182	14
Art	138	2
Business Education	1076	12
Homemaking	230	3
Industrial Arts	631	7
Science	727	8
Music	397	4
Physical Education	1627	19
Total	8666	100%

established by responsible educational leadership. Such policies include the total number of students to be assigned to the particular school plant, the curriculum content, planned student-teacher ratios for all subject fields, and the number of class periods to be taught daily. Each of these policy decisions will affect the physical planning of the school.

With the instruments available to planners now, it is possible to prepare a comprehensive statement which should give any alert architect the educational information he needs for the wise and economical planning of a secondary school to house the known, current program. Project master planning, however, involves more than the current program. It should include consideration of basic educational trends which well might alter the assignment and use of space carefully planned to meet current educational programs.

One statement of these trends was given by Koopman at a conference on planning the secondary school, as follows:

1. The educative process will assume greater prominence.
2. The scope of the educational program will greatly increase at all age levels.
3. Education for the individual will become a continuous life-long process.
4. Humanistic general education and the emphasis on citizenship will grow in importance and provide the unifying principles of both formal and informal education.
5. Specialized education will expand greatly and will be delayed somewhat.
6. Programs of education and recreation for adults will expand into a new frontier for education.
7. The family will assume an even more important role in education than in recent times.
8. There will be an increasing application of the community school policy.
9. An increasing percentage of the national expenditure will go to education.[5]

An architectural project master plan for a school cannot be developed successfully by the architect alone; nowhere is the team approach more vital. The educator cannot prepare a de-

[5] Ohio State University, Bureau of Educational Research. *Planning the Secondary School—1960 and Beyond.* Report of a Conference for School Administrators and Architects. Columbus: the University, 1956. p. 7-8.

tailed educational specification and then divorce himself from
further planning. Just as the architect should be a part of educational planning discussions, so should the educator be a part
of the architectural solution development.

Here again an understanding of the respective roles and
competencies of the educator and the architect must be clarified and maintained. While the designer must be given real
freedom to interpret the educational specifications into physical
spaces, the educator should be consulted as to whether the
designer's evolving plans are meeting the educational needs.
Budget limitations sometimes create a situation where educational and architectural appraisals of alternate design solutions
should be made simultaneously if planning is to proceed on
schedule.

A project master plan should be completed to indicate the
number, types, and relationships of all the buildings needed to
house the maximum enrolment approved by policy for the
project when completed. This complete draft is essential no
matter how much or how little of the complete plant is to be
constructed in the first step. Effective and economical planning
demands a complete master plan before any one structure is
erected. Such a procedure makes it possible to build toward an
integrated plant whether actual construction is accomplished
in one or a dozen separate contracts.

Meeting the Needs of a Changing Educational Program

One of the biggest problems in housing secondary education
is to provide a school plant that not only meets the needs of
the current program, but also will lend itself economically to
meet the needs of a *changing* educational program. Most
schools being constructed today will have a long structural
life. Since educators seem to agree that the one certain aspect
of current secondary programs is that they are changing and
will continue to change, it follows that buildings should be
designed to encourage rather than inhibit changes in the use
of building space.

The key word is *flexibility*. The word itself has been in educators' and architects' vocabularies for years but not with the same semantic depth it now has.

In the "good old days," planners knew the educational program a school building would serve because the educational needs of communities appeared static.

The occasional design pioneer who did envision the possible need for reassignment of space use found himself sorely limited by the rigidity of structural design and lack of variety in materials.

Modern technology and the wide choice of versatile construction materials, however, make it possible for planners to design great flexibility into buildings simply and inexpensively. Today the greatest barrier in achieving flexibility in school buildings lies in the thinking processes of planners.

Caudill has stated it thus: "Generally when school planners speak of flexibility of space they are referring to all four qualities of space—fluidity, versatility, convertibility, and expansibility. . . ." [6] He continues to describe each of these elements of flexibility.

Fluidity of space Caudill illustrates by describing a house with an open plan as follows:

> A house with an open plan differs from a house with a traditional plan in that the open plan affords a free flow of space in the main living area, while the traditional plan cuts up this main space into box-like rooms—a separate cubicle for the hall, one for the dining room, and one for the living room. The open plan considers these three elements as parts of a compound volume, and provides for integration of these space elements; the traditional plan chops up the space into so many isolated cubicles. . . . This new spaciousness has given educational architecture warmth, and a friendly, non-confining atmosphere. . . . No longer are classrooms cages in which to work.[7]

To many, *versatility* of space means the multi-use of space. Caudill warns about trying to make the same space serve so

[6] Caudill, William W. *Toward Better School Design*. New York: F. W. Dodge Corp., 1954. p. 139.
[7] *Ibid.*, p. 136, 137.

many purposes it serves none well. However, he heartily subscribes to the planning of as much space versatility as possible,
weighing each use against any possible educational loss. He
says:

> So this quality of versatility of space can get out of hand.
> But can we not make it work for us? Why not put it to work
> in the corridors which are used only for walking? Can we afford
> space just to walk in? Some schoolhouses have as much as
> 28 per cent of their floor areas devoted to corridors. If the space
> for these corridors was designed for more versatility, taxpayers
> would not be so reluctant to see them in their schools. The
> school planner should learn more about space and how it can
> be used for more than one purpose.[8]

Design for *convertibility* of space is one of the most important features of contemporary schoolhousing. Even the most
traditional educational program can use this feature to advantage. Two regular-sized classrooms could be converted into
one small classroom to house a small class in conversational
French and into one large classroom to house a large class in
some other subject. This could be accomplished over a week
end between semesters by having the maintenance crew move
a nonstructural space divider from the center point to the one-
third point of the total space taken up by the two regular
classrooms. Both teachers and students could work more
efficiently after the space reassignment because the French
teacher could establish a much more intimate teaching-learning environment for a conversational-type subject, while the
other teacher, possibly working with an assistant teacher, could
have more room to house his large class for better work relationships and could preserve the individual space essential to
human dignity.

This feature of convertibility offers the one great hope that
today's planners can meet the challenges of tomorrow's unknown needs. Caudill states:

> The importance of the convertible quality of space cannot
> be over-emphasized. School planners should study other build-
> ing types. If they would study office buildings, for example,
> they would find that the up-to-date office building has been

---

[8] *Ibid.,* p. 137.

designed with no definitely set partition arrangement. Of course, much thought has been given to how the partitions can be arranged for many situations, but not for just one. As tenants come and go, the partitions are changed accordingly.[9]

Expansibility of a school plant depends upon the proper placement of buildings on an adequate site and the planning of buildings so that they may be extended at minimum cost. There should be a predetermined limit to expansibility, set at the time the project master plan is made, and scrupulously observed.

The type and program of a school plant may change with changing conditions. Modification of the grade grouping organization may necessitate a radical change in the enrolment and program for a given school plant. School district reorganization will cause the use of many school plants to be altered beyond any degree that can be anticipated when they are built. Caudill concludes:

> The school plant must be designed to grow without growing pains; additions can be very expensive if provision has not been made for them. . . . But whether growth is anticipated or not, it is a good rule to plan for expansion. It pays off in savings to the taxpayer, in efficiency to the changing education process, and in pride and appreciation of a unified, beautiful plant to the pupils who must work and live in these ever growing schools.[10]

As one watches the shifts of population, particularly in metropolitan areas, it is clear that yet another element in *flexibility* should be considered in the planning of school buildings. That element is *contractibility*. Long-range planning must consider not only the possibility of space reassignment to meet changing educational needs, but also the possibility that shifting populations and enrolment cycles may dictate that a small percent of the total number of teaching stations in certain areas should be of a portable type. These classrooms should be designed to provide every educational and space refinement found in a permanently located classroom. The only difference between a portable-permanent and a regular-permanent class-

[9] *Ibid.*, p. 138.
[10] *Ibid.*, p. 139.

room should be that one is designed to be moved to other sites as needed, while the other is designed to remain on one site.

Types of Plan Solutions

School buildings have always been planned to meet someone's idea of adequacy. The fact that school-plant layout and design have changed so markedly during the past 50 years shows that responsible authorities have recognized that changing educational philosophies require changing design patterns in school buildings. At the same time, technology has developed rapidly. Each succeeding group of school-building planners was expressing function, form, and technology as it had developed up to his era. Some innovations have come as a result of the exploitation of some material or method. Some have evolved from an analysis of educational program needs. Some have been different just for the sake of being different. On the whole, however, the concepts of school design that have gained acceptance have grown out of a continuing search for better ways to meet the needs of a slowly changing educational program and to use the offerings of a rapidly developing technology. Of these two forces, the greater influence has been our advancing technology.

Perkins and Cocking describe some of the functional planning developments which have been influencing school-plant design in the present century.

> The regimented and static-desk-teacher relationship began to be replaced by informality, with mobile furniture adaptable to group discussion or project work and a varied stock of accessory facilities for painting, making toys, models, furniture, presenting plays, learning by doing.
> Among the exciting developments which began to be felt in the first quarter of the 20th century which led to fundamental changes in the entire school program were: growing acceptance that children learn to do by doing; school should help children to live better now than in some future day; pupils should have the opportunity to understand the environment in which they live; how to live with others has to be learned; schools have a stake in teaching how to make a living;

music, arts, and handicrafts may be as important as reading
and arithmetic; mental development is dependent in large
measure upon proper health and physical development; learning to work together in groups is a necessary part of one's
growth; education is concerned with the whole person and one
part affects all the rest; schools are for all the children
regardless of social or economic standing; schools are concerned primarily with present-day problems not alone those of
the past; adults can learn as well as children, and their
education is never completed; and finally, the dawning understanding that the school exists to make communities better, not
just to teach knowledge.

Such developments brought tremendous changes. More and
more pupils came to schools and remained there for years.
School programs were expanded to include provisions for
teaching health, physical education, arts and crafts, music,
shop work and trades, science of all kinds, agriculture, homemaking, and other things. Hot lunches at school began to win
acceptance and approval. Adults demanded that the school
provide a program for their needs. And thus the school became
quite a different type of institution.[11]

Many changes in educational programs during the twentieth
century came about in traditionally designed buildings. Such
buildings do not prevent changes in activities if these changes
are not too demanding on the structural or mechanical patterns
of space. The buildings, however, that defy the elements of
fluidity, versatility, convertibility, and expansibility sometimes
make space reassignment so difficult that even the dedicated
educator finally must accept some less-than-half-way compro-
mise which frustrates the improvement desired. Altho the inflexible school building cannot stop progress completely, it certainly can discourage constructive advances in curriculum and
instruction.

Campus Plan

Probably the most dramatic change in school architectural
design was the abandonment (where circumstances permitted)
of the traditional E-type building for what became known as

[11] Perkins, Lawrence B., and Cocking, Walter D. *Schools.* New York: Reinhold
Publishing Corp., 1949. p. 236.

the campus plan. The need for elbowroom to serve a vital educational program, the philosophy that physical plant had a definite relationship to the effectiveness and attitudes of the people using it, and a technology that made it possible for pioneering architects to develop simplicity and functionality as the key words in school design—all these factors produced the campus plan for secondary schools.

The compact, multi-storied, inflexible, overadorned, monumental school building gave way to a decentralized, single-story, flexible, and simple structure. Instead of the small city-block site, the spacious site of 40 to 100 acres was accepted. Highly flexible master-planned buildings stretched their finger-type, low-center-of-gravity masses in organized but free patterns, close to the earth. These schools looked and felt like an integral part of a dynamic, democratic society. They appeared to invite change rather than stifle it. They became a cooperative part of the communities they served rather than standing aloof, towering forebodingly over the clusters of lesser structures which form the crossroad communities of America.

Altho basically new in general design, the campus plan, for the most part, carried over into its more functional enclosures the same compartmental and specialized subject-content areas found in its predecessor. There was the English building; the science building; the homemaking building; and the art, social studies, and the mathematics buildings. Each was designed to serve its particular function in the educative process. These separate buildings were related to one another in a general site plan that reflected what interrelationship they had one for the other. The planning told the story that educators and architects had done much to improve the teaching-learning climate for a curriculum and philosophy that were subject centered.

There were, however, some educationally significant developments which evolved from the campus plan idea. As buildings became less centralized and more spread out, more care had to be given to interrelationships. The concept of master planning took on real significance. Building groups, especially those units designed to house such specialized subject fields as science, homemaking, and industrial arts had to be planned with a saturation enrolment in mind if the final result were to be a well-organized plant. When a fixed saturation enrolment was assigned to a school site, further thought about the need for other schools was stimulated. This need resulted in more emphasis on total community planning and development.

The decentralization of buildings and students resulted in a recognition of the need for larger school sites. The parking problem, which developed about the same time the campus plan became popular, added to the necessity for master planning sites and for enlarging them. Five or more acres of land are required in some areas just to provide parking for students' cars.

One of the more significant educational developments evolving from the campus plan was larger and better dimensioned classrooms. One-story, simple-structured buildings opened many new design approaches to architects. It became possible, for example, to introduce daylight into a building from openings in the roof as well as the walls. The variety of new building shapes that resulted from experimentation with multi-source daylight design changed the popular concept of a school building. The most educationally significant results of this new design freedom were higher levels of better distributed daylight in classrooms and wide-span classrooms. The introduction of multi-source daylight made classroom widths of 30 to 40 feet practical. The square teaching station evolved and with it the possibilities of better space relationships of students with teachers and other students.

Many secondary-school districts adopted both a wider span and a square room resulting in larger classrooms—840, 900, and some over 1000 square feet of floor area. The one-story buildings also opened up for many teachers the numerous advantages of outdoor classroom space.

Architectural and engineering changes involved in the campus plan were relatively more significant than the curriculum changes. With the abandonment of the "envelope" concept, the secondary-school building became an entirely new design problem. Basically it changed in form from a complex, vertical mass to a simple, horizontal mass. Decentralization of buildings and services created the need for more serious study of the interrelationship of major teaching and service stations such as the administration unit, the library, the auditorium, the gymnasium, the cafeteria, and parking facilities. The problem of student traffic patterns and distances between major areas also required new analysis.

Structural engineering practices changed, too. The lighter structure possible for one-story buildings encouraged the greater use of light-steel members, laminated wood arches, beams, and the like. The roof shapes designed to introduce daylight thru monitor windows and the pressure for building flexibility thru the use of nonbearing or nonstructural partition walls caused many an engineer to burn the midnight oil with a slide-rule as a partner. The development of wider building spans gave both the architect and the engineer some new design approaches.

The mechanical engineer found his problems materially changed, too. One large central heating plant often proved too awkward or expensive to meet the needs of scattered building units. In many instances it proved far more convenient and economical to develop smaller heating and ventilating systems to serve individual building units.

The electrical engineer needed to restudy electrical service requirements and distribution systems. The acoustical engineer found his problems of sound control considerably different from those in an envelope-type building.

Schools Within the School

In another recent development in schoolhousing, however, the educational implications outweigh the architectural changes. It has come about because educators in some areas, particularly where large high schools were developing, wanted a school plant that was designed around a *student-centered* rather than a *subject-centered* curriculum. The concept of the school-within-a-school was born.

Those who advocate the school-within-a-school program describe this concept as one which incorporates all the advantages of a small high school, with its attention to the individual student and his particular needs, with the advantages of the large high school with its broad, well-staffed program. Extreme departmentalization of subject areas is broken down. A cross section of students, usually from 300 to 600, representing all grades in the school, with their own teachers, work together in their own building group. Teachers in all the subject fields work together, with their small student group representing their common interest. The program is developed around large blocks of time with one teacher who is then able to be a friend, counselor, and helper to each student in his group. Nonacademic subject content is mixed in with traditional fields of study, and all teaching stations take on a laboratory atmosphere where the problem-solving approach is emphasized for all teaching-learning processes.

There may be three or four such schools-within-a-school on one campus. Altho the major portion of the school day for each student is spent with his own small group, all-school activities are planned which give each student the feeling of belonging to the school as a whole.

A few highly specialized subject areas are handled just as they are in a typical departmentalized organization. Unnecessary duplication of courses and facilities is avoided by integrated scheduling of some courses for students from all "schools." Physical education facilities are generally shared by all, but such services as administration, counseling, library, lunchroom, and student government usually are developed on a small-school basis.

Architecturally, the school-within-a-school has many of the characteristics of the campus-plan school.[12] Classrooms housing science, mathematics, art, English, homemaking, social science, and languages are grouped together in integrated building

---

[12] Architectural Record. "North Hagerstown High School, Hagerstown, Md." *Architectural Record* 120: 16-72; July 1956.

School Executive. "Winners in the Sixth School Design Competition." *School Executive* 76: 86-87; March 1957.

See also: Chapter VII, p. 196-97.

units instead of each subject field being housed in a separate building. The "school" units are related to one another and to the specialized units to form a functional and esthetically pleasing whole.

The housing implications of a school-within-a-school program are somewhat different from those of a subject-centered program. The philosophy of the school-within-a-school makes the individual student the focal point of interest and concern. The school plant itself must reflect this student accent if the program is to succeed. If the total growth and development of the individual student is the center of interest, those responsible for guiding and instructing him must communicate about him as often as practical. Each teacher must learn to know each student he works with, not only from reactions he receives from his relationship with the student, but also in terms of other teachers' interpretations of his behavior and development. Teachers and students must have as much contact as possible in and out of the classroom, yet each must have his share of privacy.

All the teaching stations serving the program for each small school must be interrelated so that there is a physical sense of unity among them. Industrial arts shops, usually set apart from the main group of buildings in a campus plan, are brought into the family group of classrooms. Administration and guidance and library services are made available within each small school. Food service is informal, with portable serving units which permit student lounge areas and sheltered patios to become pleasant social centers for serving lunch.

Imaginative planning for varied uses of all building space is required, since few areas are devoted exclusively to one type of activity. The careful placement of fixed equipment in teaching stations for such subjects as science, homemaking, and art leave generous open floor areas so that many other kinds of instructional or social activities may take place in them.

Class scheduling is often reorganized from time to time to permit total student participation in special events or occasions. The staff of such a school cannot be a group of rugged individualists, each promoting his own specialized subject field as if it were the one valid hope of civilization. A combination of personnel screening and a well-planned and executed in-service training program is necessary to develop the faculty for a successful school-within-a-school program. This cannot be a program that begins and ends; it must be continuous.

The wise planning of building facilities for teachers can aid materially in the success of this inservice training program. Since nearly all teaching stations are scheduled for use each period, the teacher's period of counseling must be spent away from his teaching station. There are no departments, hence no departmental offices. Each teaching station is reasonably close to the administrative hub of each small school; there must be a number of small, private offices for conferring with students or parents and for just getting away from everyone else. In addition, teachers have the use of a common central area for the preparation of work and correction of papers, and another common central area for relaxation and socializing. Such centers bring the teachers together frequently. The general and specific communication among staff members that comes from such association aids teachers materially in understanding themselves and their students.

Large Consolidated Schools

The housing problems presented by a large consolidated school plant (kindergarten thru Grade XII; 600-1200 enrol-ment) can best be considered by reviewing such a case. A village district operated a K-XII school plant. Several adjoining rural districts joined the village district to form a consolidated district. All students from the outlying districts were trans-ported to the one village school. This consolidation of students, administration, and tax base made it possible for the consoli-dated school to employ more competent professional personnel, to have one teacher for each elementary grade, and to operate a broader educational program in all grades, particularly at the secondary-school level.

Soon other neighboring rural districts operating one-teacher schools saw the advantages of such consolidated effort and wanted to become a part of it. They were included but the increase in enrolment finally made it necessary to build two elementary schools, one on the north and one on the south side of the village area. When the elementary-school pupils were moved out of the old building into the new schools, additional space was available for the expansion of the high-school program and enrolment. As the population continued to grow, it became necessary to provide a new senior high-school plant and convert the original building into a junior high school.

Problem: How do you plan a school building so it can serve adequately as a K-XII consolidated school and later as a senior high school and as a junior high school?

This is not a hypothetical problem. It faces architects and educators all over this country. It is a problem that exists in many areas where school-district organization is already set but where shifts in population within large districts place varying demands upon all types of school plants.

The problem has not been taken seriously enough because many educators and architects have not realized or do not acknowledge the extremely important role of the physical plant in the total educative process. They have subscribed placidly to the philosophy that a school is a school is a school.

Back to the problem, How can a single school plant be planned and constructed to meet nearly the full range of educational program needs? This can be accomplished best by studying all the implications of flexibility detailed earlier. Further help also can be gained by establishing some basic design criteria for such a school. For example, some requirements such as these should be given the designer:

- The dignity, privacy, and convenience of each general grade group housed in the total plant must be respected.
- Each general grade group such as the primary- intermediate- and secondary-grade groups must have a portion of the plant that is identified and used by them exclusively while having convenient access to common facilities designed to serve all grade groups.
- The portion of the school plant used by one grade group should be usable independently of other portions of the total plant.

• Each general area of the school plant should be expandable while staying within its general area of identification.

• Educational equipment and storage units should be portable and interchangeable so they can follow the grade level or program they serve no matter where they may be housed.

If such educational specifications were applied to a building design for this K-XII school, the resultant plan might resemble a composite of a one-story, campus-type, school-within-a-school layout. Such a plan would permit the development of groups of separate self-contained buildings, each group with its own pattern of expansion and having good relationships with common facilities, such as assembly, administration, library, swimming pool, gymnasiums, and play and recreation areas. The design of each building unit would provide for as complete a flexibility of structure and interiors as current technology and equipment permit. It would be possible to reassign space and change location of all educational equipment such as laboratory units, storage units, chalkboards, and tackboards. Each teaching station could be rearranged to provide whatever space and equipment proved necessary for the kind of program that might be housed in a building for as long as it was adequate.

The design of any school building—particularly a special type like a K-XII plant—should include considerations of any technological developments which may be applicable to the problem. In such a large school, for example, the feeding program may raise some tough administrative problems if all grades must be served by one cafeteria. This dilemma has been resolved in some instances by having the kitchen in the service area and transporting the food to groups of students in different parts of the plant. Primary and elementary classes may be served by portable food units in each classroom. Older students may be served in small multi-use areas located thruout the plant. The day of mass feeding and large food service areas married to food preparation areas is over. Such a building design feature can enhance the educational program so that the feeding program becomes a focal point for broader teaching-learning relationships rather than a nerve-harassing mass exercise in bolting down food.

Newer Housing Concepts

Educators and architects have been reassessing the second-ary-school program and plant against the probable needs of society in the second half of the twentieth century. Out of these studies have come some most stimulating and challenging proposals for a different design approach to both program and plant. Two of these new proposals have received wide publicity. One is the Random Falls idea, presented in 1956 by Shaw and Reid.[13] A second approach, the "School of Tomorrow," was developed by Caudill, Rowlett, Scott and Associates.[14] The authors of these innovations in educational program and housing are the first to insist that their proposals are not blueprints, but possible illustrations of what could be.

The Random Falls idea is described as an educational program and plant for *youth and community*.

> This proposed program for secondary education is, in effect, a partnership program. Through it, youths are helped to move from junior to full partnership with adults in a joint effort to bring maximum self-realization to each individual and improvement to the community.
>
> The proposal is developed under three headings: (1) Citizenship Development, through vocational and service contracts with local (and ultimately state and national) employers and agencies which are planned by the student and his advisors; (2) Development of the Individual's Resources, through the body of common and specialized learnings pursued primarily within the confines of the school campus; and (3) Community Service, the utilization by the student of community resources (physical and human) as well as the use of school resources (again persons as well as things) by members of the community.[15]

The plant design implications would be to create a school where the student would be placed with a single teacher for most of his formal school day; classrooms (learning labora-

[13] Shaw, Archibald B., and Reid, John Lyon. "A New Look at Secondary Education: The Random Falls Idea." *School Executive* 75: 47-86; March 1956.

[14] Caudill, Rowlett, Scott and Associates. "A School for Tomorrow—An Architect's View." *School Executive* 76: 53-68; February 1957.

[15] Shaw, Archibald B., and Reid, John Lyon, *op. cit.*, p. 52.

tories) would be provided where many learning experiences could occur in a single area; and the large school enrolment would be broken down into units of 300 students for their general education experiences.

The "School for Tomorrow" proposed a completely different architectural approach, also based upon advanced educational concepts. Caudill and his associates want the ultimate in space fluidity, versatility, and convertibility so that the plant will have, as they express it, "the timeless quality—a certain dynamics—which allows it to be adapted to any educational program, any age group, any designated period of learning. This must be, because education, like the American way of life, is ever changing, never static." [16]

This structure is designed to serve a community where the school site itself is "synthesized" with its neighborhood. The star-shaped site, with points reaching deep into the related community areas, makes no definite break between home and school. The school "Center" is a completely versatile service area where *all members of the family and neighborhood* may share almost continuous educational experience. A two-and-a-half acre concrete canopy covers a vast floor on which portable "learning laboratories" may be grouped and below which they may be stored when not needed. Powerful lifts raise the circular rooms to the floor level; when lowered their flat roofs form part of the floor.

Both these exploratory approaches serve to crystallize into definite programs and structures some of the more advanced thinking of both educators and architects which is beginning to influence practice.

Special Design Problems for Secondary Schools

Scarcity of population, shifts in population, and evolutions in school programs sometimes combine to create unique problems of educational planning and design. Several of these special situations are discussed in the paragraphs that follow.

[16] Caudill, Rowlett, Scott and Associates, *op. cit.*, p. 54.

The Small School

A definition of terms is most important in any discussion of small high schools. To people accustomed to the conditions common around metropolitan areas, a small high school might be one with 1000 students. The term *small* as used in this chapter, however, refers to a high school of fewer than 200 students. In 1952, that enrolment bracket included 13,142 schools, well over one-half of all the high schools in the United States.[17]

One of the most common and disturbing design problems presented by the small high school centers about the small sites usually provided. At first glance, this might seem to be a reasonable relationship—few students, small site. But the space required for outdoor secondary-school sports is pretty much the same for an enrolment of 200 as for an enrolment of 500 or more. Standard-dimensioned playing fields do not vary with the size of the enrolment.

The other basic problem is the need for special rooms and special services required for a well-rounded educational program. Such facilities as laboratories, shops, gymnasiums, an assembly-feeding space, music rooms, and a well-stocked library can be provided only at costs which make them prohibitive in most communities.

Educational planners have listed the disadvantages of a high school with fewer than 300 students as follows:

1. Costs per student are high for an extremely limited educational program, as many desired subjects cannot be offered, and classes in most subjects are small.

2. The expense makes it hard to employ enough teachers to provide for the proper variety of courses. Most teachers have to teach at least two fields and some subjects have to be taught without proper preparation.

3. It is hard to retain well-prepared teachers because they go to schools where they can teach full time in their preferred fields.

---

[17] U. S. Department of Health, Education, and Welfare, Office of Education. "Statistics of Public Secondary Day Schools, 1951-52." *Biennial Survey of Education in the United States, 1950-52.* Washington, D. C.: Superintendent of Documents, Government Printing Office, 1954. Chapter 5, p. 42.

4. Administration and supervision are seldom of high quality; salaries are relatively low and the principal often has to spend part time in classroom teaching.

5. If shops, laboratories, and vocational units are provided at all they are very costly in proportion to the plant as a whole and they have to go unused much of the time.

6. Supplemental services such as health and counseling often cannot be offered.

7. The limited educational program sometimes leads to difficulties with the accrediting agencies.

The curriculum handicaps cannot be fully overcome except by overstaffing, but the design of the school building can help. The first step to a reasonable solution of the problem of the small high school should be to approach it from a new angle. In the past many have merely attempted to reduce the scale of the traditional facilities provided for a large high school. Experience has established that this approach cannot succeed.

The problem of the small school needs the application of all we know about such basic elements as flexibility, fluidity, and multi-use of space. It requires close, cooperative effort between educators and architects.

One example of a fresh and successful approach to the problem of the extremely small high school is the Death Valley High School recently completed at Shoshone, California. Robert Trask Cox, the senior architect for this project, states the problem and describes the solution which was developed as follows:

A Desert High School—A multitude of unusual problems confronted the school district and architect when the high school outgrew its temporary quarters in a small two-bedroom residence. The country is wild, rough and desolate. To the east —desert as far as the eye can reach; to the west—rugged, forbidding mountains of volcanic origin; at the foothills—a highway, a warm spring and a small village. The climate is as harsh as the terrain. Blistering hot in summer, cold in winter with sand-laden northern winds in excess of 70 miles per hour. It rains almost never, but when it does, it results in a deluge.

The population is hardy and independent. The 150 people of the settlement work at the gas station, the general store, or in mines. Some are prospecting, following the trails of pioneers of a hundred years ago.

School is taught by three teachers, one of whom acts as district superintendent. The students live within a radius of 65 miles and are picked up by the school bus every morning.

The Program—To offer to the 21 students in the high school educational opportunities which are equal to those in a large city, within the extremely limited budget of the district.

The Convertible Classroom—On the surface two basic requirements seemed to be in conflict with each other. Cost-wise it was imperative that each square foot of teaching space be used during as many periods a day as possible. On the other hand, the complete high school program, inclusive of college preparatory courses, required a great number of specialized spaces and equipment.

Reconciliation of these conflicting elements was finally accomplished by designing a convertible classroom. This convertible classroom is hexagonal in shape, with movable seating, and has three adjoining alcoves for specialized subject fields. The alcoves are separated from the main classroom area by means of large slide-up panels. Each alcove can be opened when needed to become a part of the general classroom and serve as demonstration and laboratory work space. Three such units provide all the necessary classroom space; and each of the three teaching stations thus becomes a truly multi-purpose learning laboratory.

Chalk- and tackboard are located on the slide-up panels and also in each alcove. Cabinets in the main classroom provide storage for general supplies.

Classroom No. 1—Art, social studies, languages, business education, and library. Visual supervision of library from classroom No. 1. Typewriters mounted with typewriter hardware disappear underneath counter when not in use. Art, social studies and languages taught as one course.

Classroom No. 2—Home-living and senior problems; cooking and food chemistry; general science.

Classroom No. 3—Crafts, clothing, shops and college preparatory science. Outside auto shop adjoins shop alcove.

The physical education program bypasses team games for lack of pupils, and concentrates on tennis, archery, horseshoes, ping-pong, golf (on a desert course), and volley ball.

The Multi-Use Building—The building is to be used by the community for the weekly movie, social gatherings, townhall meetings, dances. School uses include indoor physical education, music, drama, lunch and student body assembly. Feeding program not provided. The toilets serve both the school and the community meetings. Shower and locker facilities form part of this sanitary unit to avoid duplication of space and fixtures. Faculty toilet and cot space doubles as health unit for use of visiting nurse.

The site improvements and buildings are laid out to fit into the natural surroundings. The J-shaped building turns its back towards the wind and creates a protected court. Addition of future classrooms will create a second court.

No public utilities are available. Water is taken from a spring that also supplies the township. The school will have its own diesel motor generator for electricity. A liquid petroleum gas tank will supply the gas.

The amphitheater is used by guest lecturers who are invited to supplement the school curriculum.[18]

Better and better small high-school plants will be provided when the educator gives the creative designer a well-detailed set of educational specifications and then lets the architect apply his knowledge of current technology as it pertains to the integrated, multi-use of space.

Building a Large Plant by Construction Increments

In many rapidly expanding communities today it is necessary to provide school plant facilities in several areas of a school district at the same time. In other communities a second, third, or even a tenth high-school plant must be provided on an increment basis because of the nature of the enrolment growth or because of limited ability to finance schoolhousing, or both.

Providing a new high-school plant by successive increments, constructed over a period of several years, presents both educational and architectural problems. The typical high-school program is operated around well-defined subject departments. In fact, most high schools are designed as a series of department-centered units. The problem of building to a project master plan based on saturation enrolment, beginning in 1958 and finishing in 1963, while housing portions of an education program and student body during some four years of construction activity illustrates what may happen in many communities. Obviously the most essential step is first to master-plan the entire program to its ultimate completion.

[18] Adapted from an unpublished report provided by Robert Trask Cox, AIA.

The educational usefulness of the occupied portions of the plant and the economic considerations of the piecemeal construction programs should be evaluated before definite policies of size and type of plant are set. When such an evaluation is made, the solution which best meets the educational and architectural problems usually takes the approach of the campus plan or the school-within-a-school.

If the program centralizes subject areas into separate buildings for science, homemaking, art, and the like, such teaching stations can be provided as needed by master planning the number and location of each type of classroom required for the saturation enrolment and building at each location only the number needed for each increment of growth. This kind of increment building is the least satisfactory because the first construction might result in four or five small building units scattered over a large building area. Each of these initial building units would be expanded once or twice as the program required. This procedure of building onto scattered small units forces contractors to move building materials and equipment to various sections of the site, resulting in awkward and costly construction conditions which might continue off and on for five or six years. The hazards and disadvantages of operating a high-school program in the midst of such inconvenience are obvious.

A more efficient method of building a large high-school plant by construction increments, when subject-area buildings are used, is to erect such buildings as whole units and assign space in them to the educational program to be housed. Thus an entire science building might be constructed in the first increment but only two of its 10 teaching stations would be assigned to science instruction. The other eight classrooms would house classes in other subjects for a year or two. As the need for more science stations became apparent, other subjects would be provided for in other buildings and gradually the science building would be devoted solely to that subject field.

This system requires each teaching station to serve several subject fields before it is assigned, at least semipermanently, to one. To convert space from one subject to another is awkward but, with adequate planning, it can be done with reasonable satisfaction. If an increment plan of this nature is followed, the specialized laboratories are usually constructed among the first buildings since, with proper planning, they can serve the academic fields.

By far the most satisfactory way to build a high school by increments is the school-within-a-school basis. The teaching-station needs for the students and program to be housed are constructed as a unit in relation to the saturation-enrolment master plan proposed. A section of the site is planned as a self-contained project. When it is complete, it can be landscaped and developed independently of the construction programs to be carried on later.

Beyond the educational advantages of schools-within-a-school, this plan permits students, teachers, and administrators to live and work in a well-ordered, completed, and adequate plant without being distracted by later building operations.

Reconstructing or Remodeling Old Buildings

There are several important factors to explore when communities are considering the rehabilitation of old school buildings. The first question goes back to the check point for all housing decisions, namely: How will such a program fit in with the over-all community development? Old school buildings generally are located in the old sections of a community. The location should influence a decision to add another 50 years of usefulness to a given school plant. What are the current and contemplated land uses of the area served by this building? What age-group students will this area be producing for the next 50 years? Since school plants serving contemporary educational programs tend to need more land space, what are the possibilities of site expansion, at least to currently recommended minimum sizes, at reasonable cost?

A second question would be how well the old building would lend itself to space reassignment to provide the kinds of teaching stations now recommended. Any investment of funds in an old building must recognize that the laboratory-type teaching station, even for English and mathematics, will be an accepted and expected feature within the lifetime of the reconstructed building. More floor space per teaching station will be required for additional equipment and storage. More floor space will be needed for the small-group and individual study stations required when class groups are broken down into working segments.

The third basic question, for study by competent architects and engineers, would be whether or not the structural system of the building would permit the space reassignment required for continued educational usefulness and could be brought up to code provisions within economic reason. A cursory examination does not tell much about structural adequacy. Experience has indicated that estimates of the cost of renovating an old building generally prove too low. Those with wide experience use a rule-of-thumb that if the estimated cost for rehabilitation is 60 percent or more of the cost of comparable new facilities, rehabilitation plans should be abandoned in favor of new construction.

By the time most administrators get well into a school-plant renovation program, they are prone to find themselves wondering, "Why didn't we tear this old landmark down and start all over?" The administrator faces a new set of decisions each week. How far toward a complete replacement job is it economical and desirable to go when rehabilitating an old school building? New electric light fixtures make the old ceiling look dingy, and besides, the room needs acoustical treatment—a new ceiling *is* the only satisfactory answer. Nothing can make an old floor look more inadequate than a new ceiling. New ceilings and floors make worn doors, thresholds, trim, sash, etc., stand out in distracting review—and so it goes. Anything less than a completely redone building leaves an unfinished appearance and some functional weakness.

One important aspect of rehabilitation is the penalty paid in the efficiency of the educational program while the work is going on. Complete rehabilitation of an old building often requires as much time as the construction of a new building. This means that students and program must be housed for long periods of time in makeshift space. The educational price paid for such interruption of normal service to students and teachers must be added to the other costs. Sometimes there is no other space available in which to conduct school, which results in expensive stopgap programs limited to vacation periods.

As yet there is no known way to rehabilitate an old school building to make it as functional as a new building. The limitations of the kinds, relationships, and adequacy of space found in a school constructed 30 to 50 years ago cannot be overcome. A renovated building cannot be as efficient an educational tool as a wisely designed and constructed new school building.

Adding to Existing Facilities

When administrators are considering adding facilitites to an existing plant, many of the same questions arise as when the problem is rehabilitation versus replacement. For example, the pattern of over-all community development is of paramount importance to either problem. How many students must be served by the school in question—now and when the ultimate community growth has occurred? Setting a policy for maximum enrolment for a given school usually is the first major decision to be made. This maximum enrolment figure should be the result of defensible and thoroly understood educational policy if it is to stand up under pressures to increase the size of the school as the community grows.

Breaking away from the traditional community center of secondary education and developing a second or new high-school plant is a matter of crisis in many communities. Facilities that should have formed beginning units of a new school plant are often tacked on to a poorly located existing school simply because the administrator and board lacked the information or courage to present the long-range housing needs to the community.

Several other factors should be considered. Educational program needs should be documented by a space-adequacy survey. After the exact number and types of teaching stations have been determined for the plant, an evaluation of space needs should be made by a reappraisal of the best possible use of the existing building area. Maybe the English and social studies departments report the need for five additional classrooms for their use. A restudy might indicate that instead of five additional classrooms for English and social studies, the additional facilities should consist of two new science stations and one new homemaking laboratory, with the old science and homemaking facilities being converted into five generously dimensioned academic classroom-laboratories.

Additional facilities should be placed on an existing school site only in accord with a master plan that reflects the saturation enrolment and construction for that site. This master plan may be an old one toward which the plant has been growing over the years, or it may be a new one replacing a previous plan because of new factors such as changes in area growth or birth-rate statistics. The new master plan should have as much study as is required to make it a valid replacement for the old master plan.

The addition of new facilities to an existing plant usually brings up the matter of architectural forms. Altho reasonable attempts should be made to tie in the new facilities with the architectural style of the existing buildings, there should be no hesitancy in adopting the architectural style that recent experience and contemporary building materials indicate will serve the educational program and site utilization best. Good planning and functional building forms should never be waived in favor of retaining a single architectural style for a school plant.

Within a period of a few months several years ago, a culmination of experience and critical analysis indicated that ground brightness instead of direct sky brightness could be used as an effective daylight source. While school building design was being modified to take advantage of this new concept, a new building material became available in the form of a neutral-colored, low-light-transmission glass (12 to 14 percent). When the alert architects put one and one together, it became possible not only to simplify school building design while creating a better visual environment, but also to incorporate space once used only for corridors into sheltered, outdoor classroom areas. The whole operation resulted in a more refined visual environment in the classroom, increased space for the educational program without increasing the area of the building, a freeing of building design and site utilization from the inhibiting influence of preferred orientation for daylighting, and an actual reduction in construction costs.

Within a short period of time during World War II, new structural members became available which made buildings of wider span economically possible. Laminated wood and light steel members represent two of these developments. School buildings designed just before World War II did not have these two structural members available. Thru their use the square classroom was made economically feasible. The square room, approximately 1000 square feet in area, has proved a far better educational space than its rectangular predecessor, and it costs no more to build. Often it costs less.

The design possibilities opened up by new structural materials were reflected in many new roof shapes and window patterns. Multi-lateral daylight sources became common. Old problems were solved and new ones created.

As today's technology is reviewed, ever widening horizons seem to be opening for the creative builder. New developments in heating, ventilating, and air conditioning make it apparent that the thermal environment is to receive long overdue consideration. New developments in electronics and plastics offer continuing challenges to the designer. Knowledge of acoustics is finding its way slowly into school design. Electric light sources are becoming more numerous and more efficient. The illuminating engineer is becoming more and more aware of the need for better control of daylight and electric light sources. All this is just the beginning.

If significant progress is to be made in obtaining buildings that serve the educational program better while making the hard-to-get housing dollar go farther and farther, the administrator must accept his responsibility for bringing the right kind of competency to bear on his schoolhousing problems at the right time. He must realize that a developing technology requires a problem-solving architectural service that keeps abreast of new materials and methods. A building can be only as good as the architectural and engineering services that created it. Two buildings completed on the same day can be 25 years apart in design concepts.

Post-High-School Educational Program

Most junior colleges operated in the same buildings as high-school programs, have had little if any consideration of their plant requirements. They were tacked on after the high-school building was constructed; they use whatever space is available. In some instances, a wing of a few classrooms is assigned exclusively to junior-college classes but more often the classrooms used by junior-college students are also used by high-school students. Thus existing facilities offer little guidance in planning. The following brief discussion is based on comments of an alert administrator of a joint program and upon observation.[19]

The physical plant appears to play an even larger part in the successful operation of such a combined program than is the case in housing any other segment of the secondary-school program. The basic housing problem in a combined high school and junior college is to create a feeling of separateness while retaining the educational and economic advantages of one overall operation and plant. Many of the elements of the school-within-a-school concept are applicable since fundamentally the idea of department-centered buildings should be abandoned in favor of small building units, each housing several subject areas. Every effort should be made to establish as many teaching stations, facilities, and general campus areas as possible to be used exclusively or nearly exclusively by junior-college students.

[19] Vaniman, Glenn G., Superintendent, Citrus Union High School District, Azusa-Glendora, California. (The high school and junior college have been operating together in this district since 1915.)

Such general facilities as the library, shower and locker rooms, and lunchroom should provide either small separate rooms or portions of large spaces that are the exclusive domain of Grades XIII and XIV. Portable food service units, portable demonstration units for science, and portable towel and equipment dispensers for physical education can be used to carry out the idea of separateness-while-together. The area of one full classroom can be designed as a separate student lounge, and offices for junior-college student government, and publication activities can be so located that no high-school student need pass within 50 yards.

Flexibility, as discussed previously in this chapter, has wide application in such a housing program. The fluidity of space must become real. Because junior-college classes often are smaller than high-school classes, partitions must never be more than a momentary barrier to space rearrangement. Whole sections of buildings may need to be reassigned in terms of space use each semester.

Close coordination between the high-school and junior-college curriculums means that many items of expensive equipment can be used by both groups. Often, special equipment purchased for one program can be used to supplement the other program and result in enrichment for both. Such possibilities suggest that storage spaces be designed and located so that a maximum use of all equipment can be realized.

The separate location or use of recreational facilities should be a planned feature of such a school. Some parents object to their high-school daughters associating with the "older men." Even tho the students appear to hold to other views, the wise administrators and the architect should do what they can to discourage them. In the past decade smoking on the campus became one of the social problems in a school of this kind. Facilities should be provided with enough separateness to permit on-campus smoking within at least part of the junior-college area and still permit adequate supervision of high-school students. Some division of the campus is necessary to successfully administer a plant that houses students with such wide spreads of chronological and social ages.

One of the most difficult problems for a junior-college program of this type is to provide a wide variety of trade and vocational courses. The industrial-arts program of the high school does not provide the facilities necessary to carry on a terminal program in trade and industrial fields. Sometimes a combined school of this type is located in a community where a work-experience program permits students to use the facilities of commerce and industry as part of their junior-college training. Where such arrangements are not possible, the junior-college curriculum tends to develop around academic courses.

Principles of Economy

A chapter on the secondary-school plant would not be complete without some discussion of cost and how to evaluate it. The best educational philosophy and planning often become compromised to a point of complete mediocrity by lack of funds, a poor use of adequate funds, or a partial, short-range analysis of the over-all cost of a building. Many times the cost of a school plant is considered only in terms of the original investment. The long-range price paid for operation and maintenance over 40 to 50 years is often overlooked in the short-sighted concern about construction costs.

Concentrated and naive concern with building costs per square foot or cubic foot probably has been responsible for the construction of many of the most expensive school buildings erected in this country. To considerations of first cost must be added the big items of operating and maintenance costs, to be met for all the years a school building serves a community.

The original cost as well as the operating and maintenance costs of a building are directly related to the quality level of that building. Gibson states that:

> The degree to which a school plant provides a proper environment for the activities that must go on in it determines its quality level; a comprehensive definition might state that quality level is the degree to which the school plant:
> (a) makes satisfactory provisions for the spaces needed to do a sound educational job now while protecting the probability that space needs of future educational programs will change;

(b) provides for its occupants the amenities which the American public associates with a good standard of living and a physical environment which promotes working comfort and efficiency;

(c) is constructed of materials which give maximum life to the buildings and ensure low maintenance costs.[20]

Any evaluation of the true cost of a school building must begin by testing the proposed plans or completed construction against such criteria of quality level. Gibson's quality-level story continues:

. . . a poor school district cannot afford to build cheap buildings. The only place money can come from to pay the constant, excessive maintenance costs of cheap construction is out of funds intended to buy a good instructional program. If these already over-stretched funds are not used to maintain buildings, the cheap school plant soon disintegrates into a health and educational hazard for the students we compel by law to occupy it.[21]

A helpful recent publication on the cost of school buildings is *13 Principles of Economy in School Plant Planning and Construction.*[22] The 13 principles are selection, educational planning, usefulness, flexibility, expansibility, exactness, simplicity, compactness, multiple use, modular coordination, repetitive design, durability, and prefabrication.

A second recent document on school building costs is entitled *Cutting Costs in Schoolhouse Construction.*[23] This readable brochure stresses education, environment, and economy as the trilateral balance to be achieved in a successful school building program. Some of the 15 means of economizing suggested raise controversial points, but each deserves the considered attention of anyone interested in this extremely

[20] Gibson, Charles D. "School Buildings: Quality Level and Cost." *Architectural Record* 116: 177; November 1954.

[21] *Ibid.*, p. 182.

[22] National Council on Schoolhouse Construction. *13 Principles of Economy in School Plant Planning and Construction.* Nashville, Tenn.: the Council (Secy.-Treas.: W. D. McClurkin, George Peabody College for Teachers), 1954. 47 p.

[23] American Association of School Administrators. *Cutting Costs in Schoolhouse Construction.* Washington, D. C.: the Association, a department of the National Education Association, December 1952. 19 p.

popular pastime. The suggestions are: cut down on the cubage, simplify the silhouettes, shorten outside walls, plan for maximum use of space, leave off the gingerbread, make use of repetitive structural units, use larger and fewer building material units, take advantage of modular coordination, design for maximum use of material, do not cheapen the fabric too much, do not pad the buildings, use speedy erection methods, take care in scheduling bid-lettings, design schools that can grow without growing pains, and get the best professional services.

When the big housing shortage hit the schools after World War II, many lay people, educators, and architects panicked into constructing cheap buildings simply because their problems looked too large to solve within the cost framework of good, average quality housing. Enough stopgap, cheap school buildings were constructed all over the United States to prove the fallacy of this solution.

The educator who had to maintain a cheap school for several years with current operating funds, and the architect who found that the client for whom he had planned a cheap building was only a *former* client, realized how costly they really were. When money-saving roofs leaked; when buildings needed a paint job within a year after occupancy; when the inexpensive heating system failed to meet minimum requirements; when poor ventilating provisions caused schools to be dismissed during a hot spell; when glaring, money-saving daylight and electric lighting systems resulted in complaints from teachers, students, and parents; when the bargain hardware failed to hold up; when the marked-down casework, made from uncured lumber, resulted in warping and unopenable doors; when all of these things and more turned up in the new school building, the school board and the superintendent could not remember the low building budget they had insisted upon. They simply blamed the architect.

Once again experience is turning out to be an excellent teacher. The fallacy of constructing cheap school buildings has become fairly well established over the nation.

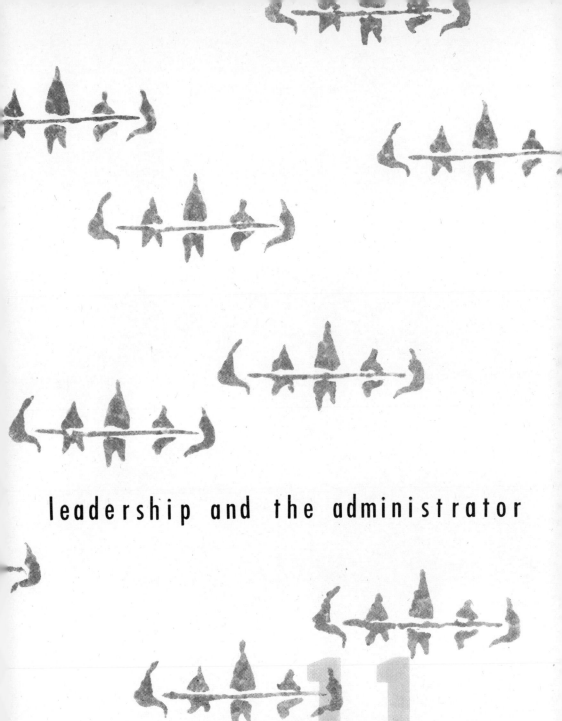

leadership and the administrator

11

leadership and the administrator

WITHOUT DISCOUNTING the essential value of the classroom teacher or the superintendent of schools, it may be suggested that, in helping young people move toward the full realization of their potentialities, no single person is in a more strategic position than the high-school principal. What power for creativity and self-realization rests in him! The total well-being of millions of youth can be favorably affected. Unfortunately, the opposite is possible also—boys and girls may suffer by the principal's inadequacies. Because the scope of his influence is so great, the principal is the center of many divergent forces. Some principals may try to avoid these pressures by standing still. However, there is no standing still. Relentless forces are moving; they compel a response. One of these forces is man's unquenchable search for knowledge, now crucially accelerated. "Knowledge is power," and the high school is the portal to knowledge for many youth.

The high-school principal, then, is in a pivotal position at the point of *articulation between the school and the society it serves.* His leadership role should be considered both in relation to the demands of society and in relation to his function within the school. In both areas he follows the same principles in dealing with individuals and groups. He needs the same strengths of personality and skills of leadership.

Relating the School to Society's Demands

At best, there will always be some lag between the requirements of society and the response to those requirements made by the educational program. The goal, however, is to diminish the gap between the need and the school's response. The procedures described in the paragraphs that follow are among the services to individuals thru which the school may meet society's needs and demands. In these the principal should take the lead.

Follow-Up Studies of Students

Follow-up studies of former students can be simple or extensive in scope.[1] They may be designed to yield information on any area of the program which the school wishes to evaluate, from guidance services to the quality and quantity of the teaching of any subject. One study dealing with the curriculum revealed that graduates thought they should have had more help in homemaking and more skill in participating in community responsibilities.

If carefully formulated, such follow-up studies can be analyzed for trends. For instance, in rural areas particularly, follow-up studies will indicate both the direction and quantity of migration of local residents. Continuous analysis of the kinds of occupations which former students—both graduates and nongraduates—are entering is essential information for any school in evaluating its curriculum.

Increasing attention is being given to longitudinal studies of students for information regarding their occupational patterns over a period of time.

---

[1] Baer, Max F., and Roeber, Edward C. *Occupational Information: Its Nature and Use.* Chicago: Science Research Associates, 1951. 603 p. Chapter 10.

Contacts with Industry

High-school graduation is more and more a requirement for employment in industry. The teaching of skills, attitudes, and understandings essential to productive employment is a legitimate concern of the school, when kept in balance with other goals. Conferences and institutes planned by representatives of industry, labor, and education can do much to provide the school with insights into the ever changing world of work. Consultants from these groups can contribute to curriculum development. Carefully planned trips thru industrial plants can help teachers gain a broader outlook on the world into which the students will go from high school.

As industry continues its interest in the supply and quality of manpower available and is increasingly concerned with training programs, administrators must be alert to the development of educational opportunities for meeting the needs of industry.

Contacts with Employment Services

One of the most fruitful but often neglected sources of information is the local or regional state employment office. Here the principal may find summaries of local trends in industrial development and employment. Regular conferences with the office manager could be significant. The local manager has information on developments affecting the labor market in all parts of the country, which may be important to local youth. The principal should foster this relationship thru the guidance counselor or personally, preferably both. Many schools are using the excellent testing service provided by the U. S. Employment Service thru the local or state office.

Participation in Regional Planning [2]

The school has an important stake in all community planning, and, furthermore, it can find effective laboratory experiences for students in community enterprises.

[2] See also Chapter IV.

In the Western Adirondacks, a number of schools participated in a survey of the economic resources of the region. Students in social studies classes made inventories of items in their communities which were essential for economic development. The facts were collected, tabulated, and used as the basis for a conference held by educational and business people. Educators were impressed with the potentialities of the local community as a laboratory for students in social studies classes. Representatives of industry were also impressed with the potential resources available for helping develop small industries. The exchange of ideas was useful to all concerned. This particular conference resulted in a decision to employ full time a person who would provide leadership for further study of local resources for economic development.

Cooperation with Other Programs of Education

The secondary-school program is built on the work of the elementary school, and, in turn, the secondary school must help students develop skills for the requirements of whatever educational experiences may follow. The administrator must do whatever possible to provide smooth transition and continuity for students, both as they come and as they go.

In developing more understanding between elementary and secondary school he can initiate conferences for teachers from both levels, preferably on questions which avoid the timeworn tendency to blame the former teacher or school for inadequacies. One group found it constructive to discuss, "How can we help our sixth-graders make the best adjustment to the seventh grade?" In this case the junior-high-school teachers looked rather closely at what sixth-grade pupils did and gathered some impressions of the emphasis and concerns of the elementary-school teachers. The elementary-school teachers inevitably were made aware of adjustments for which their pupils should be prepared.

Guidance institutes, in which problems common to all levels are considered, have been helpful. One group of schools involving all grades held a series of meetings on the improvement of reading. In this case, elementary-school teachers were prominent in explaining some of their skills in teaching reading, a subject in which many high-school teachers were admittedly deficient.

With a steadily growing percentage of high-school students going on for advanced training, the administrator must give more attention to the admission standards of colleges and technical schools.

Sometimes a subject is included in the high-school curriculum on the erroneous assumption that colleges require it for entrance. Many administrators have not yet realized that increasing numbers of institutions are evaluating and classifying new students on the basis of extensive testing programs. (The same is true of military and industrial agencies also.) The phrase *no specific requirements* often appears in descriptions of admission requirements. However, the score on a College Entrance Board examination is likely to be important in admission. Chronicle Guidance Publications publishes a useful series of charts on college entrance requirements.[3]

Interpretation of Program to the Community

Regardless of the excellence of the curriculum, some systematic interpretation to the community is necessary. When changes are needed or are under way, the necessity is even greater. Many parents are only dimly aware of things that educators take for granted. Parents need to be shown some of the trends which are the basis for changes in the curriculum. It helps parents to have the guidance program explained in detail, together with some of the factors which make systematic guidance so essential; to have the changing occupational pattern explained and to discuss its implications; and to get information on new findings regarding child development.[4]

---

[3] Chronicle Press, Moravia, N. Y.

[4] Many films, often free, are available for meetings of this kind. See: National Institute of Mental Health, Federal Security Agency. *Mental Health Motion Pictures: A Selective Guide, 1952.* Public Health Service Publication 218. Washington, D. C.: Superintendent of Documents, Government Printing Office, 1952. 124 p. *1956 Supplement,* 80 p.

In one community where parents showed hostility toward the school, the board finally decided to hold a series of meetings to improve understanding. After 10 such meetings, largely devoted to interpretation of problems of educating today's youth, the attitude of the parents changed from hostility to a reasonable appreciation. Having carefully discussed what they thought a school should do for their children, they examined the present school program and facilities, visited other schools, and made comparisons. They recognized some failures in meeting their responsibilities as parents and took steps to organize resources in the community for certain public services. Much tension and unhappiness could have been avoided had this procedure been followed earlier.

Altho parents of high-school students are not as closely associated with the school as are parents of younger children, they will usually attend study groups or other programs on problems of adolescence, trends in evaluation, and the like.

The Task Within the School

The principal's community contacts are many, but it is within the school itself—and no two schools are alike—that all his efforts find their focus.

> There is no such thing as *the* high-school principalship in America. Rather, there is a range of roles, duties, activities, and influences which form mosaics of performance which identify a position in each school as one of responsible leadership. To this position, when justified by formal appointment, we attach the title of principal.[5]

Areas of Leadership

Whatever his duties, his job requires him to function in four areas: planning, organization, supervision, and evaluation.

[5] Austin, David B., and Collins, James S. "A Study of Attitudes Toward the High School Principalship." *Bulletin of the National Association of Secondary-School Principals* 40: 104-40; January 1956. (See especially page 138.)

Planning—Logically, planning should assume first place in the long list of the principal's duties. Many principals lack effectiveness because they play by ear rather than from plans. In the complicated modern school, the principal must *anticipate events and work out necessary procedures.* The opening of school, orientation of new students and teachers, faculty meetings, setting up the school calendar, and working with lay groups—such duties require the careful planning that can lead to a calm and orderly sequence of events.

Most difficult is the development of a long-range plan covering the many segments of the educational program. Some principals have found it profitable to make a chart on which their major tasks are placed in some sequential order together with a tentative time schedule for each accomplishment with the names of individuals or groups involved. The chart may be simple; or it may be elaborate, listing many specific areas requiring attention and indicating persons involved and the relationships among areas. For instance, if the chart includes a curriculum revision project, a related problem may be clearance with parents and the state department of education. Another problem may pertain to evaluation. Thru the graphic representation, the principal can better visualize the personnel and time that will be required.[6]

Organization—We have seen that the principal must try to articulate the high school with society's requirements. To do this effectively, the principal must organize all his resources so that they function with maximum efficiency.[7] *He does not spend his time on small tasks which can be delegated to someone else who is available.*

Setting up an effective organization may be hindered by members of boards of education or school superintendents who still define the principal's function in clerical and managerial terms. Worse still, the principal himself may find security in performing clerical duties, thereby avoiding more basic responsibilities. Also, some principals fear to relinquish control over any part of their establishment.

---

[6] See also p. 194-96, regarding principal's use of time.
[7] See also Chapter VII.

In developing his organization, the principal carefully analyses his responsibilities and the resources of the personnel in his school—students, teachers, and others—and then delegates responsibilities. He should keep to himself only those duties which no one else is qualified to perform. Some principals have found it helpful to keep a diary of all their activities for several days, thereby having a more objective look at their expenditure of time and energy.

Delegation of duties solves no problems, however, if it merely sloughs off extra duties on teachers already overburdened. Principals usually need more secretarial and clerical assistance and can render a service to the school and the community by insisting on adequate help.[8] Occasionally, there are persons in the community who can give voluntary assistance on certain school duties. Whatever the plan of organization and delegation, it should be made clear to all concerned. Even in small schools it is a mistake to assume that all relationships are clear to everyone. New teachers, especially, need careful orientation to the organizational pattern and areas of responsibility.

Supervision—All agree that the principal's major responsibility is to provide leadership in developing the program of instruction. Too often, however, subordinate duties conspire to keep the principal from fulfilling this, his major task. In many small and medium-size schools there is practically no formal supervision.

What it means to improve instruction depends upon the situation. One principal spends half of each school day with his teachers in classroom visits, conferences, and committee work. Another spends little time in classrooms but much time with groups of teachers, students, and parents. In improving instruction, the whole fabric of education is involved. This includes knowing what is going on, locating areas where improvement is needed, knowing desirable practices, helping parents grow in their understanding of student needs and of desirable changes in the school program, helping teachers feel comfortable with an evolving curriculum, and bringing past

---

[8] See also Chapter IX.

gains and current needs into balance. The heart of the matter
is in pushing beyond plant, budget, and "things" to a systematic consideration and improvement of the quality and
kinds of experiences needed by all boys and girls.

What has traditionally been called supervision is increasingly
being viewed under the more inclusive term of *inservice
training*. There is no one way to begin an inservice program. A
general principle which will ensure maximum progress, all else
being equal, is that the teachers must share in decisions regarding the areas for study and work. Most teachers are aware of
deficiencies in the school program; and, with adequate leadership, they will be able to delineate a fairly inclusive list of the
problems with which parents, teachers, and students are concerned.

If he wishes to begin a program informally, he will usually
find teachers who wish to discuss some individual student.
Such a discussion makes an excellent starting point, particularly
if it is done systematically by way of a case conference.[9] By
this method, teachers develop objectivity and an understanding of the student; and soon they see that changes in his
environment and program are necessary. Thru study of the
impact on the student of his home, his community, his school,
his potentialities, and his limitations, they gradually come to
view the curriculum more objectively. They may seek to provide more flexibility and to bring about changes.

It is neither possible nor desirable to try to improve all
the program at once. Change at any point will indicate needed
changes in other areas, regardless of where the faculty begins.
For instance, an analysis of students' reading difficulties will
eventually lead to questions on such matters as grouping,
emotional factors, problems of health, and curriculum.

In initiating the program, the principal should be careful
to approach the matter with a positive outlook. Neither he
nor the teachers should assume that what teachers are currently doing is not good. For the most part they are doing the
best they can under the circumstances. The principal will do

---

[9] Hammock, Robert C., and Owings, Ralph S. *Supervising Instruction in
Secondary Schools.* New York: McGraw-Hill Book Co., 1955. 316 p.

well to remind himself that *teachers want to do the best job possible and that they have inner resources for growth.*

In its broadest sense, the inservice program includes matters not generally considered instructional, but which must be taken into account if the instructional program is to serve its purpose. The curriculum must be viewed in the larger context of the community and of the nature of boys and girls. A study of the problems of adolescents—their growth and development and the social and cultural factors affecting them—will, in turn, affect the curriculum. Furthermore, such study will go far in helping teachers and parents to see the necessity for making the high school inclusive, that is, a place where *all* youth of high-school age can find a reasonable measure of self-realization.

Supervision includes classroom visits by the principal, often neglected for a variety of reasons, including lack of time, lack of confidence, and failure to see the supervisory relationship as one which encourages the growth of the teacher, both as a person and as a teacher.

One result of imaginative supervision will be a continuous adaptation of the school to meet the needs of individual students. Much is already being done by creative teachers. But as methods for discovering individual differences are refined, the necessity for doing will become more urgent.

Traditional barriers to making individual adjustments will be met. For some, the state department of education has become a whipping boy—a psychological barrier. Many state regulations are only minimum requirements to protect against deterioration; they need not obstruct creative ideas designed to meet the needs of boys and girls. The state department is usually interested in sound experimental programs. Before excusing inaction by hiding behind state regulations, the principal should explore possible adaptations with state department personnel.

Another barrier—both real and psychological—is the limitation of a school plant. Sometimes, however, an old building has unrealized potentialities. The principal and his staff may not have given thought to the need for more flexibility of

program. Grouping within groups will be increasingly necessary as teachers move away from teaching all students the
same content. For instance, actually moving the movable
furniture in a classroom may help. Large rooms might be improved by flexible partitions. One mathematics teacher found
he could deal with a wide range of ability in one group by
placing small groups in different rooms and moving from one
room to the other.

Evaluation—With the increasing complexity of educational
programs, the matter of evaluation becomes both more imperative and more difficult. The progress of the students, the
effectiveness of the teachers, the value of the curriculum, and
the scope of the guidance program need to be continually
appraised.

Any program of evaluation, however, is contingent on a clear
definition of what is to be evaluated. The principal must continuously help the faculty and the parents to sharpen their
ability to define the purpose of the school both generally and
specifically. Only when goals are clear can the measuring
rod be applied. One of the most widely used instruments is
the *Evaluative Criteria*.[10] In using this, the faculty follows
a systematic procedure for clarifying goals and evaluating the
school's program in relation to the goals. Altho used widely
in some areas, in many others this instrument is less well
known. If the principal does not wish to go into extensive
evaluation at once, he may find sections of the *Evaluative
Criteria* useful for specific areas of his school. For instance,
the guidance program could be evaluated separately.

Compilations of standardized test scores should be used to
determine progress in specific subjects. However, care must
be taken not to make them the sole criterion of progress.
Some teachers may tend to teach for tests.

One general problem in evaluation all high-school authorities
must come to grips with soon. With the ideal of universal
secondary education almost completely in effect, the evaluation
of students based on achievement in a limited number of

---

[10] Cooperative Study of Secondary School Standards. *Evaluative Criteria.*
1950 Edition. Washington, D. C.: American Council on Education, 1950. 305 p.

academic subjects must be modified to meet the requirements of reality. Otherwise there will be a growing frustration and confusion. The St. Paul, Minnesota, schools have faced this situation by developing a reporting practice known as the "continuous growth" method.

> It rejects the concept of absolute standards for all. Each child is judged and graded upon individual growth rather than upon the ability to meet a preconceived and uniform standard. . . . *Competition has not been eliminated, only the basis of the competition has been modified.* Now pupils of superior ability [are] required to achieve on a level commensurate with innate ability and in comparison with other pupils of similar aptitudes. This kind of competition replaces the type which permits a gifted pupil to enter into academic competition with average and below-average pupils. . . . Under the latter type of competition for marks, the superior student could survive without developing his talents to full capacity. Under our present system, in which he is held responsible for achievement to match known ability, he must work harder to earn a satisfactory rating than he did before.[11]

Another shift in emphasis is also strongly indicated. Principals and teachers reflect a concern with academic achievement to the exclusion of other values in the school by classifying students as *good* or *bad.* In the light of current knowledge about motivation and in view of the spread of ability in verbal skills, it seems that the use of words carrying so much moral overtone is unfortunate. A quick learner is not necessarily a "good" student—he may be a lazy or superficial one; nor is a slow learner a "bad" student.

Scholastic ability, like any other special ability, has been unevenly distributed among boys and girls. It is morally indefensible to treat all boys and girls as tho they had the same ability but as tho some try harder than others and therefore succeed. A boy who fails to complete high school but has the initiative and administrative ability to build up a successful and useful business is not stupid even tho the school classified him as such. Until schools develop broader bases for evaluating abilities, these arbitrary judgments will continue.

---

[11] St. Paul Public Schools. *Today's Challenge: Tomorrow's Citizen.* St. Paul, Minn.: Board of Education, 1957. p. 12-13.

Leadership Procedure and Skills

It is obvious that to plan, organize, supervise, and evaluate today's complex secondary-school program effectively the principal will need to call up all his ingenuity and skill as a leader. He must have thought thru what educational leadership in a democracy means and have arrived at convictions regarding principles for action. While the principles and goals of leadership are essentially the same for any situation in a democracy, the circumstances of the secondary school suggest some procedures which the principal may find useful for making his leadership most effective. The principal:

Keeps in touch with students
Uses the social sciences
Recognizes and uses group emotion
Works as a group leader
Brings about change thru growth
Keeps channels of communication open
Serves as a counselor
Recognizes the nonteaching staff.

Keeping in touch with students—The principal must be on guard lest his many duties conspire to make him lose direct contact with students. He should attend as many student activities as possible and be genuinely interested in the program at hand. He must be available so that boys and girls may talk with him about their problems and other concerns. The more individual students he knows, the better.

In addition to personal contacts with individuals, the principal will find it useful to understand their goals and aspirations as revealed in many ways in a systematic guidance program. He should have frequent, regularly scheduled conferences with the guidance staff. Students reveal their concerns in compositions on such topics as "How I felt when I got my report card" and "When I felt most at sea." [12] Autobiographies and daily schedules charted by groups of students asked to keep a record of what they do every five minutes for an entire

---

[12] For suggestions for getting student reactions to situations, see: University of Chicago, Center for Intergroup Education. *Diagnosing Human Relations Needs*. Washington, D. C.: American Council on Education, 1951. 155 p.

day are useful when properly done and their limitations understood. Conferences with the school librarian will reveal the kinds of literature currently popular. The principal might have a weekly discussion or seminar with a group of students on topics of their choice, thereby keeping in touch with the adolescents' point of view.

Using the social sciences—The principal should be a practicing social scientist. Because the principal works primarily with and thru people, he should know and practice the findings of the behavioral sciences. Thru careful observation and analysis in recent years by means of anthropology, psychiatry, psychology, and social psychology, many aspects of human behavior now can be related to causal factors more definitely than ever before. *This means that education has become more essential than ever before in helping man direct himself, individually and collectively.* Especially has depth psychology increased our understanding of motivation, a matter of continuing concern for educators.

For the principal, nothing illustrates the importance of understanding the cause-effect aspect of behavior better than viewing the school as follows: At any given moment there is a certain amount of nervous energy distributed thruout the school in the persons of teachers and students. Each individual is responding to pressures from without and within in myriads of complicated and dynamic patterns. The school is in a state of equilibrium. *No other person can disturb this equilibrium* quite as easily or as drastically as can the principal.

By any arbitrary action, by sudden change in his method of operation, the principal may adversely affect the entire school, setting off defense-against-fear reactions. People fight back. Not being able to get at the principal directly, as in primitive combat, they resist him in civilized, subtle, but, nevertheless, destructive ways. Theoretically, thruout the establishment, the total aggressive needs of all involved will be felt. If the leadership in the school is mature, such tension can be absorbed, but under other circumstances it may not be. Some of the results may be defacement of property, absenteeism, and "headaches" in general. The mood in which the principal meets the day is an important matter to the school's morale. His actions have a decided, causal effect on many people.[13]

As a student and a practitioner of the behavioral sciences, the principal will consider and respond to the power structure within his community. *Elmtown's Youth* illustrates what this implies in terms of teacher reaction to students from different socioeconomic levels.[14] The principal understands community tensions and cultural conflicts and knows that groups from different socioeconomic levels have different value systems and behave accordingly. As the standards of conduct and of beauty may be different on opposite sides of the track, so goals and motives will vary from group to group. It is especially important that the principal provide for his teachers leadership in understanding this phenomenon.

Recognizing and using group emotion—Idealism appears to be at its height during adolescence. Age and experience have not yet blunted or qualified youth's inclination to "follow the gleam." Frequent opportunities arise for developing a healthy and unifying emotional atmosphere in the high school. This might be the most powerful and appropriate way for unifying the divergent aspects of the modern high school.[15] Assembly programs that use all the resources and emotional impact of music, art, and drama should be planned with this in mind. School traditions should be made articulate and should be assiduously respected. Care should be taken not to treat the American flag perfunctorily. Boys and girls can and should thrill at the unfathomable experiences and aspirations which it symbolizes. They need to revere it! What is suggested here is not chauvinism, but development of rightful pride in what the United States means in its fullest dimensions.

Schools can use their intercommunication systems regularly —even daily—for short devotional periods of a nonsectarian kind, utilizing inspirational music and poetry. Commencement

---

[13] Saul, Leon J. *The Hostile Mind.* New York: Random House, 1956. 211 p. (A good presentation of the dynamics of hostility.)

[14] Hollingshead, August B. *Elmtown's Youth.* New York: John Wiley and Sons, 1949. 480 p.

[15] Ulich, Robert. *Crisis and Hope in American Education.* Boston: Beacon Press, 1951. 235 p.

programs, such as many described in the bulletins of the
National Association of Secondary-School Principals, can contribute much toward developing creative emotional experiences.[16] The "our school" attitude requires more than athletic
contests if it is to touch the deeper springs of loyalty and aspiration of boys and girls.

Works as a group leader—In fulfilling his responsibility for
planning, organizing, supervising, and evaluating the program,
the principal must work with and thru groups, whether they
be in the school or in the community. Much of his success
hinges on his skill as a group leader. If he thinks of supervision in its broadest sense, that is, helping his faculty to grow
in skills and understandings necessary for their work, much of
his supervision can be done by working with groups of
teachers and parents. The principles of good group work apply
whether one works with teachers, students, parents, boards, or
citizen groups.

A new idea of leadership is being recognized. New, yet old!
Twenty-six centuries ago a wise man of China wrote:

A leader is best
When people barely know that he exists, . . .
Of a good leader, who talks little,
When his work is done, his aim fulfilled,
They will say, "We did this ourselves." [17]

This concept of leadership emphasizes the importance of
helping others realize *their own best potentials.* Human beings
strive to become what they essentially are capable of being.
The modern leader knows this, accepts it, and builds on it. He
sees himself as the catalyst of constructive forces in individuals
and groups. He finds satisfaction not only in his own achievements, but also in the discovery, unfolding, and development
of others' skills, appreciations, and understandings.

Using the problem-solving method—In any school, especially one striving for improvement and willing to make

---

[16] National Association of Secondary-School Principals. *The 1957 Commencement Manual.* Washington, D. C.: the Association, a department of the National
Education Association, 1957. 224 p.

[17] Bynner, Witter, translator. *The Way of Life According to Laotzu: An
American Version.* New York: John Day Co., 1944. p. 34-35.

changes, problems will arise that demand administrative leadership for their solution. Knowing how others have met a particular situation may help the principal in solving the problem or it may be something on which he can build an even better solution. But each school and each community has its unique characteristics to which the school must respond creatively. No single procedure will be so valuable to the principal in his leadership role as that basic skill known as *the problem-solving method.* This procedure is not new; but it is growing in acceptance as administrators increasingly use the democratic process. One of the CPEA studies asserted that "the problem-solving method should be thoroughly implanted in the administrator as *the* basic method of task performance."[18] Briefly put, the steps in solving problems are as follows:

1. Statement of the problem—definition and limitations (If the problem cannot be stated, it cannot be solved.)
2. Analysis of the problem to determine its related problems (This means identifying the key questions; also sorting out questions which take the group afield, recognizing them, and agreeing not to discuss them.)
3. Suggested solutions, with selection of the best one
4. Development of the solution
5. Putting the solution into effect—assigning tasks to individuals.

Too much cannot be said about the strategic value of this procedure. It dramatically shifts the emphasis from the concept of an authoritative father figure who knows or should know all the answers to that of a person who shows his respect for the integrity of other people by following a procedure which helps them find the solution to common problems. It means that no matter what the situation, the leader can help the group take logical steps toward setting up previously undefined goals and arriving at them. In this method the process is the key to success. Like knowledge of navigation, it enables one to find and follow a route no matter where one may be at

[18] Cooperative Project in Educational Administration, Southern States. *Cooperative Project for School Improvement and Leadership Development: A Staff Report.* Chapel Hill: University of North Carolina, School of Education, 1955-56. p. 236.

the moment. Furthermore, once the problem-solving process is familiar to a group, individual teachers tend to use it in their classrooms. Unstructured situations become less forbidding; teachers become more creative.[19]

In working with groups in problem solving, some have found it very helpful to keep two concepts in mind:

One is to help the members to begin work on a problem with *temporary noncommitment* to any solution. Once a person asserts a strong position on any issue before it has been discussed, the matter of changing his stand becomes more difficult. He is now openly identified with a point of view, and his energy goes into defending his position rather than into exploring the problem and possible solutions. Therefore, it is worthwhile for the leader to help members of the group to state problems in terms of impersonal situations and in such a way that members of the group will not say initially, "I believe in this or that. . . ."

The other concept is the *consensus* in preference to the split vote. In a democracy it is customary to decide issues by voting. When many people are involved and the relationships are impersonal, this method is adequate. However, among small groups of people more or less acquainted and intimately related, especially faculty groups, it is better to strive for consensus, that is, total agreement. This is not always possible but is an ideal toward which to strive. Whenever voting takes place, especially on vital issues, a majority always implies a possible 49 percent of the group who still remain opposed. To be sure, a mature person can adjust to this procedure, and should. But wherever possible, the principal will derive his authority from what Raup calls the uncoerced community of persuasion.[20]

Bringing about changes thru growth—In his work with groups and individuals, especially within the school, the principal tries to maintain and develop an environment conducive

---

[19] Prestwood, Elwood L. *The High School Principal and Staff Work Together.* New York: Teachers College, Columbia University Press, 1957. 96 p.
[20] Raup, R. Bruce. "Education and Power." *Teachers College Record* 51: 499-511; May 1950.

to mental health. In other words, he builds on sound psychological principles. Much of his energy goes into situations concerning people and their responses to those situations. California city superintendents place high value on *the principal's ability in exercising psychological rather than legal authority.*[21] Such psychological authority grows out of the ability to recognize and accept certain principles affecting human behavior and to follow them in such ways as these:

1. The principal sees that changes are made in an orderly manner. A basic requirement for mental health is a reasonable assurance that one's environment will remain stable. People do not resist change simply because they are conservative or hidebound. They resist it because the human organism requires a measure of stability of surroundings and procedures. They need to feel reasonably sure that tomorrow will be like today. Undoubtedly, one of the contributing factors to current anxiety is that so many people move from one location to another so frequently. Hence, it is more important to grow into change by the gradual process of viewing it from afar, sampling, and then accepting. Not only does the principal not behave in an erratic manner, but he sets up procedures whereby *people may bring about change on their terms.*

2. The principal recognizes the identification of persons with program. Many people believe that if the weakness or the inadequacy of a situation or program is logically pointed out to another person, he will respond positively and thereby change his point of view. However, it does not work out quite that way, and for a very simple reason: The person identifies himself with what he does. All his emotions are involved. This is what some psychologists call ego involvement. When we discuss a program, which seems so impersonal, what we are really discussing is the people who are participants in that program.

Each person discussing the program is really discussing himself to the extent to which the program affects him. An attack or an evaluation of a program is an attack or evaluation of people. With this in mind the principal is sensitive to the individual's stake in the change. So, wherever possible, the principal will see to it that the process of change is a gradual substitution of the objects of ego involvement. People identify themselves with the very process of change itself, so that they

[21] Walters, Thomas W. *The Job of the High School Principal as Perceived by California City Superintendents.* Doctor's thesis. Stanford, Calif.: Stanford University, 1955.

can say, "We brought about the change," or "This was my idea." In one school where a French teacher attacked any suggestion that diminished the importance of the teaching of French, directly or by implication, the principal wisely suggested that even tho the number of students taking the language in their school might be decreased, the amount of French being taught to the other students should be increased. The shift of emphasis from quantity to quality maintained the teacher's equilibrium and his sense of importance as expressed thru the importance of what he taught.

3. The principal avoids "threatening" situations. Just as the physical body may be threatened by various tangible situations of danger, so is the psychic economy of an individual threatened by less tangible situations. For example, any proposal to change the curriculum poses a vague threat to some teachers because by implication it suggests that the current program is inadequate. Parents feel threatened when their children fail in school. A teacher feels threatened when the principal visits his class or when he is suddenly called to the office. What this suggests, then, is that whenever an individual is threatened, he tends to direct his vision and energies toward the threat and often, as a result, does not function as sensibly as he might. The principal constantly asks: Is this the least threatening way to go about this?

4. He builds on the individual's needs, whether dealing with students, teachers, or others. It cannot be said too often that the principal must always keep in mind the driving and relentless psychological needs of individuals. These needs may be summed up in this way: Each of us needs to feel he is accepted, to have an opportunity to contribute to the welfare of the group, and to be given recognition for what he does. Many teachers go from one end of the year to the other without the principal's positive recognition of his efforts and achievements. The principal should develop a systematic (not automatic or perfunctory) procedure for discovering the good things his teachers do and then commending them for them personally. He can be realistic about people's limitations yet be warmly and sincerely appreciative of their good points.

In setting up procedures for bringing about orderly change, the principal needs to safeguard himself and others not only against inertia, but also against unwise changes in the program as a result of special pressures in the community. While the principal or the superintendent must make decisions and assume responsibility for them, he may also find it necessary to protect himself against the whims of people with power in the community. The school should have a clearly stated, detailed statement of its purpose, in the formulation of which the community has had a share. To this statement the school can anchor its program and from it can project changes. The school should have a well-organized procedure for initiating change.

Keeping channels of communication open—In his autobiography Winston Churchill advanced the idea that the rigidity of the Japanese language, which made communication difficult for them, played an important part in their defeat by the American forces at Midway. In a time when the high school must respond to conditions more rapidly than ever before, the principal must be concerned with communication as a leadership tool. He tries to keep the channels open both ways.

One of the best methods is frequent group meetings in which individuals feel free to express themselves. Communication is impaired in group procedures that do not allow full participation by members. It is also impaired by failure to carry out group decisions. When group work is limited largely to talk without action, individuals soon will say, "What's the use?" The channels may be considered open when individuals feel free to express themselves without fear of recrimination. But the principal must remember that it is easy to confuse his own feeling of freedom of expression with the feelings of others. As a group leader he must be alert to the extent of participation by each person. Some individuals normally find it difficult to express themselves and hence fail to communicate.

Other kinds of effective communication include well-written bulletins and frequent informal contacts with individuals. Essentially, however, the principal must see communication in broad dimensions, from the simple one-way announcement over the intercom to the intricate business of reading what the individual is trying to communicate by his behavior symptoms.

Serving as counselor—In a study cited earlier, more than 9 in 10 citizens, teachers, superintendents, and principals agreed that it was important for the principal to understand the personal and professional problems of teachers and to help them meet these problems.[22] The effective principal has always been a counselor. However, today's principal must be helpful to individuals who themselves are reacting to the demands of a complex society. To succeed, he must use as many of the known skills and insights about counseling as possible.

He cannot be expected to be a specialist in vocational or educational counseling nor to assume the duties of a psychologist. But his relationship with teachers, students, and parents is so often a counseling one that to be skilful in this will add to his leadership ability.

What, in brief, is counseling? It is a face-to-face relationship in which one person (the counselor) helps another to gain better understanding of himself in relation to some problem he is facing. This may mean gaining insight into one's motives, or gaining better perspective by seeing things more realistically, or making plans involving a new experience. During this process the principal-as-counselor listens to what the other person has to say. He lets the other person "carry the ball." When he does ask questions, they will be for clarification, not loaded to evoke an answer he wants. He will avoid making such statements as, "Don't you think it would be better if you did so-and-so?" or "Why did you do that?" He responds to feeling, recognizing that it is with this that he is essentially dealing. The setting of the interview will be relaxed and unhurried.

When does the principal counsel? Each time a student is sent to the principal for disciplinary reasons is a potential counseling situation. The principal tries to understand the student's point of view and gives him opportunity to present his side of the picture. They discuss the penalty and reach agreement on it so that the experience is truly an educational one. This does not mean the principal is "soft"; students expect and unconsciously want to pay for their misdemeanors. Discipline is not punitive, but is handled according to mental health and guidance principles.

Whenever a parent and a principal talk over a mutual problem involving a student, the principal will get further if he sees himself as a counselor. He will try to see the relationship

---

[22] Austin, David B., and Collins, James S., op. cit., p. 129.

between the specific problems which the parent brings up for discussion and the parent's inner needs as these are reflected in the interview. For example, if a parent launches out on an attack on the school or a teacher, the principal will realize that this parent may be working out some personal problem— the school problem may be only the symptom. In one situation a parent kept referring to the good school he attended as a boy —larger and better than the school in the community where he then lived. This seemed to be the parent's way of compensating for his own feeling of insecurity. He kept reminding others that he was "better" than they were by identifying himself with a "better" school.

As a counselor, the principal will also be aware of the way his own needs can be brought into the situation. For instance, he will be on guard against the effects of his need to justify himself. His needs and the parent's must be brought into balance.

Effective counseling is based on the principle that people have inner resources for growth. Given the right kind of opportunity, they can eventually solve their own problems. To provide the right setting, the principal must protect the integrity of the counselee. He does not try to manipulate people but really believes in and accepts the other person as a worthy individual. He listens carefully and patiently. He puts himself in the other person's place. He cannot listen if he is constantly trying to think up an answer to show the other person where he is mistaken. Counseling is a joint quest, not a debate.[23]

In performing his supervisory function, the principal will benefit greatly from his skill as a counselor. By following the principle of the joint quest, he can help teachers grow. By this constructive method, he asks the teacher to describe what he considers the best features of his work and makes it possible for the teacher to face areas where he needs help and to gain insight about himself with respect to areas which are threatening to him.

---

[23] For further discussion of the counseling role of the principal, see: Morris, Glyn. *Practical Guidance Methods for Principals and Teachers.* New York: Harper and Brothers, 1952. Chapter 8, "He Lets Me Talk," p. 189-223.

Recognizing the nonteaching staff—Every person employed in the modern high school has a role in developing the total potential of the school. Unfortunately, in an institution where academic status tends to play an important part, some members of the staff are unwittingly excluded from the opportunity to make their maximum contribution. The location of the custodian's headquarters in the basement of many schools tends to be equated with his place on the academic totem pole. His duties are of such a nature and are performed at such a time as to induce his chronic irritation and tension. The principal can counteract this in several ways.

One principal walks around the school with the custodian each morning and invites his suggestions regarding school maintenance, thereby cultivating a "we" relationship for all to see. The custodian has a mail box with the teachers. He is included in social affairs. The principal sends him notes of appreciation from time to time. Furthermore, the students and the teachers are helped to appreciate the contribution to their health and comfort made by the custodial staff. This is a legitimate object of education for which time should be allotted. Vigilant care should be taken not to permit boys and girls to become careless and thoughtless about the maintenance of their school home. Such training is not only desirable for the individual student but it also avoids unnecessary work for the custodians.

At every point the principal notes the importance of all nonteaching personnel by recognizing them. For instance, their names are always included in school publications with the same prominence as those of other personnel.

The Principal as a Person

We have considered the principal's role in relation to forces both without and within the school. How well he performs as a leader depends to some extent on how well he understands himself and safeguards and utilizes his own best potentialities. As a person, he feels the effect of the pressures and demands made upon him. These may change him to some extent: he may grow stronger or he may unwittingly fall back on childish, defensive behavior. As a leader it is essential that he be the most mature, well-balanced member of the group. In fulfilling this role he understands himself, sees himself as embodying an ideal, knows the range of his influence, accepts his limitations, makes wise use of his time, and maintains his balance.

Understanding Himself

The administrator should know and accept himself. This sounds much simpler than it may turn out to be. Recent discoveries have served only to underline the importance of self-understanding, especially for those who work extensively with people.[24] Those who assume responsibility for helping others to develop integrity and self-direction must be especially careful that their own problems do not get in the way.

Many a teacher's creative plans for meeting individual needs of students have died a-borning because the administrator confused his own compulsive need for order with the "danger" of setting up a new precedent or of disrupting the schedule. When local organizations make excessive demands on the school band for community affairs, the administrator may confuse *his own needs* for community approval with the musical development of his students or the school's service to the community. The principal, too, has need of approval, success, and love; and he cannot deny himself the satisfaction of these legitimate needs. However, as a "practicing social scientist" he has an obligation to understand himself and to avoid working out his needs at the expense of others.

It will help him, for example, if he can recognize when he or his colleagues or the students are being frustrated. Frustration beyond a certain point leads to aggression. Aggression takes many forms from wildly striking out to subtle, backhanded damning by faint praise.

---

[24] Linscott, Robert N., and Stein, Jess, editors. *Why You Do What You Do.* New York: Random House, 1956. 305 p.

Seeing Himself as Embodying an Ideal

Altho it may be dangerous to think of oneself more highly than one ought to think, it is equally unfortunate not to recognize one's potentialities and opportunities. The principal has an initial advantage generally coveted by men. Students, teachers, and parents believe he *should* be admired and respected. To be sure, this is not an unmixed blessing, because some people expect of him just the opposite of what others expect, and he cannot measure up to conflicting ideals. He bears the heavy responsibility of being the kind of person in whom youth and adults may see the concrete expression of high standards. He is visualized as a just, kind yet firm, person of good manners and discriminating tastes. As boys and girls develop values, the personification of these values in some adults plays an important part. Probably no single person in the community is viewed by youth so intently and critically, yet so ideally, as their secondary-school principal. It may help him if he remembers that according to Remmers and Radler between 75 and 80 percent of American teen-agers *like* school.[25]

Knowing the Range of His Influence

The principal's values, likes, and dislikes assume great weight in the community. It is no accident that the small high school which produced nine national women's ski champions has as principal an enthusiastic skier who has sponsored and taught skiing in his school. Nor is it an accident that in a school where the principal likes to travel, students take organized trips to distant parts of the United States. Nor is it just coincidental that in a high school where the principal is fond of the theater there happens to be a keen interest in drama. And so on down the line.

The principal's values and goals tend to be assimilated by his colleagues and his students. The dimensions of his life may profoundly touch the whole community. Thru him others discover unrealized potentialities. Hundreds, even thousands of

[25] Remmers, H. H., and Radler, D. H. *The American Teenager*. Indianapolis: Bobbs-Merrill Company, 1957. p. 119.

boys and girls may or may not discover some of life's richest experiences, depending on how well the principal rises to the full measure of his important calling.

Accepting His Limitations

In the national study of attitudes toward the principalship [26] no word is said to the effect that the principal must know everything there is to know in the course of instruction. But it is desirable for him to understand the dimensions of his role and how he can best utilize his potentialities. His job requires that he be a catalyst—not a walking dictionary.

To be sure, he is expected to have intellectual curiosity, but this is a far cry from encyclopedic knowledge. Many principals who avoid their supervisory responsibilities may do so because they fear that teachers will expect them to help in the teaching of specific subject content. Principles of learning may be applied to any situation. Usually, the teacher's problem will have something to do with motivation and the understanding of boys and girls and their needs. This is the "pitch" which the principal can take. Having freed himself from the fear of working in areas in which there may be technical aspects unfamiliar to him, the principal is ready to go ahead.

Making Wise Use of His Time

The art of leadership depends largely on the ability to delegate authority and responsibility to others. This frees the leader for his most important tasks. Unfortunately, in our culture, activity in itself has assumed unwarranted virtue. Keeping busy at inconsequential tasks alleviates anxiety for the principal as it does for others. *People take refuge in such busyness to escape from themselves.* It takes a degree of maturity for a principal to assume the role of the reflective, helpful counselor and planner. Many difficulties of the modern administrator may revolve around failure at this point.

---

[26] Austin, David B., and Collins, James S., *op. cit.*

The charge has been made, tho not substantiated, that the modern secondary-school administrator lacks intellectual curiosity. Certainly it is difficult to assimilate what there is to know currently and at the same time keep the wheels of the modern secondary-school organization in motion. For this reason special effort is needed to keep inviolate some regular time for reading and thinking. There is evidence that the most successful administrators are also extensive readers of serious books, professional and otherwise.

Basic to the theme of this chapter is the idea that the occupation of school administrator is a high calling and a noble profession which requires thought as well as action. The administrator is chosen for his brain power more than for his work in the halls. A half-hour each day spent with book and pencil in hand may be far more useful to his school and community than any two hours of the rest of the day.

Every effort should be made to reduce educational lag by judicious reading. For example, the four-page *NASSP Spotlight* [27] can be of tremendous value to the principal. In 10 minutes he can have the significant results of many hours of reading by a competent staff at NASSP headquarters.

Before moving in any new direction the principal can plant his feet on the ground by checking for information in the *Encyclopedia of Educational Research.* As Lyman Bryson has pointed out, one cannot argue about a fact, yet it has been noted that principals often neglect to check the research on a controversial topic before undertaking to discuss it.

The principal cannot respond to all the demands made on him. He is expected to participate in many ancillary community programs. He needs some guiding principle to help him select activities so that his energies, knowledge, and prestige will not be frittered away. He might ask himself: If I do this job, am I avoiding doing something more essential? Is this job really necessary? Is there someone else available for this job who cannot do what I am trained for?

[27] Published five times a year by the National Association of Secondary-School Principals, a Department of the National Education Association, 1201 Sixteenth Street, N. W., Washington 6, D. C. Free to NASSP members; $1 a year to others.

There are obvious tasks no one else can do such as meeting with the board of education, selecting staff, and attending faculty meetings. Selling tickets for the basketball game could be done as well by someone who has not been trained in school administration. The principal must resist the temptation to be preoccupied with the tangible aspects of administration, such as equipment, supplies, and transportation, to the neglect of the less tangible, the ends toward which these are the means— the improvement of instruction. The superintendent of schools, too, can help by protecting the principal from excessive demands on his energies.

Maintaining Balance

An ancient philosopher suggested that the good life is characterized by a sense of proportion; he called it the "golden mean." It is unlikely that any human being achieves more than an approximation of this ideal. However, leaders must make a special effort in this direction. In *The Organization Man* [28] Whyte has pointed out the subtle dangers to human personality which are implicit in our communal life. The principal must constantly appraise himself in relation to his obligations to the "organization" and to himself.

A democratic climate includes both (a) respect for the integrity of individuals and (b) knowledge and use of skills in helping people grow in directing themselves. Skills can be taught, but "where there is no spirit, the letter faileth." The principal must practice what he preaches, by a genuine concern for each individual. In general, the subtle nuances of his own attitudes and behavior are eventually absorbed by the teachers and students as the desirable pattern of behavior.

Balance, too, must be sought in relation to program. Community tradition and pressures, personal whims, gaps in program due to lag in understanding, as well as other factors, can keep the school one-sided in its emphasis. The principal must work continuously with faculty and parents to develop a

[28] Whyte, William H., Jr. *The Organization Man.* New York: Simon and Schuster, 1956. 429 p.

balanced program. Even national emergencies must be met in ways that recognize a school's full range of values. Today's emphasis on programs for the gifted is necessary; but this, too, unless handled judiciously, could become quite out of proportion.

The Superintendent's Role

The successful development of the secondary-school program depends to a large extent on the quality of the superintendent's relationship to it. His remoteness from the classroom, as opposed to his legitimate concern with the problems of the total school system, may jeopardize this relationship. At its best, this relationship is most fruitful when the superintendent observes its two contrasting features: On the one hand, he cultivates understanding and cooperates in every possible way required; and on the other, he knows when to start creative forces going and then to leave them to develop along their own lines.

Superintendent and Principal

The quality of the relationship between principal and superintendent will have a decided influence on the over-all goal of the school, that is, developing the potentialities of the boys and girls.

To insure a maximum of understanding, areas of responsibility must be clearly defined. Within the framework of the systemwide and state-mandated policies, the building principal should have the entire responsibility for what transpires within his building. When services which originate outside the building principal's office are essential to his program, there is sometimes misunderstanding regarding areas of responsibility. For instance, guidance service may operate on a shared-services basis, and the counselor may be employed by a cooperative board of which the district superintendent is the executive officer. When the counselor enters a building, he is responsible to the principal of that building, and his program is developed in accordance with the wishes of the principal. The counselor reports to the principal and follows his leadership in performing his duties. This procedure should hold for all services.

On the other hand, the principal has an obligation to cooperate in utilizing services provided by the superintendent's office. His is not a discrete empire over which he rules. The school is a part of a larger organization into which it must be integrated.

Reducing Areas of Tension

The superintendent can release or redirect the potentialities of the building principal by dealing with areas of uncertainty and threat in a statesmanlike manner. For instance, it is obvious that the building principal should be involved in selection of his staff. If he is to be evaluated on the product of the school, he should be given maximum consideration in choosing teachers. There should be standard operating procedures for all areas so that the building principal is not subject to erratic behavior from headquarters.

The principal's integrity should be respected, and there should be a clear understanding of boundaries of responsibility. If at all possible, the superintendent's office should not be located in a high-school building. The superintendent will not violate the essential courtesies in their relationship. For example, when the superintendent visits the high school, he might wait in the principal's office until the principal gets there rather than go around the school building looking for him. Furthermore, wherever the high school is the *pièce de résistance* of the local educational enterprise, the superintendent must resist the temptation to usurp its prestige on occasion and publicly identify himself too closely with its accomplishments. The building principal cannot be expected to be his best self if he must surrender the laurels of achievement to someone who has not earned them.

The superintendent, too, must be on guard against his own human frailty. If he has served as a high-school principal, he will be tempted to compare the present administration with his own and unwittingly to remember only his achievement and overlook his mistakes.

Free Exchange of Ideas

In the relationship between principal and superintendent, as in usual staff relationships, good communication is essential to understanding. Not merely written communiqués—altho these in the right kind and quantity are important—but regular and frequent opportunity is needed for face-to-face exchange of ideas and discussion of problems under conditions and procedures designed to elicit maximum participation.

For instance, one county superintendent holds regular half-day meetings approximately twice a month with the principals and other supervisory personnel. The general plans for these meetings, largely focused on improving instruction thru in-service programs, are hammered out at a three-day conference before the opening of school in the fall. At that time the group meets in a neighboring summer resort where discussion can proceed in a leisurely manner. It is difficult to estimate the value of this kind of integrating experience.

Interpretation to Board Members Necessary

At every point the expanding and diversified secondary-school program needs to be interpreted, but especially so to boards of education. Much depends on their wise and sympathetic consideration of the needs of adolescents. This is an important leadership responsibility of the superintendent.

To do this adequately, the superintendent must feel identified with the secondary program. This requires an understanding of the special problems of the secondary school and the scope and nature of programs designed to meet them, such as exploratory, pre-college, vocational, work-experience, extension, correspondence, and general programs. He should be committed to the values implied in the secondary school as an American institution which, in the midst of rapid change, is striving to meet the educational needs of all the adolescent youth of the nation.

The range of board activity runs thru a wide variety of educational problems. The superintendent has a strategic role in determining the focus of the deliberations of the board of education *thru formation of agenda.* This is a strategic leadership function. In this, as in administrative activities in general, the pull is toward consideration of the physical aspects of the program. This is a natural pull: first, because plant and equipment must be there before school can begin, and second, because these are tangible problems with which many board members feel comfortable.

However, board members are equally responsible for the instructional program. Many become keenly interested in problems of guidance, curriculum, and student health. They need help in understanding these and other features of the instructional program. One superintendent sets aside a part of each board meeting so that some feature of the educational program may be presented by a competent person. He takes every opportunity to dramatize educational problems. On one occasion he had hung in the board room a large wall chart graphically illustrating the range of reading ability found among pupils in each grade. In a short time the board was able to see some of the implications in the teaching of reading, as well as what meeting individual needs meant in this case. On another occasion board members were invited to watch a dramatization of the development and solution of an uncomplicated student problem involving a change of program thru an adequate guidance program. One board member said, "Now I know what you mean when you talk about guidance." What the superintendent does specifically will depend on the circumstances. However involved the situation, he can gradually introduce individuals and groups to wider areas of understanding. He can take individuals with him on specific missions; others can be asked for help in preparing information on specific problems.

Fitting the Secondary School into the Total Program

Because of overlapping abilities, the lines between elementary school and high school and between high school and college are valid only as administrative devices. Reference has been made to the amount and extent of overlapping in terms of student ability. Increased understanding of boys and girls of junior-high-school age leads to a demand for a more distinctive program at that level. The diversified needs, terminal and preparatory, of the senior high school require continuous study and adjustment. Growing pains are prevalent at each level. Meanwhile all these must be articulated as smoothly and effectively as possible. The greatest strain centers around the secondary-school program inasmuch as this must meet requirements from so many directions.

Only the superintendent can provide the leadership necessary to insure continuity and articulation to the entire educational program. Committees of teachers from elementary, junior, and senior high schools can clarify the problems as they see them as well as describe the goals of their schools. Some superintendents find it profitable to provide for continuous communication between elementary and secondary schools thru a variety of teacher organizations and inservice programs involving both groups. Secondary-school teachers have learned from elementary-school teachers and vice versa. Human relations are improved when teachers work together on problems of articulation.

In conclusion: A leader is one who has vision, who believes in the innate potentialities of people for helping themselves. Whether he be a building principal or a superintendent of a large county or city school system, the underlying principles on which he operates are the same, and he utilizes them in all his relationships.

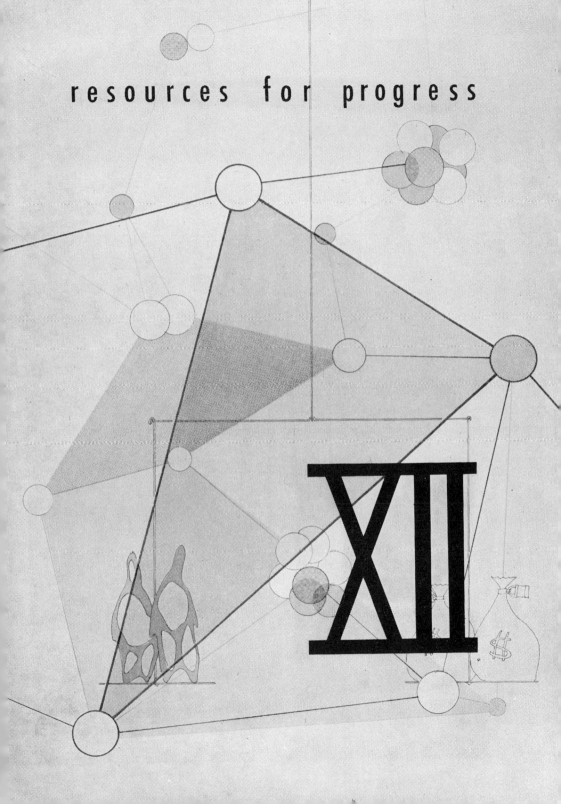

resources for progress

XII

resources for progress

To CARRY OUT the proposals outlined in this volume, people, ideas, and money will be required. Each of these three categories of resources depends upon the other two for its full effect. In the absence of any one of the three, or without a suitable balance among them, the most earnestly desired changes are unlikely to occur. For this reason the identification, development, and imaginative employment of resources are among the principal items to be considered by those responsible for creating better secondary schools.

Ideas Are the Basic Resource

In our recurring concern with the material aspects of our educational problems, we sometimes fail to remember what no teacher should forget: The power of ideas exceeds all the other forces available to man.

The financial needs of schools are real and urgent; no useful purpose is served by understating them. But the most difficult problems of education are almost always to be found in the realm of ideas. Certainly this is true of secondary education in America today. Money can help us to achieve our goals, but we can derive those goals and generate the means to approach them only on a basis of knowledge and ideas.

Fortunately there is already available a wealth of knowledge to be shared for the improvement of schools. The rapid rise of the behavioral sciences in recent decades has made possible a more systematic approach to the art of teaching and has deepened our understanding of the social and psychological setting in which learning occurs. In sociology, psychology, psychiatry, cultural anthropology, and all the other disciplines that seek a firmer knowledge of the nature of man, scholars are steadily pushing the frontiers of inquiry outward. Much of what they learn bears upon the processes of education, and many of their discoveries can be of value in the schools.

In teaching itself, research and experimentation continue in a steadily widening stream. Among the most promising inventions for gathering and disseminating new ideas in education have been the regional study councils, formed as school systems and graduate institutions have joined forces to promote the study and improvement of teaching and administration. Increasingly, tho still inadequately, local school systems and state departments are expanding their research programs to obtain better answers to local problems and to gather sound data for policy decisions.

School administrators now use research materials more regularly than they once did. The *Encyclopedia of Educational Research* and the professional journals are the well-used working tools of the abler superintendents. Graduate schools of education, state departments of education, and the Educational Research Service (of the American Association of School Administrators and the NEA Research Division) are major allies of local school administration.

Unfinished Business in Research

The progress we have made in educational research is significant, however, chiefly as a measure of what remains undone. Compared with undertakings and accomplishments in other fields, the results of research in education have been meager. If we are to build resources in research adequate to deal with the problems of secondary schools, to say nothing of other areas of education, we must radically re-examine our current practices and promptly undertake a large-scale expansion of our present establishment for educational research. The importance of education in America today makes it utterly impossible to justify the enormous differences between the support provided for educational research and that provided research in industry, medicine, agriculture, and defense. All our experience demonstrates the fact that manpower and money, wisely devoted to research and development, ultimately—and often very soon—produce results far outweighing the original investment. Yet, for a variety of reasons, we have failed to carry on research in education on a scale commensurate with our study of other major segments of our culture.

Much of the research now required is on practical instructional problems involving specific procedures in various subject areas and with different types of students. Operational research of this kind will not be generated in an ivory tower or a university library. It must be related to identified problems emerging from the critical examination of practical experience. Pure research is essential in every field and must be suitably supported in education, but only as we balance basic research with a proper concern for the practical aspects of operating schools and teaching students shall we see the improvement we desire in day-to-day instruction.

Such an approach to research can become a major source of strength for secondary education if new patterns of cooperation can be devised to tie together local school units, state departments of education, colleges, graduate schools, and other groups interested in improving education. More is involved here than the transmission of knowledge from some fountainhead down to the classroom teacher, for the nature of operational research requires that experience and information be shared. The process of talking, thinking, and planning together will be as profitable to the researcher as to the classroom teacher and may on occasion exceed in value the substantive findings of a study.

Not all the questions teachers face require original answers. Many situations would be improved thru better access to the successful experience of others who have met similar problems. In recent years promising programs have been developed to promote the exchange of good practices, but much remains to be done, not only at the national and state levels, but also within the local district. Even in a single school—often within a department—teaching can be improved by the more rapid dissemination of procedures that have proved useful.

Of the factors contributing to better secondary schools, research and curriculum development must be ranked second only to the goals toward which the program is directed. The objectives themselves will be determined by our cultural requirements and the broad purposes that motivate our nation, but the degree to which people, money, and materials may be employed effectively to attain the goals will depend ultimately upon the quality of the means we can discover or invent. To design inventions, to test discoveries, and to prepare systematic attacks upon the problems that concern us, we must depend upon the tools and procedures of research and development.

The Favorable Outlook

The outlook in educational research is now more favorable than it has been. Major foundations are supporting a variety of investigations into old and new problems. The federal government is appropriating increased sums thru the U. S. Office of Education for studies and developmental programs. Professional organizations are broadening their research activities. State and local school systems are using sound research procedures more frequently than they once did. And the universities are continuing to serve as principal channels for leadership and coordination.

The increased attention to the study and solution of instructional problems thru research is not without its hazards. Together with sound, objective efforts thru well-designed projects, we are also witnessing a number of programs that are more promotional than experimental. The delay between the development of innovations and their general application has long plagued education and as quickly as possible should be reduced, but the remedy does not lie in prematurely promoting hypotheses as tho they were validated conclusions.

It is not unlikely that the findings of some of the new studies of the nature of adolescence and the role of the secondary school will lead to new instructional theories. Indeed, we must expect that as older procedures are adapted to new situations, sharper and more valid insights will result. As in all experimentation and inquiry, however, a certain amount of error will be inevitable and it is therefore essential that teachers and administrators subject new theories and proposals to careful examination before accepting them for classroom use. Rapid communication and forceful promotion without the restraint of responsible critical appraisal could produce sweeping changes in educational practice based on little more than the desire of individual schools to keep up with the newest fashion.

Proposals for Further Inquiry

The current demands upon the secondary schools give new urgency to well-designed and adequately financed research projects in a number of fields. The nature of the problems upon which more light is needed may be illustrated by the following examples:

> • What are the most economical class sizes for given subject fields or teaching purposes?
> • In working for effective learning, what is the relation, if any, between desirable size of class and the ability level of students?
> • Would better educational results follow if schools were organized around teaching teams instead of individual teachers; for example, a master teacher working with several less experienced teachers and a group of technical or clerical assistants?
> • Is there an optimum size for a senior high school or a junior high school?

• How can the small school provide a maximum range of learning opportunities for its students?

• How can a sense of belonging be fostered best among students in a large school?

• What criteria should be used in grouping students for given educational purposes?

• How can buildings be designed for increased adaptability to program changes?

• What are the effects of light, color, sound, and space layout upon the learning and other behavior of students?

• What types and amounts of specialized vocational preparation are most conducive to job success for high-school graduates?

• What can be done in the high school to prepare young people best for further education?

• How can culturally impoverished students be motivated toward intellectual development?

• Thru what forms of organization may counseling of students best be provided?

• How may follow-up studies of former students—both dropouts and graduates—be made and used most effectively for the improvement of the program?

• What are the most effective means of providing secondary-school teachers with usable information about the individual backgrounds and specific needs of their students?

• Can valid procedures be developed for job analysis and classification of the task of secondary-school classroom teachers?

• What are the special merits of television, films, and recordings, and other similar devices? How can they be employed most effectively by capable teachers, or for learning without the personal guidance of teachers?

• How can especially able youths be motivated and their learning guided most effectively?

• How can findings of social and biological sciences be drawn upon to improve the high-school curriculum and the competence of teachers?

The Power of People

To recognize the worth of ideas is to underscore the importance of people, for only in the human mind are ideas generated or put to work. What people think, what they want, and what they are willing to work for are among the powerful elements that must be part of any new undertaking in education.

Almost everyone, from the newest high-school freshman to the wisest and most influential elder statesman, is a potential contributor to the building of a better school. In every community and in the nation, the problem is to find ways to release this energy and to apply it with good effect to the work that is waiting to be done.

The Teaching Staff

A principal and obvious source of manpower for building better schools is the teaching staff itself. In every school, teachers are engaged in the traditional tasks of classroom instruction, and it may be argued that this first function of the teacher should not be undermined by crowding his schedule and exhausting his energy with extraneous activities.

There are, however, many ways in which teachers can contribute to the improvement of the schools—employing their invaluable skills, experience, and insights—without adding to the load of their classroom work. When enthusiasm is kindled, people find ways to do, with enjoyment, what might otherwise be merely a daily chore. Needed for such performance, however, are a working climate conducive to initiative, creativity, and mutual cooperation; and a quality of leadership that enables people to clarify their common purposes and to see how their own capabilities are related to those purposes. Under such a climate and with such leadership, not only are individual effort and cooperation encouraged, but the men and women involved in the process of institutional change find themselves growing personally as well.

Citizen Participation

The great variety of tasks to be tackled in American secondary schools affords the possibility for widespread participation by citizens. At the highest level, the White House

Conference on Education in 1956 revealed one way in which the experiences and aspirations of the entire country may be drawn upon to clarify issues and to determine the extent of agreement upon broad educational questions. We are still too near the time of that Conference to weigh its worth objectively, but it seems clear that the process of nationwide discussion for which the Conference was a climax and an outlet was good for American education. Certainly, it left the American people better informed upon current issues in education and upon the value of widespread public consideration of such issues. It illuminated a source of strength available in every state and every school district for the study of problems and the examination of alternative courses of action. As a significant byproduct the Conference developed, thru the conference devices it employed, both tools and tests for the school administrator.

At the heart of such processes is the interaction among the lay members of the community, the board of education, the teaching staff, and the administrator. If any community is to capitalize fully the assets it possesses in this field, it will expect of its school administrator something more than a willingness to improvise emergency plans for public participation. Long-range consistent planning will be required, guided by the principles that are being distilled from experience.[1]

When school people and community members work together most successfully, the resources available for education are more efficiently employed and additional resources are more readily developed. Successful common effort of this sort goes beyond a generalized desire to exchange goodwill and to cooperate amicably. While it includes friendliness, its essence is an intelligent awareness of the community's obligation to set goals for schools and the professional's obligation to lead in devising workable procedures for attaining those goals. Recognizing the value of orderly, legal procedure, the most effective citizen groups channel their proposals thru the school board,

---

[1] For a discussion of these principles, see: Campbell, Roald F., and Ramseyer, John A. *The Dynamics of School-Community Relationships.* New York: Allyn and Bacon, 1955. p. 149-86.

clarifying problems and marshaling objective evidence in support of their suggestions.

Those who lead in productive school-community cooperation soon learn that great achievements in this field usually have their beginnings in smaller successes, and that such programs develop as those engaged in them gain confidence in each other and in the procedures they use. No one sequence of development or operating pattern can be applied uniformly to all situations; in every one a variety of approaches and devices will be desirable. The precise combination and emphasis required for any particular community must be determined by local leadership and by the application of local resources to local problems.

New Roles for Laymen

In addition to group action there are other ways in which citizens can give substantial help to secondary schools. Every school includes among its parents and neighbors men and women whose ability and experience can add strength and depth to the instructional program. A relatively few schools have enlisted the help of such people but in most places legal requirements regarding teaching certificates and the natural inertia that prevents experimentation have blocked their service. The waste of potentially valuable help would be deplorable under any circumstances; to forego it now, when so many schools are desperately short of teachers and when students are so urgently in need of sound instruction in a wide variety of fields, is inexcusable.

Persons other than regular teachers can assist in high-school instruction in at least three ways. They may be employed as assistants to teachers, in a status somewhat similar to that of laboratory assistants who work with teachers in science in many schools. Classroom aides neither can nor should be used to replace teachers, but evidence shows that many routine tasks now performed by teachers (at the sacrifice of professional duties) could, with adequate supervision, be handled by assistants.

A second way to bring additional help to the classroom is to employ as part-time teachers men and women possessing the required qualifications who are not available for full-time duty. In addition to relieving the quantitative shortage of teachers, this plan could improve the quality of teaching in many schools. Among former teachers or other well-qualified people willing to accept part-time assignments there are some in almost every community superior to the full-time teachers holding only emergency certificates who are now recruited as a last resort.

A third plan for augmenting the regular teaching force is to enlist as consultants, or occasional lecturers or demonstrators, members of the community who have specialized experience and competence beyond that of the regular teaching staff. In this manner it is possible to present authoritative information on current scientific and technical developments, personalized accounts of current situations in other countries, or expert demonstrations in arts and crafts. Vocational education offers a particularly good opportunity to use industrial experts who can acquaint students (and teachers) with the latest developments in particular trades and industries.[2] Ordinarily, persons invited to visit the schools for such purposes are happy to volunteer their services. If repeated requests are made of the same person, however, it may be desirable to employ him on a part-time salary or a mutually satisfactory fee basis. Some schools maintain a current directory of parents having special skills or hobbies.

Certification laws in some states may currently prevent employing, either as part-time teachers or full-time aides, a number of people who have much to contribute to school programs. Where this is true, professional leaders and lay authorities have good reason to re-examine obsolete statutes or regulations and in the light of present needs and resources, to work toward desirable amendments which will maintain adequate professional standards without inhibiting intelligently flexible staffing plans.

---

[2] See Chapter III, 100-14.

Student Assistance

The student body of every secondary school is itself a reservoir of considerable potentiality for the improvement of the school. In countless schools, students take part in school service projects ranging from policy making to simple janitorial work.

There are important psychological and sociological reasons for including students in such projects, chief of which is the fact that high-school students, as they enter adulthood, should have steadily expanding opportunities to work as adults in community institutions. Thus they are able to acquire not only the skills of civic service, but in addition that sense of personal obligation which gives purpose and direction to skill and lays the foundation for assuming increasingly responsible positions of leadership.

The types of activities in which students can profitably participate are suggested by the following list which by no means exhausts the possibilities:

Improving school grounds—By participating under expert guidance in laying out a landscape design and following thru with the manual labor required to plant and maintain the grass, trees, shrubs, and flowers, students build knowledge and skill and develop a sense of ownership of their school.

Assisting in the instruction of younger children—This activity yields valuable information about human development and the nature of the teaching process. In addition to increasing the assistance available to elementary-school teachers, such a program can serve also as a major opportunity for teacher recruitment. Here, also, legal restrictions must be observed.

Making surveys of needs and resources—As students carry on such work in connection with the school curriculum, they add substance to theory, acquire firsthand experience in human relations, and make valuable contributions to important community enterprises.

Working as volunteers in community social agencies—Thru this means students experience the satisfaction of sharing in worthwhile causes for the betterment of society and gain needed insights into human problems in their communities.

Assisting in school office routines—When school office work is carefully planned for students, it becomes more than the performance of routine chores. At its best, it builds an awareness of what education means to the community and creates deeper understanding of the function of the school. Other activities might be baby-sitting during PTA meetings, guiding visitors to the school building, serving as hosts and hostesses for community affairs, participating in civil defense work, or serving as operators of audio-visual equipment.

Amid the widespread present concern with the negative effects of unwholesome adolescent behavior, it is important to note that in the constructive activities of teen-agers lie the beginnings of positive adult behavior. It would be difficult to overestimate the benefits that can come to our schools now and in the future as the effervescent energies of high-school students are channeled toward the service of their institutions.

Education Strengthens Itself

Whatever else American schools have demonstrated, they have shown that the power of people and the power of ideas can be brought into a common focus thru universal education. The rise of our public school system was most rapid during the period when the flow of immigrants reached its greatest volume and its widest diversity. Opening their doors to all who came, the public schools helped the newcomers to find themselves and to achieve a way of life which for many of them exceeded the hopes that had brought them to a new homeland.

The power that generated this far-flung network of common schools came from no dominating central agency; it arose from the force of common aspirations and the strongly held conviction that equality of opportunity is the birthright of every American child. The effects of this development are visible in almost every facet of our life today.

Nowhere are the results of our educational efforts more sharply evident than in the compounding development of education itself. Wherever the need for schools is most urgently set forth and the effort to improve them most successful, the leadership almost invariably comes from educated citizens. In any community, the most intelligent criticism of the schools is offered by those who are well informed and well educated. The instigators of school improvement in places where schools have been allowed to lag are frequently men and women who have been educated in other, more forward-looking communities. The controls of education which were discussed in Chapter I are often influenced to a critical degree by the quality of the education received by men and women who exercise those controls.

Much of the current controversy in American education has arisen because parents want for their children better schools than they attended themselves. Whatever shortcomings our old schools may have had, they seem at least to have sharpened the discrimination of many members of the present adult generation and to have raised their level of educational aspiration. To develop intelligent criticism of the school by all its students —present and past—is a creditable accomplishment for any school system and an excellent springboard for further gains.

Educational Progress and Economic Productivity

To assert that ideas, people, and education are among our major assets for creating better schools is not to deny the importance of material resources. Good schools require money, and if we are to raise today's schools to the level of tomorrow's requirements, we shall have to devote to them substantially more money than we now do.

In a publication that has become a minor classic among those interested in tracing the relation of good education to the economic, social, and political well-being of communities, the U. S. Chamber of Commerce makes these statements:[3]

---

[3] U. S. Chamber of Commerce, Education Department. *Education—An Investment in People.* Washington, D. C.: the Chamber, 1955. 44 p.

Education is an essential means to successful self-government and the protection of our political freedom.

The group of cities having the highest education levels also was found to have the highest average per capita retail sales.

Belief in a "free market economy" was directly related to the years of school completed.

People with less than a high school education showed less economic understanding.

These variations [in average educational level among the states] suggest differences in the capacity of the adult population to produce and consume goods and services and the need to improve state school systems.

Economists and educators have repeatedly demonstrated that better educated people are more productive workers and more discriminating consumers, and accordingly that business leaders interested in the well-being of their enterprises are wise to support good schools. It is also clear that the ever rising curve of America's industrial output reveals a steady growth in our ability to finance our educational effort.

Schools as Investments

We do not say as strongly or as often as we should that the funds devoted to education are not expenditures at all, except in the narrow sense of technical accounting practice. These outlays are in fact long-range contributions to our chief capital account, investments against which no depreciation need ever be taken, for with wise management these funds compound themselves indefinitely. In the long run, good schools actually cost nothing since the benefits they produce far outweigh the allocation made for their support.

Poor schools are expensive, for they not only waste the resources of students and teachers, but also give the undiscerning patron a deceptive sense of security that blinds him to the wiser course he might have chosen. In every school district, and at the state and national levels, the truth must be repeatedly set forth: Dollars denied to schools that need them are never "saved"; instead they set off in every case a tragic chain reaction of inefficient teaching and wasted potential.

Ample documentation of our financial ability to support education can be found in the reports of our current economic strength. This volume is no place to record the details of America's economic development, but a clear summary of our prospects for the years immediately ahead was published in 1954 by the National Citizens Commission for the Public Schools. In this report the Commission said:

> In the decade ahead, in the absence of war or other unforeseen natural disasters, the United States will have a greatly expanded volume of income available for consumption, investment and savings. Education needs will grow, but relative to the growth of national income the amount involved will not be unmanageable. The money requirements can be financed by allocating to public education a small percentage of the increase in national income and productivity. The financing problem is a problem of policy, not of resources; the problem is to select the best basis on which to make a small portion of the increased national production and income available for education.[4]

Our economic ability to support good schools is unmistakably clear. Not only have our total output and our output per capita increased, but (of far greater import in our projections) our ability to convert work into wealth has forged steadily ahead. Our output per man-hour, for several years before 1948, increased annually at an average rate of about 2.2 percent per year; since 1948, gains have exceeded 3 percent per year.[5] As we move at an accelerated tempo into the era of automation and atomic energy, the rise in our ability to produce may be expected to outrun the most optimistic earlier estimates.

The National Dimension

Altho long experience with public education has amply validated the principle that strong local control under state law is the soundest basis for conducting schools in our democracy,

[4] National Citizens Commission for the Public Schools. *Financing Public Education in the Decade Ahead.* New York: the Commission, 1954. p. 1.

[5] Lipton, Milton. "Productivity Trends: III. What the Averages Conceal." *Conference Board Business Record* 13: 246-50; June 1956.

the facts of our economic life reveal just as clearly that we
cannot hope to establish or maintain schools equal to our national needs if we insist upon purely local and state support.
When local resources are insufficient to produce good schools,
local control loses its meaning.

The chief justification for federal aid is that it can place in
the hands of state and local boards funds which may be controlled locally to obtain the programs needed locally. The current need is in specific localities but the pupils served by each
local program may live out their productive lives in any part
of the United States. In a nation of such mobility as ours,
localities are not permanently kept apart by the physical distances that appear to separate them. The inescapable fact is
that the quality of education in any part of our country affects
every other part. Local public education has national consequences, and planning for it must include a nationwide
dimension.

After the fullest allowance has been made for differences
in climate and economic conditions, it is not logical to argue
that anything approaching equality of educational opportunity
is available in this nation when average current expenditures
per pupil vary from $158 in Mississippi to $482 in New York.[6]

Nor is it reasonable to assert that conscientious local effort
alone is likely to solve the problem. When the personal income
of the people of the state is divided by the number of children
of school age, the quotient is $3364 in Mississippi; $12,256 in
Delaware.[7]

The need of young Americans for sound secondary education
and America's need for adequately prepared citizens cannot be
met well enough or soon enough to cope with the emergencies
before us unless we use the federal government as well as state
and local agencies to collect and distribute tax funds in support of public education. Neither can we expect to equalize
school support by a division of taxing authority.

---

[6] National Education Association, Research Division. *Advance Estimates of
Public Elementary and Secondary Schools for the School Year 1957-58.* Washington, D. C.: the Association, November 1957. p. 29.

[7] National Education Association, Research Division. *Rankings of the States.*
Washington, D. C.: the Association, December 1957. p. 12, figures for 1955.

The situation was put well by a report from the U. S. Treasury several years ago:

> As a practical matter, the scope of revenue separation appears to be severely limited. Those taxes which might appear to be appropriate for earmarking for State and local governments would not yield enough to meet the revenue needs of these governments. . . .
>
> An essential element of the State and local tax problem is the uneven geographical distribution of tax bases, and this would be left untouched by reallocation of tax sources. Exclusive State jurisdiction over income, profits or wealth taxes, even if practicable, would not solve the problems of those States whose residents consist primarily of low-income recipients. On the other hand, some States would have a revenue-producing potential much beyond their needs, largely by accident of the geographic pattern of industrial concentration which has developed over the years.[8]

Both the difficulty and the urgency of finding money to improve education will increase as the wave of postwar children advances to the secondary level. Since the cost per pupil in high schools usually runs 30 percent or more beyond the elementary-school cost, it follows that substantial increases in local budgets will be needed to meet the increased secondary enrolments without any reference to program improvements or inflation. When we recognize the widespread demand for a higher quality of high-school education, the need for an intelligent, far-sighted approach to a national plan for financing education becomes imperative.

The Encouraging Possibility

Any sober appraisal of America's need for better secondary schools and of the means required to produce such schools leads to the conclusion that we possess the resources to do what must be done. The creative ideas, the research effort, the mediums for communication, and the programs for professional

---

[8] U. S. Treasury Department, Tax Advisory Staff. *Federal-State-Local Tax Coordination.* Washington, D. C.: Superintendent of Documents, Government Printing Office, 1952. p. 4-5.

development can be produced and marshaled for this effort as they have been assembled to accomplish less important objectives upon which America has set its mind and heart. To do what is proposed for American high schools will call for a substantially increased outlay of funds, but in proportion to our rising productivity the necessary effort will be by no means either excessive or sacrificial.

Moreover, we believe that the effort will be made, for in every part of the nation and in every segment of society a new awareness of the strategic importance of education is becoming widely evident. Larger numbers of our people, both in positions of influence and among the rank and file, are seeing more clearly than ever before that our economy, our culture, our political institutions, and our system of defense ultimately depend upon maintaining effective schools and colleges.

It would be most unfortunate, however, if we were to assume that the forces of irresistible progress have now taken over and that all is well, for altho a good outcome is likely, it is in no sense inevitable.

Many influences will affect the future of our schools and the controlling factors will vary from place to place. In every situation, however, an element of crucial significance will be the nature of the leadership that is brought to bear. Our deliberate choice of a decentralized pattern for controlling education in the United States requires leadership of a high order, not only at the national level, but in every state and community. As education leaders consider the total question of resources to power the process of change, they are being called upon to undertake the critically responsible task of identifying, assembling, and organizing the people, the ideas, and the materials required. In addition, they must provide much of the vision and insight necessary to give meaning and direction to the common effort. The extent to which such leadership is available thruout America will largely determine the speed and efficiency with which the work will be accomplished.

13

high schools for tomorrow

high schools for tomorrow

THE 1958 Yearbook Commission affirms that we must not only sustain the gains made in secondary education in the past, but also that we must now develop and maintain a program of universal secondary education which affords to *each* American youth the maximum opportunity for achieving self-realization and social effectiveness. This goal demands that the quantity and quality of secondary education be greatly extended so that all the abilities of all our youth are properly developed. The mission of the secondary school is to be a dynamic force in perpetuating and refining our democratic society.

Progress Toward Universal Secondary Education

Chapter I summarized the current provisions for the education of youth. It was pointed out that nearly 9 in 10 American youth are now attending school. Nearly 90 percent of these youth go to tax-supported and publicly controlled schools, while the rest attend a variety of independent and parochial schools.

One distinguishing feature of America's current pattern of secondary education is the wide diversity of organization, facilities, program, services, and financial support among our nearly 30,000 schools. There is no typical secondary school. Progress toward the attainment of universal secondary education varies tremendously among institutions. In some communities the high school may graduate as few as 10 to 15 percent of those who enter, while other schools may have an extremely high proportion who graduate. Substantial numbers—about 4 in 10—are failing to graduate from high school.

The secondary school of tomorrow will retain until graduation all normal youth, who will take advantage of the many opportunities provided in an increasingly effective educational program. The institution providing this demanding and challenging education is likely to be the comprehensive secondary school, serving the many purposes of society and youth, including the common purpose of integrating education to insure social stability and balance, and the several purposes of individual pupils for the realization of their vocational, educational, and avocational goals.

An Appraisal of the Modern Secondary School

An evaluation of the modern secondary school which seeks to serve the needs of its youth population and to meet the demands of an ever changing society may forecast some of the dimensions of the secondary school of the future.

Significant Accomplishments

The achievements of the modern secondary school are numerous and consequential when contrasted with the attainments of the historical secondary school. While this Yearbook is concerned primarily with the future role of American secondary education, frequent reference has been made to the progress toward and current provisions for an adequate and effective program of universal youth education. This section discusses some of the most significant accomplishments of secondary education in our times.

The American people have come to believe that education contributes to the general welfare and that youth represent our greatest national resource. While there is a too limited understanding of the purpose and function of youth education and inadequate support of its program, the public is committed to the upward extension of the "common" school thru high school.

The goals of secondary education have been broadened from a narrow concept of serving merely the interests of an intellectual and social elite to the responsibility for guaranteeing to all normal youth the opportunity to achieve their personal and social goals thru education.

A steady increase is seen in the percent of youth receiving the benefits of an expanding and improving program of secondary education. Enrolments in Grades IX thru XII, taken as a percent of the population aged 14 thru 17 years, rose from 11 percent in 1900 to 32 percent in 1920, 73 percent in 1940, and nearly 80 percent in 1956-57. In terms of the numbers of students, secondary-school enrolments thruout the country nearly doubled in each of the six decades preceding 1940. Today it is estimated that 88 percent of all youth of high-school age are enrolled in school. In the past 60 years more than four years have been added to the average school experience of the typical American youth. This common acceptance on the part of the school and society of the responsibility for the education of all youth is one of the impressive hallmarks of our faith in the importance of education.

While there have been no sweeping reforms in the curriculum of the modern secondary school, the educational program is broader, more flexible, and more functional than the typical curriculum in the past. Effective curriculum revision and improvement have resulted from the addition of courses to meet more adequately the abilities, needs, and interests of students, and from changes in objectives, content, and instructional procedures in existing courses. Greater emphasis is being placed upon educational outcomes in terms of attitudes, ideals, and appreciations. Some schools are experimenting with newer curriculum designs, including the core curriculum, and re-organized patterns of general and specialized education. Better leadership, better school-community cooperation, and the use of research and other resources are a few of the many contributing factors that some schools are utilizing in curriculum development.

Educational services have been greatly extended in most secondary schools. Guidance and personnel work have received increased emphasis as more attention is given to the individual student as the focus of the school's efforts. The activity program in many schools is extensive and makes valuable contributions to the development of worthwhile educational goals. Health service, the library, food service, and transportation are among the special services considered essential in the total program of a growing number of secondary schools.

Both professional and nonprofessional school personnel have played important roles in building confidence and support among citizens for expanding opportunities for youth. Teaching has become a profession, requiring able, trained persons who must understand the needs of youth and know how to teach as well as what to teach. Educational leadership of a high level has become the best index of the administrative effectiveness of the building principal.

Many communities are constructing physical plants which not only meet the needs of the current program, but also are adaptable to the demands of a changing program. Successful community planning for new building facilities requires good working relations among the administrator, the architect, and the public. Rehabilitation and additions to existing buildings are being made to serve educational purposes. Many communities are expending larger amounts on new and improved instructional materials to facilitate the success of the educational program and the efficiency of the staff.

These and other accomplishments characterize an increasing number of our secondary schools. They point the way to new means of providing challenging opportunities for all youth who will be enrolled in the secondary school of the future.

Unrealized Goals

Secondary education has its critics inside and outside the profession. Some critics say that the school has failed to meet adequately the newer role demanded by today's complex society and economy; they point to the lag between the requirements of modern society and the limited offerings of a traditional program. The wide gap between what is known in theory and what occurs in actual teaching in the average classroom is another basis for concern. Other critics are convinced that universal secondary education is an unrealistic and impractical goal; they believe that the financial burden of educating all youth is too great and that educational opportunities, at least in the upper years of high school, should be restricted to a selected portion of American youth.

Many citizens do not understand or support the basic goals and philosophy of universal youth education. Educators have not met their responsibility in interpreting the indispensable role of universal secondary education to the public. Educated men and women are America's most valuable resource; its people cannot fail to meet the cost of educational services for a greater proportion of youth and an improved quality of education for all boys and girls of high-school age.

The challenging goal of guaranteeing to all normal youth the opportunity to achieve self-realization and social effectiveness is not being attained in the vast majority of our secondary schools. Instead, the accumulation of a four-year block of 16 Carnegie units is still the prevailing gauge of educational growth and development. Too much of our practice is unrelated to the philosophy and purposes of youth education, the ever pressing demands of our economy and culture, and the needs of young people. A functional, purposeful program of secondary education is a goal yet to be realized in most communities.

While increasing percents of all youth are receiving the benefits of secondary education, there are many restrictions of educational opportunity for various segments of our school population. One of the great unsolved problems is to educate all levels of ability, interest, and aspiration. We have planned the difficulty of our curriculum for the middle 50 percent, but the types of courses are more suited to the interests of the upper 40 percent.[1] Limited opportunities to challenge our gifted youth, restricted services to the mentally and physically handicapped, and inappropriate offerings for youth of nonacademic ability and interest are among the inadequacies.

One major weakness of the secondary school in many communities is an outmoded, entrenched curriculum which fails to serve effectively the needs of students and the requirements of modern living. Romine states that the typical curriculum in a sizable number of secondary schools:

> Is oriented to the past.
> Lacks a cooperatively developed, well-understood, and actively coordinating philosophy of education.
> Places emphasis upon academic information and skills as educational objectives.
> Is organized largely in terms of subject-centered courses.
> Is based largely upon adopted textbooks.
> Is developed largely by individual teachers.[2]

Even in communities where steps have been taken to effect changes and improvement, the defense of the traditional program continues. Significant innovations in curriculum structure and content are reported only by the venturesome few.

The number and extent of school services are not uniformly available. In a 1951-52 survey of guidance and counseling activities, the U. S. Office of Education found that out of 24,000 schools responding only about 4000, or 17 percent, had someone on the staff who devoted half time or more to guidance activities. In those few schools, the counselors, many of them without specialized training, were serving an average of 524 students each.[3] In many schools the counselors lack enough time for guidance activities and are without suitable

---

[1] Leonard, J. Paul. *Developing the Secondary School Curriculum.* Revised edition. New York: Rinehart and Co., 1953. p. 553.

[2] Adapted from: Romine, Stephen A. *Building the High School Curriculum.* New York: Ronald Press Co., 1954. p. 20-26.

[3] Jones, Arthur J., and Miller, Leonard M. "The National Picture of Pupil Personnel and Guidance Services in 1953." *Bulletin of the National Association of Secondary-School Principals* 38: 105-59; February 1954.

materials. Other educational services, including the library, health services, the cafeteria, and transportation, are either not available or not adequate in many schools.

Schools have not discovered the appeals and motivations that arouse youth to feel that our free society will soon be a trust in their keeping, to preserve and enhance. Youth need greater assistance from the school in the development of moral and spiritual values by which they may live. Cynicism, indifference, conformity, and lack of self-discipline are all evidences that the school has not met this responsibility for many youth.

Edmonson, Roemer, and Bacon highlighted the shortcomings and weaknesses in our modern secondary school as follows:

1. In most states there are large numbers of school districts that are too small to provide an adequate program of education, especially on the high school level.

2. Educational agencies, such as schools and colleges, have never been as adequately financed as their increasing responsibilities and programs would warrant.

3. Secondary education has not been made effectively free to all boys and girls, many of whom have been forced to drop out for financial reasons.

4. The college preparatory objective has so dominated the thinking of high school teachers that adequate planning for the noncollege group of students has been retarded.

5. The higher prestige claimed by the academic subjects has placed vocational courses and health instruction [and other so-called nonacademic offerings] at a distinct disadvantage.

6. The health program of the schools has not achieved marked success in the development of desirable health habits or the elimination of physical handicaps.

7. Schools have not developed adequate plans for providing work experiences for young people.

8. In some schools, the individual student has received so little special consideration that failures, lack of mastery of essentials, and poor school adjustments have become common, with resulting problems of juvenile delinquency.

9. Educational procedures and practices in schools have been so thoroughly standardized that adjustments to new needs have been slow and difficult.[4]

---

[4] Edmonson, J. B.; Roemer, Joseph; and Bacon, Francis L. *The Administration of the Modern Secondary School*. Fourth edition. New York: Macmillan Co., 1953. p. 577-78.

This summary of the more common limitations of the secondary school as it operates in many communities emphasizes weaknesses that must be overcome by the secondary school of the future.

The Secondary School of the Future

An enormous and essential task faces secondary education. It is the unfinished business of sustaining and diffusing the many achievements of the modern school and of moving forward to complete an effective program of universal youth education. This program must provide the kinds and quality of educational experiences that will develop effectively all the abilities of all American youth. The secondary school will then assume in full its indispensable role in our democratic society.

Studies and Reports about the Future School

Various efforts have been made to describe a Utopian school, and other attempts have depicted a changing school drawn from best current practice in selected secondary schools. Major publications of national policy-making groups in education have suggested, and frequently advocated, many dimensions of a novel and dynamic school. These are excellent examples:

Association for Supervision and Curriculum Development. *What Shall the High Schools Teach?* 1956 Yearbook. Washington, D. C.: the Association, a department of the National Education Association, 1956. 230 p.

Commission on Life Adjustment Education for Youth. *Vitalizing Secondary Education.* U. S. Department of Health, Education, and Welfare, Office of Education, Bulletin 1951, No. 3. Washington, D. C.: Superintendent of Documents, Government Printing Office, 1951. 106 p.

Cummings, Howard H., and others. *A Look Ahead in Secondary Education.* Report of the Second Commission on Life Adjustment Education for Youth. U. S. Department of Health, Education, and Welfare, Office of Education, Bulletin 1954, No. 4. Washington, D. C.: Superintendent of Documents, Government Printing Office, 1954. 105 p.

Harvard University, Committee on the Objectives of a General Education in a Free Society. *General Education in a Free Society.* Cambridge, Mass.: Harvard University Press, 1945. 267 p.

John Dewey Society. *The American High School: Its Responsibility and Opportunity.* Eighth Yearbook. New York: Harper and Brothers, 1946. 264 p.

National Association of Secondary-School Principals. *Planning for American Youth.* Revised edition. Washington, D. C.: the Association, a department of the National Education Association, 1951. 64 p.

National Education Association and American Association of School Administrators, Educational Policies Commission. *Education for All American Youth: A Further Look.* Revised edition. Washington, D. C.: the Commission, 1952. 402 p.

National Society for the Study of Education. *Adapting the Secondary-School Program to the Needs of Youth.* Fifty-Second Yearbook, Part I. Chicago: University of Chicago Press, 1953. 316 p.

Trump, J. Lloyd. *New Horizons for Secondary School Teachers.* Urbana, Ill.: University of Illinois, Commission on the Experimental Study of the Utilization of the Staff in the Secondary School, 1957. 36 p.

Educational periodicals frequently publish articles on the future secondary school. Shaw and Reid proposed a totally new type of program and designed a new type of plant to house the program they advocated.[5] Their "Random Falls Idea" has produced much discussion. A symposium of challenging articles on the high school of tomorrow was prepared by the staff of Teachers College.[6]

These many contributions to the design and program of the school for the future emphasize the importance of an intensive restudy of the secondary school. They not only recommend promising practices now in effect in some communities, but they also propose new frontiers that are neither in existing

---

[5] Shaw, Archibald B., and Reid, John Lyon. "A New Look at Secondary Education: The Random Falls Idea." *School Executive* 75: 47-86; March 1956.

See also chapter X, p. 278-79.

[6] Teachers College Record. "High Schools for Tomorrow." *Teachers College Record* 56: 355-411; April 1955.

patterns of secondary education nor in many discussions of the problems of youth and their education.

Requisites for the Future Secondary School

As this Commission reviews its own thinking as well as the recommendations of these many other groups, it sees eight essential characteristics of the secondary school of the future. Secondary education in some communities today may exemplify one or perhaps more of these qualities, but few if any schools could rightfully claim to meet the description in full.

1. *Our society will accept its responsibility for universal youth education and will provide adequate support for education thru high school for all youth and a program thru the fourteenth year of schooling for many youth.*

This concept of education for all youth recognizes the responsibility of our society to establish and maintain an educational system, at public expense for the vast majority of students, that will insure equality of educational opportunity for all levels of ability, need, and interest. The selective character of the secondary school and its relatively low holding power will cease to be problems as the school and the community make changes in policy and program to guarantee the fullest development of our nation's greatest assets. This expanded program of secondary education will necessitate a substantial increase in expenditures for schools. The need for a comprehensive plan for financing education which involves the federal government as well as state and local agencies must be recognized.

2. *School organization will facilitate the realization of the purposes and functions of education for all youth.*

Organizational patterns of grade groupings and of faculty specialization will be developed to provide greater flexibility and diversity as a means to encourage rather than to retard the development of adequate educational programs and services. No one organizational structure will be predominant; patterns will vary in terms of state and local customs and needs. The comprehensive high school promises to be the best instrumentality to guarantee the growth of democratic attitudes and social unity and the development of the abilities of all youth, if its program is sufficiently flexible and diversified to meet all individual needs. The internal organization within a particular school will follow no common pattern; it will be adaptable and functional as it serves youth.

3. *The individual student will be the focus of the school, which will be fully oriented to his needs and will be effective in facilitating his growth and development.*

The school will discover each youth's potentialities and will provide suitable learning experiences in the school and in the community to develop these potentialities to the maximum degree. Teachers and other members of the school staff will know the students as individuals. The home will understand the role of the school and will contribute effectively in areas of parental responsibility and cooperation. Guidance personnel will be an integral part of the staff of each secondary school, directing and coordinating the many guidance and counseling services to students.

Mass education will continue only as a memory of the traditional school. Reaching the needs of all youth will characterize the school of the future. *Substance* and *process* will be regarded not as protagonists in rival educational circles but as related means to the development of the individual as a mature, integrated person.

4. *The curriculum of the secondary school will develop new designs, content, and methods to provide the learning needed by both youth and society.*

The traditional curriculum will be displaced by a structure providing a balanced program of general education and specialized education. There will be a greater standardization of curriculum content in view of the increasing mobility of our population, growing recognition of the force of education in our national welfare, and new and improved materials of instruction developed by educational organizations and other professional agencies. There will be increased emphasis upon intellectual achievement based upon every individual student's interests and motivations. Improved teaching methods, enhanced by many electronic and mechanical aids, will result in more effective instruction.

The place of technical and vocational education as part of specialized education will be clarified and strengthened. Increased emphasis will be given to technical skills that are common to a variety of occupations. Retraining will be provided for adult workers whose former skills become obsolete due to automation and other shifts of technology. The increasingly higher qualifications required for American industrial employment will place a premium on technical and managerial skills, training for which may be provided in part thru community or junior colleges.

The expanded and enriched program of the future secondary school will meet the challenging demands of our modern society and the many diverse educational needs of a rapidly increasing youth population. The emerging curriculum will develop the competencies and attitudes in youth that will prepare them to live fully and to work effectively in a complex and dynamic society.

5. The staff of the school will attain status and prestige comparable to other professions as their professional competencies are utilized effectively in the achievement of the purposes of secondary education.

The school of the future will differentiate among the professional, semiprofessional, and nonprofessional tasks that must be performed to insure an adequate educational program, and these tasks will be related to the purposes of instruction. The teacher's role will be stimulating and challenging and will demand a high level of professional competence, as well as a professional level of remuneration.

Professional consultants in many specialized areas will be available to help the teacher in his increasingly complex task. In addition, trained clerical and technical assistants will be provided to help teachers with nonprofessional duties.

Educational leadership will be the primary responsibility of the principal to the end that all the resources of the school contribute to quality education for all youth.

6. *The physical plant and instructional resources will be so designed and selected as to make their maximum contribution to youth education and community living.*

The secondary-school plant of tomorrow will be designed to facilitate a changing program of youth and community education. Elements of flexibility, versatility, convertibility, and expansibility will insure that school buildings will serve the needs of youth and society. The school environment will promote healthful growth in body, mind, and spirit.

All kinds of instructional materials will be available to teachers. Some of these resources will be housed in the school's instructional materials center, and many others will be essential equipment in each teaching laboratory.

7. *Home-community-school responsibilities will be understood, and each agency will perform its function in the education of youth.*

Able leadership will develop and utilize the many resources available to effect school improvement and community betterment. The school has an important role in community life that demands professional leadership and participation. The democratic school calls for a high level of cooperative study, planning, programming, and evaluation by both lay and professional groups. The community school is one effective approach that is building better communities for youth and adults.

A re-examination of the responsibilities of the home, the community, and the school for the education and welfare of youth will indicate the problem areas of need and support. In some areas the decision will be made to utilize the joint efforts of many community agencies, including the school. In other service areas the school will be assigned sole responsibility, and in still others the home and the community will perform the necessary functions. A sound determination of policies and procedures for the school's role in youth education and welfare is predicated on this thoro examination of responsibilities.

8. Continued experimentation and evaluation will show the way to new and improved methods and procedures to be utilized in the dynamic secondary school.

Many areas of research and experimentation will be investigated and the results used in a continuous program of revision and improvement. Staff members will be assigned definite responsibilities in research; all teachers will be encouraged to experiment in their search for new and better methods of instruction. Evaluation will be an essential part of each school's educational program. The appraisal program will include all aspects of the educational effort, including the physical plant, the curriculum, the staff, the learning process, and the results in terms of behavioral outcomes. The public will be regularly informed of the strengths and weaknesses and the successes and failures of the program. Educational leadership is charged with this responsibility. According to the Educational Policies Commission:

> To locate the differences between educational theory and practice, to arrange these differences according to their importance, to probe for their causes, to prescribe for their removal, and to appraise the results of the entire process—these are the persistent tasks of educational leadership.[7]

Other Forces

Earlier chapters have summarized the important nationwide social and economic influences and the products of our society and its organization that are significant in their impact on sec-

[7] National Education Association and American Association of School Administrators, Educational Policies Commission. *Policies for Education in American Democracy.* Washington, D. C.: the Commission, 1946. p. 277.

ondary education. Current influences which are a result of the official concerns of our government are also reflected in our secondary schools. These trends are having their direct effects upon our plans and decisions about the goals of secondary education, the tasks of the modern secondary school, and present provisions for youth education.

A statement of these potent forces was made by the President's Committee on Education Beyond the High School:

> Revolutionary changes are occurring in American education of which even yet we are only dimly aware. The Nation has been propelled into a challenging new educational era since World War II by the convergence of powerful forces—an explosion of knowledge and population, a burst of technological and economic advance, the outbreak of ideological conflict and the uprooting of old political and cultural patterns on a worldwide scale, and an unparalleled demand by Americans for more and better education. . . . The gap between this Nation's educational needs and its educational effort is widening ominously.
>
> America would be heedless if she closed her eyes to the dramatic strides being taken by the Soviet Union in post-high school education, particularly in the development of scientists, engineers, and technicians. She would be inexcusably blind if she failed to see that the challenge of the next 20 years will require leaders not only in science and engineering and in business and industry, but in government and politics, in foreign affairs and diplomacy, in education and civic affairs. A responsible exercise of our Nation's role in world leadership also requires a broadened citizen interest in and understanding of foreign relations and world affairs.[8]

These challenges are sure to prove major determinants in the destiny of secondary education as well as higher education. The magnitude and complexity of these problems will commit the secondary school to new and more difficult tasks. It is imperative that these changes and forces which will influence the direction of secondary education in the future bring forth our maximum efforts to meet our nation's educational needs.

[8] President's Committee on Education Beyond the High School. *Second Report to the President.* Washington, D. C.: Superintendent of Documents, Government Printing Office, July 1957. p. 1.

A Program of Universal Secondary Education
and America's Future

This Yearbook Commission believes that the achievements of the modern secondary school should be recognized as worthy of our highest praise. The untiring and fruitful efforts of the past and present have nurtured and guided the secondary school thru a period of growth and maturation. This relatively young institution has now come of age and is ready to assume the grave responsibilities and obligations of maturity. This new and demanding role of universal secondary education is intertwined with America's future. As the early school contributed to the development of democracy, the secondary school of tomorrow will be a dynamic force in the perpetuation and refinement of our free society. America's destiny is in the minds and hearts of its youth.

ACKNOWLEDGMENTS

The Yearbook Commission wishes to recognize and thank the following agencies and persons who helped in the preparation of this book:

Kistner, Wright & Wright—Art work by FRANK T. SATA, part-time Junior Designer for the firm, and student of architecture at the University of Southern California. His designs for cover and chapter titles were made under the direction of HENRY L. WRIGHT, FAIA, a member of the Yearbook Commission.

American Association of School Administrators—Liaison on planning, HELEN HODGE COX, assisted by JERE KUPECKY.

NEA Research Division—Secretarial and editorial assistance by BERNICE BRIGHAM and HELEN BRONHEIM. Editorial assistance by BEATRICE CRUMP LEE. Assistance on typing and proofreading by VALDEANE RICE, JEANNIE BIGGS, HELEN BRIGUGLIO, GLENNA KING, WALLY ANNE SLITER, and LILLIAN YANG. Indexing by HELEN BRONHEIM.

NEA Division of Publications—Editorial services by JESSE S. COWDRICK and CARRIE G. GRIMSLEY. Proofreading by ELIZABETH NELSON and MARCIA H. OSMAN.

Judd & Detweiler, Inc.—Printing under the general direction of C. B. DEETER.

RECENT AASA YEARBOOKS

OFFICERS 1957-58

AMERICAN ASSOCIATION OF SCHOOL ADMINISTRATORS

President

PHILIP J. HICKEY, Superintendent of Instruction, St. Louis, Missouri

President-Elect

C. C. TRILLINGHAM, Superintendent, Los Angeles County Schools, Los Angeles, California

Vicepresident

J. CHESTER SWANSON, Professor of Education, University of California, Berkeley, California

Executive Committee

HOBART M. CORNING, Superintendent of Schools, Washington, D. C.
MARTIN ESSEX, Superintendent of Schools, Akron, Ohio
NATT B. BURBANK, Superintendent of Schools, Boulder, Colorado
WENDELL GODWIN, Superintendent of Schools, Topeka, Kansas
THE PRESIDENT, PRESIDENT-ELECT, and VICEPRESIDENT, ex officio

Executive Secretary

FINIS E. ENGLEMAN, 1201 Sixteenth St., NW, Washington, D. C.

Secretary Emeritus

WORTH McCLURE, 2122 California St., NW, Washington, D. C.

Associate Secretary

SHIRLEY COOPER, 1201 Sixteenth St., NW, Washington, D. C.

*Executive Secretary, Committee for the Advancement of
School Administration*

HOLLIS A. MOORE, JR., 1201 Sixteenth St., NW, Washington, D. C.

371

INDEX